Women, Violence and Postmillennial Romance Fiction

This book interrogates the significance of the revival and reformulation of the romance genre in the postmillennial period. Emma Roche examines how six popular novels, published between 2005 and 2015 (*Twilight, Fifty Shades of Grey, Gone Girl, Sharp Objects* and *The Girl on the Train*), reanimate and modify recognisable tropes from the romance genre to reflect a neoliberal and postfeminist cultural climate. As such, Roche argues, these novels function as crucial spaces for interrogating and challenging those contemporary gender ideologies.

Throughout the book, Roche addresses and critiques several key attributes of neoliberal postfeminism, including a pervasive emphasis on individualism and personal responsibility; an insistent requirement for self-monitoring, self-surveillance, and bodywork; the celebration of consumerism and its associated pleasures; the prescription of mandatory optimism and suppressing one's 'negative' emotions; and the endorsement of choice as a primary marker of women's empowerment. While much critical attention has been devoted to those attributes and their pernicious effects, Roche argues that one crucial repercussion has been largely overlooked in contemporary cultural criticism: how these ideologies function together to effectively sanction gender-based violence. Thus, Roche exploits textual analysis to demonstrate the subtle ways in which neoliberal postfeminism can augment women's vulnerability to male violence.

Emma Roche completed her doctoral work at Maynooth University, Ireland, in 2021. Her research areas include gender studies and genre studies, with a particular focus on contemporary popular fiction.

Routledge Advances in Popular Culture Studies
Series editor
Lorna Piatti-Farnell

This interdisciplinary series is our home for cutting-edge popular culture research. It includes monographs and targeted edited collections that provide new insights into a variety of topics, theories, and cases from around the world.

Women, Violence and Postmillennial Romance Fiction
Emma Roche

Women, Violence and Postmillennial Romance Fiction

Emma Roche

LONDON AND NEW YORK

First published 2023
by Routledge
4 Park Square, Milton Park, Abingdon, Oxon OX14 4RN

and by Routledge
605 Third Avenue, New York, NY 10158

Routledge is an imprint of the Taylor & Francis Group, an informa business

© 2023 Emma Roche

The right of Emma Roche to be identified as author of this work has been asserted in accordance with sections 77 and 78 of the Copyright, Designs and Patents Act 1988.

All rights reserved. No part of this book may be reprinted or reproduced or utilised in any form or by any electronic, mechanical, or other means, now known or hereafter invented, including photocopying and recording, or in any information storage or retrieval system, without permission in writing from the publishers.

Trademark notice: Product or corporate names may be trademarks or registered trademarks, and are used only for identification and explanation without intent to infringe.

British Library Cataloguing-in-Publication Data
A catalogue record for this book is available from the British Library

ISBN: 978-1-032-34406-5 (hbk)
ISBN: 978-1-032-34407-2 (pbk)
ISBN: 978-1-003-32200-9 (ebk)

DOI: 10.4324/9781003322009

Typeset in Times New Roman
by Apex CoVantage, LLC

Contents

Acknowledgements — vii

Introduction — 1

Dominus Obsequious Sororium 1
'Silly Novels by Lady Novelists' 5
"Somebody's Trying to Kill Me . . . and I Think It's My Husband" 11
Re-Reading the Romance 14
Reference List 17

1 The *Twilight* of Postfeminism — 19

What Choice Have I? 19
What a Girl Really Wants (but Is Ashamed to Admit)? 21
Prince-Like Vampires and Paranormal Romances 26
Eager for Eternal Damnation 34
Reference List 40

2 *Fifty Shades* of Neoliberalism — 43

'Feminists for Orgasms?' 43
Affective Dissonance 46
Consent Is a Grey *Area 54*
Reference List 62

3 Happily Never After — 64

'Vagina-Dentata Dames'? 64
The Cool Girl 68
Making a (Neoliberal) Monster 73
Everyone Loves the Dead Girl 75
'Well, If It Isn't Nancy Drew' 80
Intimate Terrorism 84
Reference List 90

4 Hell Hath No Fury 93

Female Rage and the Postfeminist Masquerade 93
"The Powerful Illusion of Delicate Girlhood" 97
Mean Girls 103
"I Wish I'd Be Murdered" 110
Reference List 117

Conclusion 119

All the Rage 119
Reference List 125

Index 126

Acknowledgements

First and foremost, I would like to thank Dr. Michael G. Cronin for his advice, encouragement and guidance. Without him, I'm positive I would never have been able to shape my ramblings about popular fiction into a semi-coherent argument. Michael's commitment to this project has been unwavering, and while I cannot adequately express my gratitude to him in words, I hope he recognises the profound impact he has had on my life and work.

I extend my thanks to my colleagues in the English Department of Maynooth University, especially those who devoted their time to reading excerpts of this project. Thank you for your crucial input and guidance. I must also thank Maynooth University's Graduate Studies Office who generously funded my research. Thank you, as well, to the readers and editors at Routledge for their ongoing support and much valued input.

To Seán, thank you for dispelling my self-doubt, for being so certain I could do this. Thank you for listening to me moan and, of course, for allowing me to play Hotel Transylvania on a loop to ease my worries – all night, every night. And finally, to my family – my Mam, Aubrey, Dad, 'Nanny Maureen', baby brother Rían and perfect dog Sindy – thank you for all the sacrifices you have made for me. I love you more than anything, and I hope I've made you proud.

Introduction

Dominus Obsequious Sororium

In October 2020, Keith Raniere was sentenced to 120 years in prison for crimes including sex trafficking, fraud and forced labour. The leader of NXIVM, a group described as a pyramid scheme turned sex cult, Raniere has since been the subject of widespread media attention. But the most salacious story from the case concerns a secret sub-sect of his group termed Dominus Obsequious Sororium, or DOS, loosely translated by its members as 'Master Over Slave'. Headed by Alison Mack, a former teen actress who achieved fame in the television series *Smallville* (2001–11), DOS was a woman-only branch of NXIVM that promoted sadomasochism. Disturbingly figured as a sorority, the group was divided into 'pods' of 'sisters' or 'slaves' who were controlled by a 'master'. Upon joining a pod, these women had to provide 'collateral' including nude photographs, financial documents or videoed 'confessions' of their darkest secrets. This collateral, they were told, functioned as a demonstration of their life-long commitment to the group – their 'vow'.

Once approved as members, the women were obliged to partake in an initiation ceremony and unwittingly 'branded' with Raniere's initials. A cauterising iron was used to create this 'brand', leaving a permanent scar on their crotch. Forced to seek permission to sleep and eat, these women were expected to check in with their 'masters' several times a day. They were also required to habitually weigh themselves and their daily food, taking 'progress' photographs to illustrate their weight loss. This behaviour, they believed, facilitated their personal growth by allowing them to bolster their self-control. It later transpired that the 'sisters' had been groomed for sex with Raniere, their weight loss a means of satisfying his proclivity for slender women.

Like everyone else on the internet, it seems, I was transfixed by the Raniere case and by DOS in particular. Watching *The Vow* (2020–present), an HBO docuseries which follows several former high-ranking members of NXIVM who have disaffiliated from the group, I wondered: how were more than 100 women convinced to join an organisation which required their subjugation as 'slaves' and encouraged them towards self-denial and starvation in pursuit of 'empowerment'? In this current cultural moment, where women in the Western world have potentially more freedom and agency than ever before, why was subordination and self-punishment such an attractive option for a group of well-educated, middle- to upper-class modern women?

The Vow introduces us to several of those women, including Bonnie Piesse and Sarah Edmondson, who recount their experiences at NXIVM or DOS. Attractive and affluent, Piesse and Edmondson are self-proclaimed 'artists', fledging actresses in pursuit of their big break. But beyond these superficial connections, the women also share a common feeling of

DOI: 10.4324/9781003322009-1

inadequacy and self-doubt – of not being 'good' enough. Throughout the series, they gesture towards their distress, low self-esteem, body issues, discontent, anxiety and powerlessness. These feelings, they tell us, were exacerbated by the heightened visibility of misogyny in US culture – exemplified by the inauguration of Donald Trump in 2016.

Piesse and Edmondson identify their decision to join NXIVM in relation to those feelings, believing that the group, and specifically its Executive Success Programme (ESP), would be the solution to all their problems. Couched in business language, ESPs were promoted as their way of self-optimising – becoming the very best versions of themselves. Repudiating low self-esteem and unhappiness as 'limiting beliefs', blocking their pathways to success, Piesse and Edmondson were taught to take full responsibility for their emotions and behaviour. Self-pity and victimhood, they were told, were evidence of deficiencies in their characters, destructive feelings inhibiting their personal growth. And so, by learning how to govern those destructive feelings, rectifying their 'deficiencies' via self-discipline and bodywork, the women would be able to self-optimise – achieving personal and professional success.

While Piesse managed to escape NXVIM before her initiation into DOS, Edmondson was less fortunate. In *The Vow*, she recalls her experience of being 'branded', haunted by the smell of her burning flesh. Scandalous and shocking, this story, at a cursory glance, might be interpreted as an anomaly, a disconcerting but abnormal occurrence. Joining a sadomasochistic cult is, admittedly, a departure from the norm. Yet, as I watched Piesse and Edmondson attempt to delineate their trauma, I began to recognise a familiar cultural pattern: how women are repeatedly motivated to individuate their problems and privatise their suffering. Throughout this book, I interrogate and critique that pattern as a product of neoliberal and postfeminist culture, arguing that it has devastating consequences – especially for women.

Rising to prominence in the 1980s – under the Reagan administration in the USA and Thatcher's premiership in the UK – neoliberalism is characterised by the pursuit of policies such as privatisation, promotion of globalised free markets and free trade, and replacement of the democratic welfare state with a managerial state which contracts out welfare provision to the market. But as Rosalind Gill, Christina Scharff and other critics argue, neoliberalism also functions as a hegemonic political rationality – a central organising ethic of contemporary society shaping the way we live, think and feel. Extending market values to all spheres of life, Gill and Scharff interpret neoliberalism as a calculated technology for governing subjects, constituting them as autonomous, self-managing and enterprising (2011, 5). With its relentless focus on individualism, neoliberal ideology rejects that there are socio-economic factors dictating our lives. Like NXIVM's ESPs, it posits only personal solutions to structural issues in the form of hard work and self-transformation.

According to Gill, there is a powerful resonance between neoliberal and postfeminist ideologies, operating on at least three levels. Firstly, both ideologies are structured by a current of individualism that has "almost entirely replaced notions of the social or political, or any idea of individuals as subject to pressures, constraints or influence from outside themselves" (2007, 162). Hyper-individualising, these ideologies necessitate personal solutions to injustices inherent in the social structure of our culture, such as the gendered wage gap and sexual harassment. Secondly, the hegemonic ideals of neoliberalism and postfeminism are practically indistinguishable, privileging autonomous, entrepreneurial, self-regulating, self-reinventing and free-choosing subjects. The third, and perhaps most significant, connection is that these ideologies are specifically gendered, interpellating women specifically, and more intensively than men, to work on and transform their bodies, regulate every aspect of their conduct and present these actions as freely chosen.

In this book, I use the terms 'neoliberalism' and 'postfeminism' in tandem to indicate an ideological bloc and to emphasise what I perceive to be their innate similarity. Following Gill's logic, I believe that postfeminism has been at least partly constituted through the pervasiveness of neoliberal ideals and functions as a kind of gendered neoliberalism. Occasionally, however, I use the term 'postfeminism' independently. This is to stress a key distinguishing factor between them: unlike neoliberalism, postfeminism has an unusual, often contradictory but nonetheless *explicit* relationship with feminism.

Coinciding with the re-entrenchment of conservatism in the USA and the UK, the term 'postfeminism' first surfaced during the 1980s as a way of describing an antifeminist 'backlash' against second-wave feminism circulating in the popular media. Since then, critics including Angela McRobbie have cautioned against this conflation of postfeminism with antifeminism, proposing that it has a more complicated relationship with feminism than the 'backlash' thesis allows. According to McRobbie, postfeminism broadly encompasses a set of assumptions – widely disseminated within popular media forms – having to do with the pastness of feminism, "whether that supposed pastness is merely noted, mourned or celebrated" (2008, 2). It positively draws on and invokes feminism, only to suggest that equality has been achieved – thus installing a whole repertoire of new meanings which emphasise that feminism is a spent force. With its implicit assumption that feminism's work is done, postfeminism's dominant discursive system perpetuates the idea that gender issues are less urgent and deploys a lexicon of female empowerment – 'girl power' – to validate this 'reality'. All the while, as McRobbie argues, vengeful patriarchal norms have been culturally reinstated (55).

And so, I use the term 'postfeminism' to denote that 'double entanglement' of feminist with antifeminist rhetoric. Otherwise, I combine 'neoliberalism' and 'postfeminism' to designate their homogeneity as outlined earlier. As we will see, this book addresses, and critiques, several key attributes of 'neoliberal postfeminism'. These include a pervasive emphasis on individualism and personal responsibility; an insistent requirement for self-monitoring, self-surveillance and bodywork; the celebration of consumerism and its associated pleasures; the prescription of mandatory optimism and suppressing one's 'negative' emotions and the endorsement of choice as a primary marker of women's empowerment. While much critical attention has been devoted to those attributes and their pernicious effects, I propose that one crucial repercussion has been largely overlooked in contemporary cultural criticism: how the combination of these ideologies effectively sanctions gender-based violence.

Highlighting the scale and reality of gendered violence in our culture, the World Health Organization has recently estimated that one in three women worldwide have been victims of gendered violence while 38% of murders of women are committed by a male intimate partner (2021). Current statistics on rape convictions are equally alarming. According to the Rape, Abuse and Incest National Network, less than 6% of perpetrators are successfully convicted in the USA – despite the increase in reports of sexual attacks (2020). Likewise, in Ireland, the Central Statistics Office maintains that around 11% of reported rapes result in criminal charges (2019).

As these figures suggest, gender-based violence is still frighteningly prevalent in the Western world. Yet, I propose that the entrenchment of neoliberal postfeminism has further compounded that issue. Those ideologies, I argue, function together to make women solely responsible for their own wellbeing and self-care, inculpating them for their 'negative' feelings. This obfuscates any socio-political factors contributing to those feelings, encouraging women to privatise their suffering and find personal solutions to all of their problems. But, as Piesse's and Edmondson's stories so powerfully illustrate, the deleterious impact of that incitement should not be minimised. Rather, it can augment women's vulnerability to male violence.

As this book will demonstrate, neoliberal postfeminism functions as a tool of patriarchy to silence women's critical voices, denying them an outlet for expressing their pain whilst stifling any critique of the structures engendering that pain. At the same time, those ideologies discursively reassure women that gender inequity is an antiquated notion, nullifying the need for feminism or collective political action. Still, I propose that feminism was never totally *erased* by neoliberal postfeminism. Rather, as we saw with DOS, its rhetoric was polluted by that dominant ideology and weaponised to subjugate and silence women.

Promoted as a 'sorority', a sisterhood of female friends intimately bonded together, DOS exploited a feminist lexicon to indoctrinate its members into the group, thus entrapping them within a state of perpetual victimhood and making them vulnerable to male abuse. In other words, DOS corrupted feminist rhetoric – the desire for solidarity and relationality between women – for misogynist ends. That corruption, I propose, is another malefic effect of neoliberal postfeminism, critiqued throughout this book, which bolsters the sanctioning of gender-based violence.

Crucially, gendered and sexualised violence is a key recurring theme in the novels under study. Those novels include Stephenie Meyer's *Twilight* series (2005–8), E.L. James's *Fifty Shades of Grey* series (2011–12), Gillian Flynn's *Gone Girl* (2012) and *Sharp Objects* (2006), Paula Hawkins's *The Girl on the Train* (2015) and Megan Abbott's *Dare Me* (2012). The novels were written by women, about women, and had a mostly female readership. They were worldwide bestsellers, with lucrative film and television adaptations, and clearly resonated with modern audiences. At the same time, however, the novels were widely condemned for pleasurably representing forms of violence against women, accused of glamorising and eroticising female suffering.

This unusual paradox – the dissemination of popular literature produced by women for women which fetishises gendered violence – has been a central concern for critics of the novels. The critics have asked: what does it mean that women are producing those kinds of novels? And why were they so popular – especially amongst women? While these questions are certainly valid, I am reluctant to posit a totalising hypothesis about readers of popular fiction. Instead, I argue that these novels are best understood as striking manifestations of neoliberal and postfeminist culture and ideology. Read in this way, the novels function as crucial spaces for interrogating and challenging those hegemonic gender ideologies – specifically how they can sanction violence against women.

Marketed as disparate genres – domestic noir, crime fiction, psychological thriller, erotica and YA romance – I interpret these novels as contemporary reiterations of the popular romance formula, reanimating recognisable tropes from chick lit, the modern gothic romance and the Harlequin romance. As will be demonstrated, those tropes have been modified by and for a neoliberal postfeminist cultural climate. However, they are utilised in different ways and to different effects. Meyer and James exploit 'romance' to promote the hegemonic ideal of neoliberal postfeminism as empowering and pleasurable for women. In stark contrast, Hawkins, Abbott and Flynn subvert those long-standing tropes to critique that ideal, exposing it as a dangerous fantasy facilitating women's subjugation.

This subversion of romantic tropes notably coincides with a shift in the dominant *tone* of the genre. Once light and cheery, it becomes dark, despairing and utterly discomforting. Undermining readerly expectations of 'romance', affects like happiness, positivity and confidence are superseded by rage, disaffection and desolation. Yet, I argue, this tonal shift is not as sudden or as sharp as it appears. Rather, while the feeling that something has gone terribly wrong is *palpable* in Flynn's, Hawkins's and Abbot's novels, those unsettling affects are also perceptible in the *Twilight* and *Fifty Shades* series. Embedded into the fiction and suppressed by the dominant tone, these affects are often difficult to detect. Nevertheless, they repeatedly surface in unusual and peculiar forms, troubling any straightforward interpretation of those novels. And so, this book explicates these tonal shifts and attempts to understand their significance, arguing that the increased tangibility of affects like anger and alienation in popular fiction during the postmillennial period registers something crucial: a kind of cultural disenchantment with neoliberal postfeminism and its ideals.

'Silly Novels by Lady Novelists'

In *Gender and the Media* (2007), Rosalind Gill defines popular romantic novels as novels in which a love story is central to the narrative and which have an emotionally satisfying happy ending (194). Within this broad definition of the popular romance genre exists a wide variety of sub-genres, including the historical romance, the regency romance and the sci-fi romance. One of the most profitable and prolific of these sub-genres is the 'Hard' romance or, as it is now more frequently termed, the Harlequin romance. This type of novel was popularised in the late 1950s by the Canadian publishing company Harlequin Enterprises Ltd., the UK equivalent of which would be Mills and Boon. With an almost exclusively female readership comprising women of all ages, these novels originally cost little over a dollar in the USA and were commonly distributed via mail subscription.

According to Gill, the basic plot of the Harlequin romance can be summarised as follows:

> A young, inexperienced, poor woman meets a handsome, wealthy man, ten or fifteen years her senior. The hero is mocking, cynical, contemptuous hostile and even brutal, and the heroine is confused. By the end, he reveals his love for her and misunderstandings are cleared away.
>
> (195)

In other words, these plots are traditionally constructed around a series of obstacles that must be overcome before the hero and heroine can reconcile and fall in love. By progressing through their initial hostility, the Harlequin lovers are typically transformed. While the brutish hero is softened into an emotional being with a heart, the heroine procures a new, often elevated, social position. These stories, Gill observes, also have recurring settings, usually enchanted spaces where the heroine is socially dislocated – "perhaps on holiday, having gone away from friends or family to recover from a traumatic event, or even waking from a coma" (195).

Prototypically, the Harlequin romance centres on a protagonist who embodies the feminine stereotype of passivity: the pure and virginal heroine. This heroine is invariably depicted as a young and innocent damsel in distress, desperately fighting to protect her 'purity' against the attacks of a fearsome rakish hero who may or may not reform. This heroine must love the Harlequin man no matter how viciously he treats her. He may despise or abuse her, physically or emotionally, but she must persevere. Working to ameliorate the situation whilst simultaneously preserving her virginity and virtue, the Harlequin heroine suffers and struggles throughout. But she is ultimately rewarded for her resilience with the gift of true love – a 'happily ever after'. In awe of her tenacity and 'goodness', the hero eventually succumbs to his feelings and confesses his unwavering devotion by the narrative's conclusion.

Further underscoring the genre's exaltation of virtuousness, another typical but far more sombre Harlequin plot involves a heroine who prematurely succumbs to the hero's sexual advances and who, by the novel's end, dies a penitent and often painful death. In these novels of seduction, the heroine or 'whore' is punished for her acts of transgression and, in death, is reconciled with her own passivity. Samuel Richardson's *Clarissa* (1748) – referenced throughout both the *Fifty Shades of Grey* series and the *Twilight* series – is a notable literary precursor of this plot.

With the emergence of second-wave feminism in the 1960s and 1970s, popular attitudes towards 'romance' began to shift. The genre was commonly regarded with antipathy and dismissed as a seductive trap fetishising women's subordination to men. Feminist critic Germaine Greer was particularly critical of 'romance', famously dubbing the genre "dope for dupes" (1970, 192). Likewise, Shulamith Firestone attempted to reformulate our understandings of 'romance' by figuring it as a kind of false consciousness, a cultural tool of male power making women complicit in their own subjugation (1971, 139). However, two seminal publications sought to complicate a straightforward interpretation of the genre as inherently 'bad' or antifeminist. In *Loving with a Vengeance* (1982), Tania Modleski resisted the dismissal of 'romance' and sought to understand the reasons behind its popularity. By reformulating its patterns through a psychoanalytic framework, she interpreted romance narratives as pleasurable, Freudian revenge fantasies.

In these fantasies, the heroine is neither passive nor masochistic but omnipotent – the centre of the hero's world. This omnipotence, Modleski proposed, precipitated a redistribution of power. The 'tormented' male hero was *disempowered* by his all-consuming obsession with the remarkable heroine and her wonders while the heroine was concurrently *empowered* by the conviction that she could bring the hero to his knees. It is this privileged knowledge of the heroine's influence over the hero that Modleski pinpointed as the defining pleasure which romantic fiction offered to its heterosexual female readers.

Drawing on Modleski's arguments, Janice Radway's *Reading the Romance* (1984) details her textual analysis of a series of Harlequin novels in conjunction with an interview-based study of a group of proudly committed romance readers dubbed the Smithon women. Arguing for their sophistication, Radway dismissed the habitual repudiation of female readers of romance as unintelligent dopes by highlighting how the Smithon women were 'cleverly' able to decode the iconography of romantic cover art and the jargon of back-cover blurbs to determine the most suitable option for their needs. Radway also underscored how these women placed considerable emphasis on the educational benefits of their reading, suggesting that romance novels both bolstered their historical and geographical knowledge and enabled them to model 'reading-behaviours' for their children.

According to Radway, the Smithon women were less concerned with the textual features and narrative details of specific romantic plots. Rather, they consistently stressed how reading was an act of pleasure in and of itself – an act which provided them with a fantasy escape from the dreariness of their everyday realities and the pressures they felt in attempting to maintain their domestic spaces. And so, by enabling the Smithon women to satisfy their own private pleasures, Radway posited that the reading of romance might best be understood as a compensatory act, allowing the female reader to carve out time for herself and to address needs which are otherwise not met by patriarchal institutions and their engendering practices.

Radway's position, however, is ultimately ambivalent. As Gill highlights, Radway is critical of the Harlequin novels, highlighting their tendency to present some of the problems of life in a patriarchal society only to resolve them through an idealised depiction of heterosexual love (199). At the same time, she engages with Modleski's more optimistic psychoanalytic reading of romance by finding a pleasurable interpretation of the genre as a wish fulfilment fantasy. Empowering their readers to live vicariously through the heroine, Radway argues that Harlequin novels allow women to satisfy their innate desire for unconditional love – a desire which, in actuality, is often not met – via the escapist act of reading romance. But this kind of problematic reading rests on the reductive assumption that love and romance *are* the driving forces behind women's desires. More pertinently, while Radway refuses to condemn the romance reader outright, she also resists fully assimilating herself to their position and maintains a critical distance throughout. This critical distance, I believe, creates a gulf between Radway as a 'good' feminist and the Smithon women as 'bad' feminists, suggesting that feminism and the reading of romance are antithetical. By extension, it is implied that adopting feminist principles would deny those women the pleasure of their desires. As we will see, this implication becomes all the more pervasive in the late 1990s to coincide with the emergence of a new era of popular romance novels: 'chick lit'.

Critical responses to the romance genre and its narrative conventions have evidently been varied and complex. While some critics, such as Greer and Firestone, chose to condemn the genre outright, feminist critics such as Modleski and Radway were reluctant to write off this space of feminine pleasure or, at the very least, are committed to understanding its inherent complexities. Nonetheless, with thousands of publications since its conception and millions of subscribers worldwide, Harlequin romances and their mass market appeal draw attention to the continued popularity of cultural texts whose plots are centred on female suffering and patterns of gender-based violence. At the same time, these texts position their readers as voyeurs who, though sympathetic, may take pleasure in female victimisation.

Like those Harlequin romances, my chosen novels have been widely condemned for their gratuitous depictions of gender-based violence. More pertinently, they were accused of encouraging readers to enjoy or even revel in women's suffering. While I certainly recognise that these criticisms have merit, addressing them directly in each chapter, I propose that they are oversimplifications, ignoring the complexity of the texts and the multiple points of disjuncture within them. Still, rather than diminishing in importance, Gill suggests that the popular romance genre has undergone a rapid intensification and gained ever greater significance in the years since Modleski's and Radway's seminal texts (194). 'Romance', she argues, continues to be one of the key narratives through which Western women are interpellated or inscribed as subjects. Confirming its tenacity in the face of social and cultural changes – including high rates of divorce, the growth of new family forms and the rise of liberal feminism – Gill proposes that the saturation of romantic narratives in contemporary popular culture is no coincidence. Rather, this surge could point to a new and developing backlash against feminism as the genre attempts to adapt its themes without having to jettison the formula's innate traditionalism.

Contrary to Gill's hypothesis, Stephanie Harzewski suggests that chick lit draws on but dramatically revises the popular romance formula, updating its narratives to evolve alongside a developing feminist landscape. According to Harzewski, chick lit's attitude towards, and depiction of, female sexuality notably differ from earlier, more conservative iterations of the romance genre. For example, while chick lit narratives are often structured like a prototypical Harlequin romance, culminating in the heroine's romantic union with 'Mr Right', they simultaneously deviate from the traditional formula by dispensing with the genre's "cardinal one woman one man tenet" (2011, 28). Chronicling a succession of Mr Not-Rights, these narratives modernise the Harlequin heroine's quest for true love by 'realistically' depicting contemporary dating practices.

Likewise, Harzewski observes how chick lit is underpinned by a new rhetoric of sexual liberation. Underscoring the genre's purported revision of its sexual politics, she notes how chick lit assimilates graphic descriptions of sex and sexuality into the central romantic plot and persistently emphasises the female protagonists' erotic gratification. By foregrounding a heroine actively in pursuit of sexual pleasure, these narratives starkly contrast the Harlequin romance and its prototypical reticence. In those novels, the heroine was forced to conceal her sexual desire, feigning innocence and modesty to secure 'true love'. Conversely, as Harzewski argues, heterosexual female desire is the driving force of these chick lit plots.

Unlike their Harlequin predecessors, chick lit novels have a distinctly urban setting. Often, they follow a 20- or 30-something, white, middle- or upper-class, British or American, college-educated, heterosexual singleton as she attempts to establish her career and balance the pressures of her professional and social life – all while pursuing love and romance in a 'big city', most commonly London or New York. Deviating once more from the popular romance formula, these 'evolved' chick lit narratives highlight the challenges faced by modern women who are struggling to successfully navigate the twin realms of love and work. And so, plots which centre on the heroine's workplace obstacles, confronted and negotiated throughout, usually run concomitantly with her romantic endeavours as "the quest for self-definition and the balancing of work with social activities are given equal or occasionally greater attention then the central romantic conflict" (Harzewski, 29).

Alison Winch has identified another key difference between chick lit and the classic popular romance narratives. In what she terms the 'womance' or woman-centre romance, Winch observes a subset of chick lit centred not on a heterosexual relationship but on a group of female friends. In these narratives – typified by Candace Bushnell's *Sex and the City* anthology (1997) – the heroine's male love interest is usually marginalised or rendered redundant. Depicting the ups and downs of 'girlfriendships', these narratives focus on the intimate relationships between women, prioritising 'sisterhood' over romance (2013, 90).

By foregrounding sexually liberated, socially active and professional career women, chick lit – and its attendant gender politics – certainly seems remarkably feminist in comparison to its Harlequin predecessor. Yet Rosalind Gill and Elena Herdieckerhoff have challenged this straightforward interpretation of chick lit as fundamentally feminist. Drawing on 20 books published between 1997 and 2005, they queried the purportedly progressive politics of chick lit, arguing that – in contrast to the discourses of girl power which circulate throughout the genre – chick lit subtly reanimates Harlequin stereotypes of passivity and patterns of female suffering for the modern age (2006, 494).

Gill and Herdieckerhoff's scepticism was influenced, in part, by feminist critic Imelda Whelehan, whose research focused on perhaps the most significant figuration of chick lit's new romantic heroines: Bridget Jones. While Helen Fielding's *Bridget Jones's Diary* (1996) is often credited with giving birth to chick lit as a sub-genre, Whelehan attributed its success to its 'that's me' phenomenon, whereby Bridget was interpreted less as a fictional character than as a representative or typical figure for 30-something women in a late-twentieth-century zeitgeist (2002, 12). Taking place over the course of one year, *Bridget Jones's Diary* opens with Bridget's new year's resolutions. Enthusiastic about 'improving' her life, she commits to finding a better job, losing weight, cutting down on her alcohol consumption, developing an 'inner poise' and securing a serious, committed boyfriend.

Bridget's quest for personal and professional success, however, is conflated with the surveillance and regulation of her body. A defining attribute of chick lit novels, this conflation is evident throughout Fielding's novel. For example, in one particularly revealing diary entry,

Bridget underscores the 'unnaturalness' of her feminine identity as something which requires constant work and vigilance to maintain, asserting that

> being a woman is worse than being a farmer; there is so much harvesting and crop spraying to be done: legs to be waxed, underarms shaven, eyebrows plucked, feet pumiced, skin exfoliated and moisturised, spots cleansed, roots dyed, eyelashes tinted, nails filled, cellulite massaged, stomach muscles exercised.
>
> (Fielding, 30)

Habitually measuring and noting her weight, calorie count and alcohol intake, Bridget obsessively enters into a regimental programme of self-monitoring – all in order to achieve the 'success' she so desperately craves. While this punishing behaviour is depicted as freely chosen, evidence of Bridget's empowerment and autonomy, it is not necessarily promoted as aspirational for the reader. Instead, the mocking tone of Fielding's novel implies that Bridget's self-monitoring practices are best interpreted as a humorous satire of modern women. But Whelehan queries the banality of these purportedly satirical representations, condemning them for reproducing and modernising a well-established paradigm of female suffering from the romance genre.

Gill and Herdieckerhoff have also identified another key, recurring feature of chick lit: the heroines' ambivalent relationship with feminism. On the one hand, chick lit heroines usually exhibit some kind of feminist consciousness – be it implicitly or explicitly. Influenced by second-wave feminist rhetoric, they understand the importance of female independence and 'girl power'. On the other hand, there is constant tension in these narratives between those feelings of feminist responsibility, the heroine's obligation to be a 'good' feminist and her understanding of feminism as inhibiting her pursuit of traditional feminine pleasures. This tension is most clearly discernible in *Bridget Jones's Diary* during one of Bridget's many attempts at self-empowerment.

Fed up with the villainous Daniel's 'fuckwittage', his inability to commit to a serious relationship with her, Bridget terminates their romance. Interpreting her actions as a feminist display of self-assurance, she attempts to bolster her 'empowerment' by reading a seminal feminist text: Susan Faludi's *Backlash* (1991). A mere 12 hours later, however, Bridget crumbles and unabashedly admits her misery, confessing that she deeply misses Daniel and feels dissatisfied by the outcome of her 'empowered' act of dismissal. In this context, Fielding's narrative suggests not only that Bridget's feminist feelings of confidence and power are illusory but also that her commitment to feminism is actively impeding her happiness. What Bridget really wants, the narrative implies, are the traditional feminine pleasures found in a monogamous, committed, heterosexual relationship. Thus, Bridget exploits her newfound feminist freedom of choice to re-embrace traditional femininity, superseding feminism in the process.

According to Gill and Herdieckerhoff, repudiating feminism in favour of traditionalism is a perceptible pattern throughout the chick lit genre – most notably in relation to female sexuality. Far from being virginal, most of the heroines of contemporary chick lit are portrayed as sexually experienced and in pursuit of erotic pleasure. They actively pursue their love interests and usually feel comfortable initiating sexual contact with men. Gill and Herdieckerhoff, however, are dubious about the genre's seemingly liberated attitudes toward female sexuality, arguing that it is only within the confines of a monogamous, romantic relationship that the heroine can achieve 'true' sexual gratification (495). And so, by having the heroine *enjoy* sex for the very first time with the hero, confessing the failings of her previous sexual experiences, chick lit presents women's sexual liberation as dissatisfying. This simultaneously promotes 'coupledom' as pleasurable for the reader.

Diane Negra further troubles the genre's progressive veneer, arguing that chick lit's endorsement of traditionalism – often at the expense of feminism – is a calculated strategy that romanticises female subordination for modern readers (2008, 28). In some respects, Negra acknowledges that the female protagonists of chick lit are markedly different from traditional romantic heroines, who are rarely career driven and instead use romantic alliance to attain security, social mobility and power. Whether in low-paid or low-status jobs – such as waitress, shop assistant or housekeeper – or figured as high-flying, business women, chick lit heroines are invariably depicted as employed or at the very least ambitious, committed to the idea of a career. While this portrayal of young women as determined and enterprising appears to subvert conventional notions of femininity synonymous with the romance genre, Negra argues that chick lit ultimately delegitimates these career-focused heroines by presenting them as unhappy or unfulfilled.

In what she terms 'retreatism', Negra observes how the genre's most successful professional women – prototypically depicted as cold, calculated, ambitious and ruthless – often have an epiphany, realising that their lives are deficient without the love of a man. In these narratives, the heroine's devotion to her career is presented as an obstacle to her happiness. Lonely and dissatisfied, she chooses to return to her hometown – symbolising her retreat from the professional sphere. This 'retreat', however, has a catalytic effect, restoring her 'innate' traditional values and remoulding her behaviour to felicitously fit with conventional ideals of femininity. By turning away from the professional sphere and returning home, the chick lit heroine is refigured as emotional, caring, loving and considerate – attributes which are presented as incongruous with the workplace. Thus, as Negra underscores, the achievements of second-wave feminism are taken into account only to be repudiated, dismissed as discordant with women's 'authentic' desires.

As we have seen, chick lit narratives commonly required their heroines to supersede or denounce feminism in pursuit of pleasure. In accordance with postfeminist ideologies, these narratives reconstructed feminism as a vituperative, regulatory rhetoric inhibiting the 'conventional' desires of modern women. By superseding feminism, chick lit heroines could freely enjoy traditional feminine pleasures like marriage and motherhood – pleasures which had apparently been 'outlawed' by feminism. According to Gill, the prevalence and popularity of these narratives in the early 2000s signalled a new era of retro-sexism, characterised by the contradictoriness of its constructions of gender. For example, in the popular media,

> confident expressions of girl power sat troublingly alongside reports of epidemic levels of anorexia and body dysmorphia, while graphic tabloid reports of rape were placed cheek and jowl with adverts for lap dancing clubs and telephone sex lines.
>
> (2007, 11)

In this context, chick lit aimed to smooth the cracks in a complicated political surface by endorsing a neoconservative return to traditionalism.

However, a new space for women's writing emerged in the mid-2000s aiming to expose chick lit's shiny veneer of perfection as both illusory and potentially dangerous. Described by literary critic Paula Rabinowitz as "the romance genre gone awry," domestic noir sought to dismantle the traditionalism ideologically represented throughout chick lit by revealing what lies beneath, highlighting that something sinister is at the heart of neoliberal and postfeminist culture and confronting its readers with that reality (2016).

"Somebody's Trying to Kill Me . . . and I Think It's My Husband"

The term 'domestic noir' was coined in 2013 by novelist Julia Crouch in response to the limitations of the psychological thriller label. Since then, other terms such as 'chick noir', 'domestic thriller' or 'marriage thriller' have also been applied to the fiction. According to Crouch, the genre

> takes place primarily in homes and workplaces . . . is based around relationships and takes as its base a broadly feminist view that the domestic sphere is a challenging and sometimes dangerous prospect for its inhabitants.
>
> (2013)

Written primarily by women and with a mostly female readership, it centralises the female experience and foregrounds themes like family, motherhood, children, marriage, love and sex.

Concerned predominantly with exposing the dark secrets that lie at the heart of ostensibly happy relationships, domestic noir narratives have a clearly recognisable and formulaic pattern: they usually follow a heroine's investigation of her husband, who she suspects wants to kill her, and the subsequent disintegration of their toxic marriage. These narratives invariably trouble hetero-patriarchal relations of power, emphasising the lethal potential of domesticity for their exclusively female protagonists. As such, they closely resemble what Joanna Russ terms the modern gothic novel – a crossbreed of Charlotte Bronte's *Jane Eyre* (1847) and Daphne Du Maurier's *Rebecca* (1938).

According to Russ, the basic plot of the modern gothic can be summarised as follows:

> To a large, lonely and usually brooding house comes a heroine who is young, innocent, shy or inexperienced. She forms a personal or professional connection with an older man, a dark, magnetic, powerful and sardonic super-male, who treats her brusquely, derogates her, scolds her, and otherwise shows anger or contempt for her. The heroine is vehemently attracted to him and usually is just as vehemently repelled or frightened. She is not sure of her feelings for him, his feelings for her, whether he loves her, hates her, is using her or is trying to kill her.
>
> (679–80)

Like domestic noir, these stories typically centre on a young woman's investigation of her potential lover or husband. As she attempts to decode his unusual or dubious behaviour – determining if he truly loves her or is a threat to her – the young woman often exposes an immoral or criminal activity on his part such as fraud, murder or infidelity. Autonomous and agentic, the female protagonists in these novels starkly contrast the archetypically passive Harlequin heroines, actively investigating and unravelling the mysteries at the centre of their narratives. Russ, however, is sceptical about their subversive potential, arguing that once the mystery is solved and all misunderstandings are cleared, the status quo is ultimately restored. The heroines reconcile with their dominant husbands and re-adopt their 'subordinate' roles as doting wives. Thus, as Russ contends, these women conclude their narratives in a position practically indistinguishable from their Harlequin counterparts.

While Modleski acknowledges that the modern gothic is markedly similar to a Harlequin romance, often overlapping in terms of plot and narrative structure, she is inclined to disagree with Russ's thesis. Instead, she suggests that the genre more fully expresses, and provides an outlet for, women's most intimate fears about the claustrophobic nature of their existence (75). According to Modleski, modern gothic narratives offer female readers a fantasy way to resolve any ambivalence towards their significant others, enabling them to confront their anxieties about the unequal distribution of power in heterosexual relationships. And so, for Modleski, these novels can function to connect the personal to the political.

Critics Avril Horner and Sue Zlosnik also recognise the subversive potential of the genre. Looking specifically at du Maurier's *Rebecca*, they argue that modern gothic novels destabilise the narrative expectations of classic romances – thus disrupting traditionally prescribed social roles (1998). Often cited as a key precursor of domestic noir, *Rebecca* continues the gothic tradition of husband-with-a-secret novels. It follows a nameless female narrator's investigation of her furtive new spouse. As the narrator attempts to adjust to married life with him, she becomes increasingly obsessed with his enigmatic former wife and determined to uncover the mystery of her death. Describing *Rebecca* as "an unpleasant and rather grim study in jealousy, with nothing of the exquisite love story her publisher claimed it to be", du Maurier explicitly juxtaposed her novel with traditional romantic fiction (cited in H&Z, 102). Yet, throughout the course of its narrative, the heroine constantly highlights how her expectations about relationships have been informed by 'romance'. She thinks of "all the heroines of fiction who looked pretty when they cried," suggests that her husband's kiss was "not as dramatic as in books" and contrasts the reality of her own relationship with popular romantic narratives where "men knelt to women and it would be moonlight" (du Maurier, 44–57).

The narrator's romantic naivety is celebrated and exalted by her husband, Maxim, who persistently monitors and attempts to regulate his wife's 'curiosity'. These attempts to prolong her innocence, however, can also be interpreted as attempts to maintain the power imbalance between them. By preserving her ignorance, Maxim is able to cloak or camouflage the narrator's subordination in their relationship, denying her an outlet to express her fears, anxieties and discontent. Thus, the narrator's compulsion to investigate her husband – to uncover the truth of the secret he hides from her – coincides with her increasing awareness that those romantic ideologies have sanctioned her subjugation.

With female curiosity as the driving force of its plot, *Rebecca* clearly draws on and evokes a key underpinning narrative of modern gothic texts: *Bluebeard* (1697). In this classic French folktale, a brutish man forbids his new wife from entering his chamber of secrets. Riveted by this mystery, however, the heroine disregards her husband's directive – only to discover the dismembered bodies of his past wives. While this disturbing discovery functions as a cautionary tale for inquisitive women, *Rebecca* highlights the subversive potential of female curiosity. As part of her quest for knowledge, the nameless narrator is forced to reconsider her credulous acceptance of traditional gender roles as promoted by popular romances, questioning if those romances, and their fairytale depictions of heterosexual relationships, naturalise male domination and female subordination. It is this dismantling of the romance genre and its associated ideologies that is most explicitly reanimated in contemporary domestic noir.

Aesthetically and structurally, domestic noir narratives strongly resemble popular romances – specifically chick lit. As Victoria Kennedy observes, its female protagonists are similarly metropolitan, associated with arts and media, and are committed to maintaining their monogamous, romantic relationships (27). Like chick lit, the central and peripheral conflicts in these novels usually concern a heroine's anxiety about one or more of the following: "her body, sex life, 'biological clock', annoying mothers, being alone, money, men and finding love" (Harzewski, 34). However, while chick lit protagonists are often depicted as struggling to self-actualise – both professionally and personally – the heroines of domestic noir have already reached their goals. These women are usually married and financially stable and generally have (or had) fulfilling careers. In this way, domestic noir narratives begin where chick lit plots end, calling into question a modern feminist dilemma: what happens when being everything and 'having it all' isn't enough?

In spite of these superficial similarities, chick lit and domestic noir are notably different in *tone*. While anxieties about contemporary womanhood are played to comedic effect in chick lit, domestic noir novels are often darker, full of desolation and despair. For example, as Kennedy observes, concerns about motherhood permeate the chick lit genre (26). Typified by popular texts like Sophie Kinsella's *Shopaholic and Baby* (2007), its heroines are usually desperate to conceive or worried about the impact of a child on their professional and romantic lives. These concerns, however, are easily allayed, and the desire to procreate is happily satisfied by the narrative's conclusion. Conversely, concerns about maternity are figured as destabilising or debilitating for domestic noir's protagonists. Consumed with worries about their biological clocks, these women are typically plagued with reproductive anxiety, overwhelmed by feelings of guilt and shame in relation to their infertility or childlessness.

Undermining prevalent postfeminist discourses ubiquitous throughout chick lit, domestic noir troubles the idea that gender equality has been achieved and thus that feminism is no longer needed. As we will see, the women in these novels usually find themselves, in spite of their purported freedoms, entrapped within social systems which replicate the problems faced by previous generations of women. Dissatisfied with the inequity in their relationships and enervated by contemporary beauty ideals, these women begin to recognise that their feelings of power, agency and autonomy are illusory – that they are being constrained by those hegemonic gender ideologies.

The genre also calls into question the supposed security of domesticity and its related comforts, examining how marriage and relationships can negatively impact a woman's economic status. In what might be interpreted as a direct response to the 'retreatism' promoted by chick lit – the return to conservative traditionalism – domestic noir novels often highlight the consequences of a career woman's withdrawal from the professional sphere. In these novels, a formerly independent woman, who has left her job to rear her children or maintain her marital home, gradually realises her uncomfortable dependence on an untrustworthy spouse and begins to question the imbalance of power between them. The novels explicitly reference the 2008 economic crash, with characters being made redundant, reiterating anxieties about wealth and class status and thus undermining chick lit's endorsement of coupledom as a site of security and pleasure for women.

Using its settings and characters to create an image of white, Western and middle- or upper-class life, domestic noir is empowered to deconstruct the romance genre's idealised images of domestic bliss. As Kennedy observes, these novels are irrefutably cynical in nature, offering only gruesome solutions to the social, economic and romantic unhappiness they illuminate (28). In contrast to popular romances, which elide the often insidious realities of monogamy and domesticity, these novels create psychological portraits of modern women crumbling under the pressures and expectations of contemporary gender ideologies. In this way, they function as chick lit's nightmarish sequel, re-costuming its tropes to trouble the banality of gendered dynamics of power.

Unable (or unwilling) to conform to hegemonic ideals of femininity, domestic noir's protagonists persistently push against traditionalism and reject their prescribed social roles. Unlike the prototypical heroines of chick lit, they are often depicted as criminals, murderers and even cannibals – contemporary reiterations of the femme fatale. Popularised in hardboiled detective fiction, the femme fatale is a long-standing archetype of the monstrous feminine which emerged during the early twentieth century in response to growing anxieties about women's liberation and the 'New Woman' of the post-war period. Often characterised as an independent woman who controls 'gullible' men with her overt sex appeal, the femme fatale is calculated and cunning, a master of manipulation. But, as Samantha Lindop observes, her inability to capitulate to the expectations of her gender – to be passive, modest and chaste – causes her downfall (2015). Discredited in favour of a more virtuous female rival, an embodiment of idealised femininity, she is ultimately vilified and unable to achieve her ambitions and schemes.

The women of domestic noir invariably manipulate and murder to achieve their goals. But unlike their monstrous literary predecessor, the femme fatale, these women are usually depicted sympathetically. As Kennedy observes, the motives for their crimes are rendered relatable or at least easy for the reader to comprehend: these women are tired of being cheated on, kept financially dependent and having their desires and needs subordinated by men (32). And so, domestic noir narratives encourage their readers to actively root for the women suffering at the centre of these texts, motivating them to identify with those women and their refusal to accept societal injustices. More pertinently, by highlighting the realities of living in a patriarchal society, these novels might facilitate a feminist reclamation of the femme fatale, subverting the archetype to critique hegemonic gender ideologies.

Re-Reading the Romance

If, as McRobbie argues, relations of power are made and remade within "texts of enjoyment" or popular fiction, then the examination of recent evolutions in the romance genre feels all the more crucial (21). Explicating those evolutions, this book highlights how familiar romantic tropes are reanimated, modified and progressively transformed in popular fiction during the postmillennial period. Looking specifically at the *Twilight* series, Chapter 1 highlights how Meyer reanimates and modifies a familiar archetype from the modern gothic romance: the Byronic hero. As we will see, this archetype has been widely critiqued for fetishising and romanticising traditional notions of 'normative' masculinity which naturalise male domination and sexual aggression. Embedded into the structure of feeling, the threat of male violence was certainly palpable in those modern gothic romances. Yet Meyer heightens that threat by transforming the prototypical Byronic hero into a *vampire* – a supernatural 'prince charming' whose sexual desire is inexorably intertwined with a persistent potential for violence.

Meyer re-costumes a predatory monster as a romantic hero, an attractive suitor for a vulnerable teenage girl. In doing so, she bolsters the eroticisation of male violence synonymous with the modern gothic romance. But I propose that her most *hazardous* contribution to the genre is to combine that eroticisation with the neoliberal and postfeminist rhetoric of choice-as-empowerment so pervasive in her fiction. This combination, I argue, not only naturalises violently gendered power dynamics but also risks eroticising subordination as the 'right' *choice* for women and girls.

Nevertheless, the narrative persistently draws attention to the limitations of that rhetoric, highlighting how those ideas individuate the central protagonist, Bella Swan, figuring her as wholly responsible for, because she has freely chosen, whatever befalls her. This individuation obfuscates the structural issues determining her subordination and makes her more susceptible to the violence of men. Silencing her critical voice, that rhetoric also denies Bella an outlet to express her pain and suffering. And so, by explicating those pernicious effects, this chapter raises an important question: are these discourses of personal choice as empowerment and personal responsibility as agency synchronous with neoliberal postfeminism, disguising the reinstatement of oppressive gender roles and entrapping women within a perpetual state of victimhood?

Like *Twilight*, the *Fifty Shades of Grey* series endorses the hegemonic ideal of neoliberal postfeminism as empowering and pleasurable, promoting capitulation to this ideal as the primary pathway to success, happiness and sexual fulfilment for the heroine, Anastasia Steele. It does this, I argue, by exploiting the conventions of the Harlequin romance – thus romanticising that ideal as aspirational. Simultaneously, however, tonal discrepancies in its affective register undermine or even subvert that valorised ideal, alerting the reader to its limitations, oppressiveness and contradictions. As we will see, those discrepancies gesture towards a troubling reality: that these hegemonic ideologies are sanctioning and facilitating gender-based violence.

Thus, Chapter 2 explicates affective dissonances or gaps in James's narrative. Employing a framework influenced by Rachel Greenwald-Smith, I argue for the subversive potential of those gaps as aesthetic forms of resistance to dominant systems of power. By highlighting the recurrent discrepancies between the expectations raised by dominant ideological formations and Anastasia's affective responses to these formations, I attempt to trouble the series' endorsement of neoliberal postfeminism as unambiguously empowering for women.

In addition, this chapter examines some of the *atypical* aspects of affects, arguing that the series' unusual structure – its amalgamation of two seemingly disparate genres – creates a lacuna in the affective register. This lacuna, I propose, has an alienating effect on readers, allowing them to secure enough critical distance from the text to reconsider the banality of the kind of romance it promotes. As will be demonstrated, these affective gaps rupture the narrative's fetishisation of hegemonic gender ideologies. In doing so, they force the reader to think critically about the dynamics of power underpinning contemporary heterosexual relationships.

In Chapter 3, I shift my focus to popular domestic noir novels – *Gone Girl* and *The Girl on the Train*. These novels, I argue, exploit key tropes and archetypes from the romance genre to enact a pointed critique of neoliberal postfeminism. By reanimating the prototypical chick lit heroine for the postmillennial period, Flynn highlights how contemporary gender ideologies encourage women to adopt a masquerade of femininity that supports dominant systems of power, subjugating them through rhetoric of female empowerment. Similarly, Hawkins redeploys a classic trope from the modern gothic romance, the uncanny double or doppelgänger, to emphasise an important connection between the entrenchment of neoliberal postfeminism and ubiquity of gender-based violence in our culture.

Further underscoring the injurious effects of neoliberal postfeminism on women, the novels also subvert another popular archetype of femininity: the female monster. In Flynn's novel, these effects are *pathologising*. Conventionally female monsters in literature incited fear by refusing to be subjugated within the dominant patriarchal system. But what makes Amy Elliot Dunne monstrous is her superhuman dedication to being normatively feminine. As we will see, her desire to satisfy those gendered ideals effectuates her monstrosity and ironically provides her with the optimal tools to enact her plot for revenge. And so, by contextualising Amy's motivations in relation to that desire, the narrative subverts the archetype of the female monster, implying that monstrous behaviour is a coherent response to the stifling constraints of contemporary femininity.

Conversely, Hawkins's protagonist is coded as monstrous because she cannot satisfy those gendered ideals. At a cursory glance, this appears to reproduce popular myths about monstrous femininity, suggesting that women who deviate from the norm must be abjected.

However, the *form* of Hawkins's novel simultaneously troubles that straightforward interpretation. In attempting to conform to the expectations of her gender, thereby obscuring her 'innate' monstrosity, Rachel Watson loses authority over her own narrative voice. As will be demonstrated, this loss is aesthetically expressed; Rachel's narrative is populated with frustrating lacunas, tentative language and disjointed timelines. These aesthetic effects, I argue, formally convey to the reader how contemporary gendered ideologies have disempowered Rachel – thus enabling her ex-husband to manipulate, control and abuse her. As such, the form of the novel reinforces Hawkins's critique of those ideologies as harmful.

The novels also cleverly exploit the conventions of crime fiction, and reader familiarity with those conventions, to augment their critique of neoliberal postfeminism. As we will see, Flynn and Hawkins are actively critical of these conventions, specifically their reification of female victims into caricatures of idealised femininity. Bolstered by neoliberal and postfeminist tenets of individualism, this reification individuates and depoliticises acts of violence against women. However, the novels refuse to simply reproduce those conventions, subverting them to raise a crucial question: is it coincidental that at a time in which women are being increasingly controlled and subjugated by neoliberal and postfeminist ideologies, we are seeing more and more of these narratives about missing or dead girls?

As they gradually recognise how contemporary gender ideologies have deleteriously impacted their lives, Amy Elliot Dunne's and Rachel Watson's anger becomes palpable. However, as will be demonstrated in Chapter 4, neoliberal and postfeminist ideologies have 'safety valves' for mediating and misdirecting that rage, ensuring that critical attention is diverted away from a profoundly corrupt status quo. Both *Sharp Objects* and *Dare Me* foreground adolescent female characters who markedly resemble the protagonists and antagonists of chick lit jr. – a popular subgenre of chick lit marketed towards teenagers. Struggling under the weight of contemporary gender ideals, these girls become increasingly angry and resentful over the course of their narratives but are denied a structural basis for expressing those feelings. And so, their rage is misdirected – turned inwards against the self or outwards towards other women.

Chapter 4 thus explores the consequences of that misdirection. By analysing copious descriptions of female bodies in pain, it highlights how women's rage – when individualised as a personal issue and removed from its socio-political context – can become *embodied*. These visceral descriptions, I argue, reiterate the limitations of neoliberal postfeminism and the kind of empowerment it offers to contemporary Western women. At the same time, the novels highlight how those ideologies have altered the affect of female friendship, corrupting the intimate relationships between women. They do this, I propose, by subverting a familiar archetype of monstrous femininity from chick lit jr. – the mean girl.

These novels reanimate that literary archetype to refute popular myths about adolescent girls and their 'innate' monstrosity, disrupting the idea that girls are inherently competitive with and aggressive towards each other. As we will see, the novels redeploy the 'mean girl' to critique how hegemonic gender ideologies condition women to project their rage onto the bodies of other women. In doing so, they raise an important question: if women are forced to resolve their rage on the bodies of other women, what kind of 'sisterhood' can actually be achieved under neoliberal postfeminism? The novels also refuse to understate the destructive potential of those myths about adolescent femininity, demonstrating how they can make girls more susceptible to the violence of men. As such, this chapter argues that the misdirection of female rage functions as a tool of patriarchy, facilitating the individuation of women's suffering and thus enabling hegemonic structures of power to remain intact and evade critique.

White, middle to upper class, attractive, slim and young, the women at the centre of these texts are mostly homogenous. As the privileged subjects of neoliberal and postfeminist culture, they are assumed to be empowered, agentic and free. And so, they are reassured by popular discourses that they should feel happy, contented and confident – optimistic about their lives and life potential. Like the women of NXIVM and DOS, however, these characters are plagued by feelings of disaffection and subjugation, struggling to reconcile those 'ugly feelings' with that discourse telling them that 'all is well'.

Throughout this book, I explicate and examine these 'ugly feelings', arguing for their subversive potential. As will be demonstrated, these affects not only undermine the 'feelings rules' of neoliberal postfeminism but also challenge the benevolence of those hegemonic gender ideologies by highlighting their deleterious impact on women. Nevertheless, the female protagonists in these novels are forced to individuate, privatise, conceal or repudiate their 'ugly feelings'. Thus, the novels confront readers with a troubling reality: that women are denied an outlet to express their pain and suffering as a condition of their neoliberal postfeminist subjectivity. This book interrogates the consequences of that denial, highlighting how it can sanction and facilitate gender-based violence.

Reference List

Abbott, Megan. *Dare Me*. Picador, 2012.
Bronte, Charlotte. *Jane Eyre*. Smith, Elder & Company, 1847.
Bushnell, Candace. *Sex and the City*. Warner Books, 1997.
Central Statistics Office. "Recorded Crime Detection 2018." 3 Dec. 2019, www.cso.ie/en/releasesandpublications/ep/p-rcd/recordedcrimedetection2018.
Crouch, Julia. "Genre Bender." *Julia Crouch*, 25 Aug. 2013, www.juliacrouch.co.uk/blog/genre-bender.
Du Maurier, Daphne. *Rebecca*. Victor Gollancz, 1938.
Faludi, Susan. *Backlash: The Undeclared War Against American Women*. Crown Publishing Group, 1991.
Fielding, Helen. *Bridget Jones's Diary*. Picador, 1996.
Firestone, Shulamith. *The Dialectic of Sex: The Case for a Feminist Revolution*. William Morrow and Co., 1971.
Flynn, Gillian. *Gone Girl*. Crown Publishing Group, 2012.
Flynn, Gillian. *Sharp Objects*. Orion, 2006.
Gill, Rosalind. *Gender and the Media*. Polity Press, 2007.
Gill, Rosalind and Christina Scharff. *New Femininities: Postfeminism, Neoliberalism and Subjectivity*. Palgrave Macmillan, 2011.
Gill, Rosalind and Elena Herdieckerhoff. "Rewriting the Romance: New Femininities in Chick Lit?" *Feminist Media Studies*, vol. 6, no. 4, 2006, pp. 487–504. doi: 10.1080/14680770600989947.
Gough, Alfred and Miles Millar. *Smallville* (Warner Bros. Television). The WB, 2001–2011.
Greer, Germaine. *The Female Eunuch*. McGraw-Hill, 1970.
Harzewski, Stephanie. *Chick Lit and Postfeminism*. University of Virginia Press, 2011.
Hawkins, Paula. *The Girl on the Train*. Doubleday, 2015.
Horner, Avril and Sue Zlosnik. *Daphne du Maurier: Writing, Identity and the Gothic Imagination*. Palgrave Macmillan, 1998.
James, E.L. *Fifty Shades Darker*. Vintage Books, 2012.
James, E.L. *Fifty Shades Freed*. Vintage Books, 2012.
James, E.L. *Fifty Shades of Grey*. Vintage Books, 2011.
Kennedy, Victoria. "Chick Noir: Shopaholic Meets Double Indemnity." *American, British and Canadian Studies*, vol. 28, no. 1, 2017, pp. 19–38. doi: 10.1515/abcsj-2017-0002
Kinsella, Sophie. *Shopaholic and Baby*. Bantam Books, 2007.

Lindop, Samantha. *Postfeminism and the Fatale Figure in Neo-Noir Cinema*. Palgrave Macmillan, 2015.
McRobbie, Angela. *The Aftermath of Feminism: Gender, Culture and Social Change*. Sage Publications, 2008.
Meyer, Stephenie. *Breaking Dawn*. Atom, 2008.
Meyer, Stephenie. *Eclipse*. Atom, 2007.
Meyer, Stephenie. *New Moon*. Little, Brown Company, 2006.
Meyer, Stephenie. *Twilight*. Atom, 2005.
Modleski, Tania. *Loving With a Vengeance: Mass Produced Fantasies for Women*. The Shoe String Press, 1982.
Negra, Diana. *What a Girl Wants? Fantasising the Reclamation of Self in Postfeminism*. Routledge, 2008.
Noujaim, Jehane and Karim Amer. *The Vow* (HBO Documentary Films). HBO, 2020.
Perrault, Charles. *Bluebeard*. Barbin, 1697.
Rabinowitz, Paula. "Tupperware and Terror: The Rise of Chick Noir." *The Chronicle of Higher Education*, 3 Jan. 2016, www.chronicle.com/article/tupperware-and-terror.
Radway, Janice. *Reading the Romance: Women, Patriarchy and Popular Literature*. University of North Carolina Press, 1984.
Richardson, Samuel. *Clarissa: Or, The History of a Young Lady*. 1748.
Russ, Joanna. "Somebody's Trying to Kill Me and I Think It's My Husband: The Modern Gothic." *The Journal of Popular Culture*, vol. 6, no. 4, 1973, pp. 666–691. doi: 10.1111/j.0022-3840.1973.00666.x.
"The Criminal Justice System." *RAINN*, 4 Feb. 2021, www.rainn.org/statistics/criminal-justice-system.
"Violence against Women." *World Health Organisation*, 9 Mar. 2021, www.who.int/news-room/fact-sheets/detail/violence-against-women.
Whelehan, Imelda. *Helen Fielding's Bridget Jones's Diary*. Continuum, 2002.
Winch, Alison. *Girlfriends and Postfeminist Sisterhood*. Palgrave Macmillan, 2013.

1 The *Twilight* of Postfeminism

What Choice Have I?

In 'Vampires Suck! Twihards Rule!!! Myth and Meaning in the *Twilight* Saga', Carol Donelan suggests that if one were to mention Stephenie Meyer's *Twilight* series to almost anyone other than its 'diehard fanbase', the reaction would be invariably negative. While the saga's four novels – *Twilight* (2005), *New Moon* (2006), *Eclipse* (2007) and *Breaking Dawn* (2008) – were worldwide bestsellers, the franchise has been widely disparaged. Scholars have been critical of the problematic and objectionable politics of gender, sexuality and class embedded in the narratives. Meanwhile, escalating numbers of *Twilight* anti-fans – commonly known as 'twitters' – have inspired the production of a series of spoof films, including *Vampires Suck* (Jason Friedberg and Aaron Seltzer, 2010) and *Breaking Wind* (Craig Moss, 2012).

Nevertheless, the saga was enormously popular, and its influence is impossible to ignore. Including its five film adaptations – *Twilight* (Catherine Hardwicke, 2008), *New Moon* (Chris Weitz, 2009), *Eclipse* (David Slade, 2010), *Breaking Dawn, Part 1* (Bill Condon, 2011) and *Breaking Dawn, Part 2* (Bill Condon, 2012) – current figures suggest a gross profit of 4.9 billion dollars worldwide. The novels have been translated into 50 languages, spent 302 weeks on the *New York Times* bestsellers lists and encouraged the proliferation of copious fan fiction websites including twilightmoms.com and twilightfanfiction.net. The saga's popularity also managed to transcend its targeted demographic of teenage girls. As Sara K. Day notes, particularly avid adult fans of Meyer's vampire hero can even procure a "*Twilight*-inspired sex toy that sparkles in the sun and can be placed in the freezer for a more authentic experience" (28).

While the mainstream press berated the reactions of girls and women to the *Twilight* series – dismissing its popularity as nothing more than a consequence of 'feminine hysteria' – Melissa A. Click, Jennifer Stevens-Aubrey and Elizabeth Behm-Morawitz sought a 'diagnosis' of this phenomenon. Working specifically from a feminist perspective, their research tried to understand why American women of all ages and classes – themselves included – were so deeply affected by a story about the romance between a mortal teenage girl and a sparkly vampire. More pertinently, Click, Stevens-Aubrey and Behm-Morawitz queried why a narrative espousing conservative and regressive gender norms – especially about female sexuality – had become so popular when women and girls in the Western world were experiencing more freedom and agency than ever before (2010).

One reason they postulated for the series' popularity was the ease with which readers could identify with its central female character. Bella Swan, the novel's primary narrator, is a reassuringly familiar figure. She mirrors the passive, plain and socially awkward teenage girls and women of the classic novels of development. Following a quintessential bildungsroman story-arc, the series details Bella's attempts to navigate her burgeoning sexuality and her love for the vampire, Edward Cullen. While she endeavours to negotiate the terms of the supernatural world, ultimately choosing to forsake her future as an adult subject and her human identity, Bella's voice remains credibly authentic. Her self-deprecating tone and low self-esteem prototypically depict the discomfort of developing adolescence.

According to Click, Stevens-Aubrey and Behm-Morawitz, Bella is written as an 'every girl' or shadow character with the novel's sparing descriptions of her facilitating and encouraging reader identification. Through Bella, they argue, the reader is able to "experience the painful vicissitudes of adolescence all over again" (14). For Meyer, Bella's lack of interiority was a calculated decision. She purposely withheld a detailed description of her protagonist so that the "reader could more easily get into her shoes" (Meyer, 2010). Meyer's use of first-person narration further enables the reader to occupy Bella's subject position, effortlessly inserting themselves into the text.

Yet scholars and fans alike have been universally critical of the saga's female protagonist: she has been denounced as a retro-sexist reanimation of the classic romantic heroine. Bella spends most of her narrative obsessing over her hero's enigmatic behaviour. Consequentially, as feminist critic Anne Helen Peterson emphasises, she has "few distinct traits, talents or interests to sustain or define her apart from her all-consuming devotion to a man" (54). Peterson also highlights her discomfort at the way in which Meyer's protagonist resolves her anxieties through marriage and motherhood, underscoring how it is only in and through companionship and subordination to a male partner that Bella's self-worth is fully realised.

Bella's lack of self-confidence has been repeatedly highlighted by critics as one of the *most* problematic aspects of the *Twilight* saga. Cautioning against identification with Meyer's protagonist, Anthea Taylor argues that Bella's willingness to sacrifice everything, including her life, to be with her lover endorses a disturbingly masochistic position for the series's predominantly female readers. Masochism is certainly operative throughout the saga, and it manifests in a multitude of ways:

> In the physical dangers and eroticised pain characterising Bella's relationship with Edward; in her acquiescence to his protectionism; in the way her identity comes to be defined solely though her interactions with him; and in her desire for death to literalise the idea that they will be together forever.
>
> (Taylor, 33)

Yet, according to Taylor, the potentially negative consequences of Bella's masochism should not be understated: it risks normalising and rationalising the patriarchal control of women by men for its susceptible adolescent fanbase.

While much has been made of the fact that Bella actively *chooses* to partake in an unequal and at times abusive relationship with Edward, critics questioned why a masochistic position, and an 'undead' subjectivity, could be utopian sites of possibility for a teenage heroine in the early twenty-first century. Given the general assumption that the position of women and girls in contemporary society has radically improved, how are we to understand the choices Meyer wrote for Bella as anything other than regressive? Moreover, why did this seemingly retro-sexist narrative become so popular, particularly amongst women?

In light of this condemnation of the narrative's conservative and traditionalist undertones, Meyer tackled the criticism of her heroine head-on. Reproducing a postfeminist rhetoric of freedom of choice with respect to work, domesticity and parenting, she explained on her website that the life choices she wrote for Bella do not render her antifeminist. Rather, "feminism is about being able to choose" (Meyer, 2010). These comments, and the *Twilight* phenomenon more broadly, illuminate crucial tensions within feminism in the early millennial period. Critical responses to the texts were polarised and characterised by a potent ambivalence. While feminist media critics struggled with the 'dirty pleasure' of loving *Twilight*, they concurrently recognised that the narratives were in many ways culturally regressive and anti-feminist and affirmed patriarchal values. As Peterson summarises, the fact that readers were indirectly encouraged to "pine after men, cook for their dads, marry and have babies out of high school and to 'just say no' before the wedding ring is on their finger" simply could not be ignored (61).

By amalgamating these two seemingly disparate ideologies – feminism with conservative traditionalism – Meyer's saga is one of the most striking manifestations of neoliberal and postfeminist culture in recent years. Throughout her narrative, Meyer fetishises and romanticises neoliberal and postfeminist ideals of subjectivity as empowering and pleasurable for the reader. She does this by reanimating key tropes and archetypes from the modern gothic romance. However, as we will see in this chapter, the narrative simultaneously highlights the limitations of these ideologies – particularly the rhetoric of choice as a marker of female empowerment. By repeatedly underscoring how sacrifice and suffering are necessary prerequisites of Bella achieving her desires, the narrative troubles any straightforward interpretation of Meyer's protagonist as unambiguously empowered. On the contrary, we will see that this rhetoric of choice-as-empowerment entraps Bella within a perpetual state of victimhood. That rhetoric obfuscates the structural issues determining her subordination, ensuring that she remains silent and withholds her critique of patriarchal hegemony. Thus, in attempting to understand why this seemingly regressive series has resonated with so many women, this chapter will highlight key moments in the text which rupture the narrative's endorsement of neoliberal postfeminism.

What a Girl Really Wants (but Is Ashamed to Admit)?

From the outset, Meyer's narrative engages with the inherent contradictions of navigating one's femininity in a climate of neoliberal postfeminist logic. Best articulated through the anxiety she experiences at the prospect of her early engagement and teenage marriage to Edward, Bella's aversion to marriage is clear: she consistently refuses Edward's persistent proposals and struggles to reconcile him with her image of 'husbands' as typically dull or commonplace men. Figuring marriage as a dated residue, Bella is embarrassed at the prospect of narcissistically engaging with the spectacle of a traditional white wedding. She cringes at the very thought of wearing an extravagant bridal gown and chooses to abdicate all ostentatious wedding planning responsibilities to her soon-to-be sister-in-law Alice.

In stark contrast to Edward's deep matrimonial desires, Bella has been taught by her feminist mother to strive for personal achievement and independence before marriage. Hypercritical of young women who choose to marry before establishing their careers – a choice which she describes as worse than "boiling live puppies" – Renee persistently stresses to Bella the importance of education, emphasising that intelligent and mature women attended college before settling into any long-term relationships (*Breaking Dawn*, 7). And so, influenced by her mother, Bella's ideas about marriage neatly align with second-wave feminist rhetoric. Throughout the course of the narrative, she demonstrates an awareness that, historically, marriage has been synchronous with the abdication of female ambition and understands that it should not be a woman's sole purpose in life. Bella also contextualises her reluctance to marry Edward in relation to this sense of feminist responsibility, admitting that she is hesitant to repeat the same "cornucopia of life-altering mistakes" as previous generations of women who had prioritised heterosexual romance and domesticity over their careers – a generation of women for whom she suggests that marriage signalled "the ultimate doom" (*Breaking Dawn*, 6).

Despite this awareness of how she 'should' behave, what Bella fears most is not settling down too young or reneging her college experiences but rather the judgement of her peers, family and friends. In anxious anticipation of the gossip that will *inevitably* surround her 'foolish' early marriage, Bella asserts:

> I'm not that girl, Edward. The one who gets married right out of school like some small town hick who got knocked up by her boyfriend . . . do you know what people would think? Do you know what century this is? People don't just get married at 18 . . . not smart people, not responsible, mature people. . . . I'm sure this sounds like some big joke to you, but really . . . it's just so . . . so . . . so . . . embarrassing.
>
> (*Eclipse*, 244)

For Bella, it is the fear of societal judgement which acts as a suppressant of her desires. She grimaces at the thought of her mother's horrified expression at the news of her impending nuptials and imagines that it would be easier to inform her friends of her decision to 'die' and become a vampire than to become Edward's wife. Entangled in a discourse of shame, Bella's discomfort is revealing: it figures the feminist incitement towards independent achievement as a burden which weighs heavily on her.

Similarly, the narrative persistently undermines Bella's outward expressions of distaste for all things 'superficially feminine' by insisting that she paradoxically yet subconsciously desires these traditional structures. For example, while Bella is initially overcome with rage when Edward tricks her into attending her high school prom, she is later surprised by her pleasurable response to the event, reluctantly acknowledging that dressing up in a glamorous gown and dancing with Edward has somehow made her happy.

Likewise, Bella's initial trepidation about wearing an engagement ring is dismissed as illogical:

> "I suppose you don't want your ring now?" I had to swallow before I could speak. "You suppose correctly." "Do you want to see it?" he asked . . . "No!" I almost shouted, a reflex reaction . . . I gritted my teeth together to keep my illogical terror from showing. . . . Nestled into the black satin, Elizabeth Masen's ring sparkled in the dim light. The face was a long oval, set with slanting rows of glittering round stones. The band was gold – delicate and narrow. The gold made a fragile web around the diamonds. I'd never seen anything like it. "It's beautiful." I shrugged, feigning a lack of interest. . . . He held my hand out, and we both examined the oval sparkling against my skin. It wasn't quite as awful as I'd feared, having it there.
>
> (*Eclipse*, 456–8)

While Edward is evidently eager for his fiancé to wear her ring, Bella is clearly reluctant. She is terrified at the prospect and consistently pushes against Edward's wishes. But once Bella has seen the ring, she is instantly enamoured by it. As highlighted by her comprehensive description of the ring's aesthetic, and her glowing assessment of its beauty, she is overcome with feelings of pleasure. Nevertheless, the fact that Bella feels compelled to *perform* a kind of indifference to the ring – to conceal her pleasurable reaction to it – implies that her feelings of feminist responsibility to reject all markers of 'feminine superficiality' are impeding her capacity for self-gratification.

This suggestion that Bella subconsciously desires traditional structures is reinforced by her shifting perspectives on marriage. Though she had been initially reluctant to marry Edward, she practically *sprints* down the aisle with eagerness on her wedding day:

> All I really saw was Edward's face; it filled my vision and overwhelmed my mind. . . . Suddenly it was only the pressure of Charlie's hand on mine that kept me from sprinting head-long down the aisle. . . . In that moment, as the minister said his part, my world, which had been upside down for so long now, seemed to settle into its proper position. I saw just how silly I'd been for fearing this. . . . I looked into Edward's shining, triumphant eyes and knew that I was winning too. . . . I didn't realise I was crying until it was time to say the binding words.
>
> (*Breaking Dawn*, 18–19)

Cementing the narrative's endorsement of a return to traditional gender roles, Bella confesses that her feelings of instability have ultimately been resolved through heterosexual union. As Edward's wife, she believes she has *finally* found her rightful position in the world. Bella's attestation of her absolute certainty that she has made the right decision by marrying Edward – in conjunction with her confession that she had been ridiculous to delay her nuptials – also emphasises her feelings of pleasure. Yet, by stressing how she has achieved this satisfaction through matrimony, Bella's feminist sensibilities are once more framed as an impediment to her self-optimisation, figured as an obstacle which she needed to overcome in order to achieve true happiness.

Although marriage as a legal, cultural and political institution has been taken apart, critiqued and modernised by first- and second-wave feminism, Rosalind Gill notes how weddings have become considerably more magnificent and increasingly ubiquitous in postfeminist popular culture (2007, 218). North America and Europe have become saturated with wedding imagery in films, sitcoms and news about celebrity marriages, while an entire section of the magazine industry is now devoted to bridal wear and wedding etiquette. Gill also highlights how other prevalent markets, like the toy market, are contributing to this cultural preoccupation with marriage. She cites Barbie's possession of "no fewer than thirty wedding dresses" as one particularly potent example of how matrimonial desires are being inculcated into the minds of millions of little girls from an alarmingly young age (219). For Gill, this inundation of wedding-centric content points to a troubling reality: while postfeminist discourses maintain that the aims of second-wave feminism have been achieved, conservative social ideologies, figuring marriage as a necessity for women, are being concurrently and pleasurably renewed.

Continually expressing her antipathy towards the grotesque grandeur of the wedding ceremony Alice has designed for her, Bella identifies bridal pageantry as oppressive and restrictive. She is reluctantly dragged from her bedroom for an intensive bridal makeover and subsequently resists looking at herself in the mirror out of fear that the image of herself in a wedding dress will provoke a panic attack. Yet, in spite of her protagonist's revulsion, Meyer lingers interminably on the details of Bella's big day. Excessively recounted across more than 15 pages, the Cullen household is wholly transformed in preparation for her wedding ceremony. It is filled with hundreds of thousands of twinkle lights, 10,000 flowers and white gossamer ribbons and is infused with the scent of orange blossoms and lilacs. Although Bella outwardly rejects this bridal pageantry, interpreting it as unreasonably excessive, Meyer's inclusion of these intricate descriptions allows the reader to unashamedly take pleasure in these markers of feminine superficiality. In doing so, the narrative implies that in spite of the progress of feminism, what the – presumptively or indicatively – female readers of the series really want is permission to succumb to traditional feminine pleasures.

According to Angela McRobbie, what is distinctive about postfeminist culture is that feminism is taken into account only to be repudiated – rejected as a kind of false consciousness which does not accurately represent women's authentic desires (2008, 12). In line with McRobbie's postulation, Bella recognises that her social world has been fundamentally altered by feminism. And so she feels a sense of obligation to be a 'good' feminist, initially refusing to adopt any gendered role that might be interpreted as regressive or retro-sexist. At the same time, however, the narrative persistently reminds the reader that those feelings of feminist responsibility are actually impeding her pursuit of self-gratification and pleasure. In other words, feminism is figured as a historical structure which is no longer relevant and which must be superseded in order for Bella to get what she wants.

While this depiction of Bella appears to promote and perpetuate a decidedly postfeminist rhetoric, the narrative simultaneously draws attention to the problematic nature of postfeminism. By reformulating feminism as an oppressive 'common sense' – and frequently reinforcing this point – the novels force us to consider what, if anything, distinguishes postfeminism from antifeminism? Where is the actual line between these purportedly opposed ideologies? The characterisation of Bella's 'frenemy' Jessica, the saga's reanimation of the classic romantic female foil, illustrates clearly the ambivalent relationship between those two positions. Gregarious, selfish and vain, Jessica is immediately rendered unlikeable for the reader. She is also figured as less 'desirable' than Bella by the male characters in the series: Edward has taken no notice of her, while her love interest, Mike, consistently expresses a clear preference for Bella. Repeatedly emphasising her lack of success with men, the narratives juxtapose Jessica's flirtatious enthusiasm with Bella's self-effacing 'humility'. But while Bella's self-degradations are coded as desirable in the texts – attracting the often unwanted attention of multiple suitors including Mike, Tyler, Eric and Jacob – Jessica's confidence is rendered unattractive, a direct threat to her chances of 'true love'.

The narrative's dichotomisation of Jessica and Bella clearly valorises passivity and modesty as cardinal traits of successful femininity. In line with postfeminist ideologies, it exalts culturally prescribed modes of femininity for modern women. Yet by implying that Jessica's lack of success in romantic relationships can be accredited to her feminist self-confidence, along with her unfettered autonomy, the narrative blurs the lines between postfeminist and antifeminist rhetorics. Through its juxtaposition of Jessica and Bella, the narrative does not simply 'take feminism into account' but launches an overt attack on female empowerment. It tells readers that they must modulate expressions of their feminist self-confidence in order to 'secure' a man. Thus, in spite of its distinctly postfeminist appearance, the narrative's dichotomisation of these girls demonstrates the ease with which postfeminist discourses can be co-opted for antifeminist ends. As the narrative illustrates, these discourses can be actively antagonistic towards feminism to the point that postfeminist and antifeminist rhetorics become practically indistinguishable.

The novels' depiction of female sexuality further highlights how an antifeminist agenda has been sublimated into postfeminism and subsequently repackaged as female empowerment. Although Bella's recalcitrant sexual urges are underscored throughout, the saga presents as a bizarre allegory for chastity. It celebrates yet simultaneously discourages the adolescent exploration of erotic love. Infamously labelled by critics as 'abstinence porn', the series' lengthy postponement of Bella's sexual gratification is notable: it takes 250 pages of brooding tension before Bella is given permission to have her first kiss and a further 1,500 pages before she is empowered to lose her virginity.

While this decision to have Bella save sex for marriage appears to affirm Meyer's 'abstinence-only' message, her narratives are highly eroticised and brimming with desire and longing. Refusing to shy away from detailing her protagonist's commitment to the pursuit of pleasure, the saga is populated with 'comprehensive' descriptions of Bella's burgeoning sexual urges. In particular, Meyer focuses on Bella's struggle to control herself around Edward. Overwhelmed by the "unexpected electricity" between them, she consistently fights to resist the maddening temptation to reach out and touch him at every opportunity or to attempt to initiate a forbidden kiss (*Twilight*, 230). These palpable sexual impulses become so potent that they infiltrate Bella's dreamscape. Unable to sleep, she begins to toss and turn restlessly at night as a result of her heightened sexual frustration.

Upending traditional paradigms of active-male/passive-female sexuality, it is notably Bella – and not Edward – who aggressively pursues sexual fulfilment throughout the series. While Bella is eager to experience sexual pleasure, Edward is committed to saving himself for marriage. The lovers frequently clash over these opposing views, which figure as a key obstacle to the success of their relationship. In a reversal of the generic conventions of the gothic romance, Bella persistently attempts to persuade Edward to consummate their love. Acknowledging that traditionally their roles would be reversed, she confesses that those attempts make her feel like "a villain in a melodrama . . . trying to steal some poor girl's virtue" (*Eclipse*, 443). Nevertheless, Bella's pursuit of pleasure is unwavering, and she has no difficultly in articulating her sexual desires. She repeatedly and confidently asserts that she wants nothing more than to lose her virginity to Edward – more than food or water or oxygen. In this way, Meyer's narrative situates Bella firmly within the postfeminist era as a sexually liberated girl who is determined to experience pleasure on her own terms.

Yet, as McRobbie notes, postfeminism's celebrated freedoms, including sexual liberation, often come at a price: they are usually predicated on the reinstatement of vengeful patriarchal norms (55). And so, while Bella remains committed to her pursuit of pleasure, it is only by occupying a subject position of a wife that she can fully satisfy her sexual urges. From this perspective, the narrative figures her capitulation to a traditional gender role as her primary pathway to sexual empowerment.

More pertinently, Meyer's distinctly erotic language fetishises this capitulation for the reader:

> I took another step through the waves and leaned my head against his chest. "Don't be afraid," I murmured. "We belong together." I was abruptly overwhelmed by the truth of my own words. This moment was so perfect, so right, there was no way to doubt it. His arms wrapped around me, holding me against him, summer and winter. It felt like every nerve ending in my body was a live wire. "Forever," he agreed, and then pulled us gently into deeper water . . .
>
> (*Breaking Dawn*, 33)

Though the event itself is actually elided from the text, the description of the prelude to Bella's first sexual experience underscores how her sexual gratification has been heightened by her role as Edward's wife. By highlighting how 'perfect' this moment is between them, and emphasising Bella's feeling of certainty about it, the narrative implies that Bella has been justified in choosing to postpone her sexual gratification. Re-deploying the recurring motif of electricity, Meyer's descriptions of Bella's physical responses during this moment – her pleasurable bodily sensations – further stress her satisfaction. These 'titillating' descriptions, I propose, eroticise matrimony for the series' readers, promoting conservative traditionalism as a site of possibility and pleasure.

Meyer's erotically charged style is decidedly postfeminist since it encourages and celebrates Bella as an active sexual agent. But as we have seen, an anti-feminist agenda is often concealed within this rhetoric and repackaged as female empowerment. Therefore, the question must be asked: if Bella is forced to negotiate the terms of her own pleasure within the limitations of a patriarchal hegemony – if she can only satisfy her desire as someone's wife – how are we to distinguish between postfeminist and antifeminist ideologies? Still, by demonstrating how these rhetorics are often indistinguishable from one another, I propose that Meyer's narrative opens up a space for us to think critically about postfeminism and its inherent limitations, confronting the reader with the possibility that postfeminism is essentially antifeminism in an even more pernicious guise.

Prince-Like Vampires and Paranormal Romances

The series' promotion of conservative traditionalism and retro-sexist gender roles, in line with postfeminist ideologies, is facilitated by reanimating and modifying some recognisable tropes of the romance genre. The saga's plot, for example, follows the narrative structure Janice Radway identified in *Reading the Romance* (1984). Meyer has also been accused of 'textual vampirism' because of her repeated allusions to classic romance narratives such as *Romeo and Juliet* (1597), *Pride and Prejudice* (1813) and *Wuthering Heights* (1847). Critics have argued that her saga is sustained by, yet simultaneously gives new life to, canonical love stories. Yet in its blending of romance with the supernatural, I propose that the series is best understood as a seminal example of a sub-genre of the contemporary gothic romance – the 'dark fantasy' or 'paranormal romance' – specifically aimed at a young adult readership.

Characteristically, the paranormal romance domesticates supernatural creatures, mainly vampires and werewolves, and re-signifies the classic monster figure as an ideal lover for an adolescent girl. In spite of its apparent novelty, however, Joseph Crawford argues that the genre has a long-standing literary history, fusing elements from eighteenth-century gothic romances with the classic Austenian courtship novel (2014). Notable for her generic innovations, Ann Radcliffe's novels recast the archetypical gothic hero as a fearful, sentimental heroine desperately attempting to escape the clutches of a brutal, abusive and predatory villain. Credited with creating the gothic romance, Radcliffe's narratives often followed this female protagonist's fraught journey towards marriage. Similarly, Austen modified the late eighteenth-century courtship novel by transforming it into a novel of mutual education. Rather than having a female protagonist who had to distinguish between the right and wrong choice of partner, her novels told stories of lovers who educated and reshaped each other.

According to Crawford, the modern gothic romance ultimately derived from the combination of these two models. In the process, the prototypical gothic villain was reframed as a troubled, 'Byronic' hero whom the heroine had to redeem. Like the villains and demons of classic gothic fiction, the gothic romance hero is often depicted as a cruel and mercurial man with an active disregard for the laws of society. He is dangerous, violent and governed only by his idiosyncratic moral code. But in contrast to his more nefarious literary predecessors, the Byronic hero is usually portrayed as remorseful. Eternally at odds with his own Machiavellian nature, he is motivated specifically by his desire to redeem himself in the eyes of his beloved heroine.

For Crawford, the commercial success of Charlotte Bronte's *Jane Eyre* (1847) marked the point at which this hero, ubiquitous in gothic fiction, became a staple of the gothic romance. As a wealthy, powerful and temperamental man who often abuses and denigrates those around him, Rochester typifies the gothic romance hero. When he falls in love with an impoverished, strong-willed and unconventional young woman, Rochester's hostility is placated. Through the strength of Jane's love and her unyielding devotion, he is 'redeemed' – transformed into a more agreeable man. Thus, as Crawford observes, Bronte's novel popularised and solidified the 'redemption narrative' as a defining attribute of the modern gothic romance.

While elements of the supernatural are certainly present in Bronte's formative novel, it wasn't until the late 1970s that authors of vampire fiction sought to transform their monsters into redeemable romantic heroes. Archetypically, the vampire was figured as an elusive and solitary predator; a hideous, human-like loner who existed on the parameters of society. Often depicted as a monstrous relic of the past – as in F.W. Murnau's *Nosferatu* (1922), Carl Dreyer's avant-garde *Vampyr* (1932) and Bram Stoker's *Dracula* (1897) – this prototypical vampire was a menacing creature who threatened the stability of the dominant social order. Harmony could only be restored in these traditional vampire narratives once this creature, and the threat it symbolised, had been vanquished.

Anne Rice's *Interview with the Vampire* (1976) is widely conceived to be the benchmark for turning this vampire paradigm on its head. Bringing the figure of the sympathetic, conflicted vampire anti-hero to a mass audience for the first time, her novels disrupted the conventions of classic vampire literature. In contrast to the archetypical vampire, often depicted as a grotesque creature with decaying flesh and talon nails, Rice's vampires were notably beautiful and highly eroticised. Still, they were hardly traditional romance material. Though they were rich and powerful, as romantic heroes usually are, they were also disturbingly violent and amoral.

According to Crawford, it was Lori Herter's David de Morrissey series – *Obsession* (1991), *Confession* (1992), *Possession* (1992) and *Eternity* (1993) – which crystallised the transformation of Rice's new vampire anti-hero into a 'romance-hero-plus'. Endowed with supernatural powers, Herter's protagonist amplified the qualities of the traditional romantic hero because he was more experienced and stronger than any mortal man. De Morrissey also had no particular disposition towards violence. Instead, he was concerned predominantly with securing and maintaining a fulfilling romantic relationship.

Reshaping the vampire into a romantic hero, transformed through the redemptive power of love, Herter's innovations were unquestionably influential. Thereafter, vampires began to undergo a significant shift in representation. For instance, the eponymous protagonist of Stoker's *Dracula*, commonly recognised as the *most* influential of all vampire narratives, was transformed into a demon lover. While canonically Dracula was motivated predominantly by his hunger for power and blood, revisionist versions of this classic narrative, including Francis Ford Coppola's *Bram Stoker's Dracula* (1992), foregrounded an anti-hero who was consumed by his romantic obsession with a woman that reminded him of his long-lost love.

By the late 1990s, as Colette Murphy notes, these vampiric paramours were no longer merely the subjects of horror stories and cult classics but had become the new standard for perfect romance (2011). Indeed, television series such as Joss Whedon's *Buffy the Vampire Slayer* (1997–2003) and its associated spinoff series *Angel* (1999–2004) solidified the re-costuming of the vampire into a quintessential romantic hero. Angel, Buffy's sporadic vampire lover, was depicted as a "modern-day Prince charming with an immortal twist" (Murphy, 57). Broody and romantic, he consistently prioritised helping Buffy and her gang of "Scoobies" to maintain the social order in Sunnydale – often at his own expense.

While the overwhelming popularity of *Buffy* inspired a significant number of 'copies' – including Richelle Mead's popular young-adult novel *Vampire Academy* (2007) and CW's *The Vampire Diaries* (2009–17) – it notably differed from earlier iterations of the paranormal romance: it foregrounded an active and agentic female protagonist who disrupted the genre's typically traditional gendered power dynamics. In Buffy, viewers were offered a female protagonist that policed those who preyed upon the feminised. As 'the chosen one', a vampire slayer, she signified strength, resilience and confidence. Buffy's agency was also notably the driving force of the narrative, ultimately enabling her to save the world.

However, A. Susan Owen highlights how Whedon's series simultaneously reified heteronormative gender roles and fetishised traditional markers of feminine beauty. Buffy is recognisably coded as slim, youthful, blonde and beautiful. In other words, she is presented as 'normatively' attractive and aspirational for her predominantly female audience. Additionally, in spite of her agency, Buffy is often reliant on assistance from Angel – a paternal protector figure epitomising traditional ideals of masculinity. By continually eroticising and fetishising Buffy's 'saviour' as the embodiment of perfected masculine appeal, Owen maintains that *Buffy* ultimately reaffirmed heteronormative scripts.

In its unusual blend of themes of female empowerment with a paradoxical reinstatement of traditional gender roles, *Buffy* – and the paranormal romance genre more generally – might best be understood as a product of a postfeminist culture. They certainly exemplify the inherent contradictions of postfeminist ideologies. On the one hand, these paranormal romances seem to celebrate 'girl-power' and have produced a considerable number of strong female characters including Buffy Summers, Elena Gilbert and Rose Hathaway. On the other hand, they continue a long-standing pattern, ubiquitous throughout the gothic romance genre, of fetishising and romanticising retro-sexist gender norms, which concurrently undermines their promotion of female empowerment.

More pertinently, this re-inscription of traditional gender roles continues to influence how gendered violence is depicted in the genre. The threat of male violence was embedded in the structure of feeling in the classic gothic romances. However, this threat is explicitly expressed and intrinsic to the character of these new romantic vampires. Their sexual desire for the vulnerable heroine is also, inescapably, a desire to kill her and drink her blood. And so, by centring their narratives on these vampire suitors whose sexual desire is inexorably intertwined with a persistent potential for violence, the paranormal romance genre perpetuates traditional notions of 'normative' masculinity, which naturalise male domination and sexual aggression.

The genre's articulation of violence with desirable masculinity is not a particularly unique phenomenon. Rather, we are repeatedly confronted, via the media as well as other cultural systems, with narratives in which boys and men struggle to contain their nature, their purported predisposition towards violence. But the figure of the vampire as a lover certainly *amplifies* these notions. As Tracey L. Bealer suggests, vampiric bodies literalise a toxic version of masculinity: "their phallic fangs are fatally penetrative, while their preternatural strength renders them capable of brutal physical violence" (2011, 140).

Edward's internal struggle, his sexual attraction to Bella and overwhelming desire for her blood, is certainly foregrounded from the outset in Meyer's series. Marked by its undercurrent of potential violence, Edward's furious expression and antagonistic stare destabilise and bewilder Bella during their first meeting. Heightened by her observation that he has clenched his fists so aggressively that his tendons have become exposed, she confesses that she is frightened of the hostility she feels emanating from him. In fitting with the gothic tradition, Bella is preoccupied for much of the first novel with trying to understand the reasons behind this hostility. The routine of her school day centres on whether Edward will be present in their biology class, and he begins to feature in her dreams.

As Bella escalates her investigation, refusing to abandon her quest for answers, Edward is revealed as a quintessential gothic romance hero: he is struggling against his baser urges and his ontological status as a 'monster'. While the narrative repeatedly underscores his integrity and morality – he is disgusted by the thought of drinking human blood, for example – Edward insists that he is inherently malevolent. Prone to unpredictable bouts of intractable rage, he warns Bella that he is the world's greatest predator and exclaims that he is closer to a villain than a hero. He also consistently entreats Bella to understand that she should fear him by stressing just how easily he could accidentally kill her.

The narrative constantly draws attention to Bella's intrinsic awareness of the threat that Edward poses. Meyer describes Bella's pulse quickening and her spasms of fear in his presence. Yet Meyer has her protagonist rationalise Edward's nature and moral character. Though Bella acknowledges his potential for violence, she maintains that he is not beyond redemption, justifying Edward's violent temper as an unfortunate and unwanted consequence of his monstrous nature, which he must consistently fight to control. From this perspective, the novels appear to reassert a troubling trope of hegemonic masculinity which naturalises male violence and aggression. Further, by contextualising Edward's hostility within this familiar archetype from the classic gothic romance, the narrative neutralises the threat he poses and obscures the reader's understanding of his behaviour as problematic.

However, the series also has moments which undermine its apparent naturalisation and romanticisation of male violence. The relationship between Sam Uley and Emily Young, for example, is particularly revealing. Functioning as textual doubles for Edward and Bella, Sam is the 'alpha' of Jacob's new werewolf pack, and Emily is his loyal and devoted girlfriend who tends his home and cooks for his 'betas'. The relationship between them is significant as it is presented as one of the most successful in the saga. Noting the depth of their connection, Bella aspires to be part of a relationship like this. But when Bella first encounters this werewolf pack, she offers an intricate and disturbing description of Emily's physical appearance:

> The right side of her face was scarred from hairline to chin by three thick, red lines, livid in colour though they were long healed. One line pulled down the corner of her dark almond-shaped right eye, another twisted the right side of her mouth into a permanent grimace. . . . With the sleeves of her lavender shirt pushed up, I could see that the scars were extended all the way down her arm to the back of her right hand.
>
> (*New Moon*, 331)

Later, when Bella questions him about Emily's injuries, Jacob reveals that Sam, in the midst of phasing into a werewolf for the first time, was responsible for this violent attack:

> You know how she got hurt. . . . Well, weirdly enough, that was sort of how they resolved things. Sam was so horrified, so sickened by himself, so full of hate for what he'd done. . . . He would have thrown himself under a bus if it would have made her feel better. He might have anyway, just to escape what he'd done. He was shattered. . . . Then, somehow, *she* was the one comforting *him*, and after that . . .
>
> (*Eclipse*, 124)

As with Edward, Sam conforms to the generic characteristics of the gothic romance hero. At odds with himself, his behaviour is figured as a consequence of his inherently monstrous (or masculine) ontology and not as a reflection of his 'true' character. Perpetuating a 'he-just-could-not-help-it' myth echoed throughout contemporary rape culture, Sam's responsibility for the attack is deflected onto forces outside of his control, forces which are associated with a hyperbolised version of 'essential' masculinity. Additionally, Jacob's insistence on Sam's profound remorse – in conjunction with his justification that he was alone and without support as the first werewolf to transition in their pack – furthers the narrative's absolution of Sam's crimes.

Bella's response to the 'incident' is also particularly disquieting. Shuddering at the thought of how *Sam* must feel every time he looked at Emily's face, she is moved to compassion for the perpetrator and not his victim. Privileging the male point of view, Bella does not offer the reader a mirroring thought for Emily's suffering. Instead, through Meyer's use of first-person narration, readers are encouraged to identify with Bella and thus to adopt her empathetic position. In other words, as with Bella, readers are ultimately motivated to sympathise with the perpetrator of violent attack that has left a woman permanently scarred.

The Sam and Emily 'episode' certainly augments the narrative's romanticisation and normalisation of violence as an essential aspect of masculinity. Further, it does so whilst disturbingly encouraging the women who are suffering at the hands of these 'persecuted souls' to empathise with their abusers. At the same time, Meyer's descriptions of Emily's disfiguration are arguably jarring for the reader, undermining the narrative's promotion of those archaic gender norms, sanctioning and naturalising male violence, as pleasurable and benign. In other words, by drawing attention to the damage that has been done to Emily's body, the saga forces the reader to question the purported benevolence of these norms.

Still, Meyer's female characters are clearly 'rewarded' for persevering in their abusive relationships:

> The front door opened, and Sam stepped through. "Emily," he said, and so much love saturated his voice that I felt embarrassed, intrusive, as I watched him cross the room in one stride and take her face wide in his hands. He leaned down and kissed the dark scars on her right cheek before he kissed her lips. . . . This was worse than any romantic movie; this was so real that it sang out loud with joy and life and true love.
>
> (*New Moon*, 333)

Here, in spite of the reminder of Emily's trauma, readers are encouraged – via a rhetoric of true love – to recognise that she has found her soulmate. Similarly, the uniqueness of the connection between Edward and Bella is underscored by her mother, Renee. Drawing on discourses of destiny and fate, she exclaims that she's never seen a bond so strong between two young lovers and maintains that there is some kind of unbreakable, gravitational pull keeping them forever in each other's orbits. In this context, the series appears to suggest that male aggression, if endured, can be worthwhile. Emily's permanent disfiguration and Bella's untimely 'death' were just the price they were willing to pay for everlasting love.

This romanticisation of male violence as something that must be endured in order to procure a soulmate is a well-established feature of the romance genre and has been almost universally critiqued. But in attempting to explain the continued popularity of those narratives in which heroines are mistreated or abused by their prospective lovers, Tania Modleski offers an alternative reading of 'romance', positing that the genre offers its predominantly female readers a pleasurable, fantasy resolution to the mystery of masculine aggression (1982). These narratives, she argues, allow their readers to engage in a fantasy in which they can reinterpret the hero's often deplorable actions as evidence of the depth of his love for the heroine. And so, offering a pleasurable explanation for the quotidian brutality of the male hero, Modleski maintains that the romance genre reassures its readers, transforming male violence from a manifestation of contempt into a demonstration of love.

Julia Wood, among others, has emphasised the limitations of Modleski's argument, refusing to dismiss the genre's potential to licence women's oppression by romanticising and naturalising violently gendered power dynamics (2001). As with Wood, I am reluctant to ignore the potential ramifications of the genre's recoding of violence and male domination as romantic. More pertinently, I believe that its potential to be hazardous has only *intensified* in recent years. When harnessed with neoliberal and postfeminist discourses of choice as a form of empowerment, contemporary reiterations of the genre risk not only naturalising patriarchal dominance within intimate relationships but eroticising subordination as the 'right' *choice* for women and girls.

Throughout the *Twilight* saga, Edward engages in behaviour which might be best characterised as a kind of intimate partner abuse: he stalks Bella by surveilling her home; he forces her to eat and take medication against her will; he uses physical force to restrain her during arguments; and he isolates her from her friends and family. Yet conforming to the traditions of the gothic romance, Meyer's narrative persistently recodes Edward's despotism as romantic and aspirational, converting it into a source of readerly pleasure. In one particularly revealing episode, for example, Edward suddenly materialises just in time to prevent Bella's imminent assault by a gang of violent thugs, forcing him to admit that he has followed her to Port Angeles on her 'girls-only' shopping trip. Neither discomforted nor disturbed by this confession, Bella is flattered by Edward's behaviour, interpreting it as emblematic of his affection for her. She is also soothed by his solicitousness, feeling safe and reassured. This pleasurable response, I propose, affirms Modleski's theorisations of the romance genre, recoding Edward's unwarranted surveillance of Bella as 'romantic' for the series' readers. In addition, by foregrounding Bella's innate vulnerability in the moments before her attack – she is incapacitated by terror and admits she wouldn't have stood a chance in defending herself against her assailants – the narrative implicitly *justifies* Edward's stalking, further obscuring its insidious undertones.

Over the course of the narrative, Edward becomes increasingly overbearing and controlling. Facilitated by his supernatural gift to hear the thoughts of others, he constructs a web of surveillance around Bella, eavesdropping on her conversations with friends, tracking her whereabouts and watching her while she sleeps. Under the guise of her own protection, Edward forbids Bella from visiting her werewolf friends. He also enlists the help of his 'psychic' sister Alice to monitor Bella's every thought. While Bella sporadically expresses her frustration with him, admitting that his shielding arms had begun to feel like restraints, the narrative ultimately romanticises and eroticises Edward's behaviour by recoding it as 'sexy'.

Indeed, the series is populated with 'titillating' descriptions of Edward's flawless physique: his dazzling smile; his perfectly sculpted, Adonis-like body; his devastatingly inhuman beauty. Meyer exhausts every superlative in the dictionary to emphasise that he is "the most perfect person on the planet" (*Eclipse*, 35). Literalising the proverbial 'you take my breath away', Bella is often so disarmed by Edward's potent physical attractiveness that she quite literally forgets to breathe around him. On one occasion, she even faints from asphyxiation after he attempts to kiss her. These descriptions, I propose, not only conceal the more pernicious aspects of Edward's behaviour but also fetishise his authoritarianism as pleasurable for the reader.

Still, as Modleski comprehensively demonstrated, this pattern of eroticising male violence has a long-standing literary history and is a staple characteristic of the romance genre. Yet

I would argue that Meyer's distinctive contribution to the genre is to *combine* that eroticisation with the rhetoric of choice, female agency and empowerment so pervasive in her fiction. She adapts this rhetoric from neoliberal and postfeminist discourse, which makes feminism synonymous with individual choice and specifically with a conception of choice that is paradigmatically consumerist. This discourse, I suggest, individuates women, making them wholly responsible for, because they have freely chosen, whatever befalls them – even if that is the violence of men.

Reflecting those pervasive discourses, much narrative space is given to establishing Bella's 'empowered' right to choose. For instance, Edward initially takes responsibility for Bella's safety by opting to avoid her entirely. But he quickly fatigues of those efforts and instead exhorts her to choose whether or not she wants to embark on a relationship with him. And so he outlines for Bella the risks involved that relationship. In a series of thinly veiled threats, he advises her that it would be more prudent for her if they were not friends, urging her to take personal responsibility for her own safety. Likewise, in advance of their risky rendezvous in a secluded forest, Edward issues several specific warnings about the dangers of spending an afternoon together, encouraging Bella to inform her friends and family of her plans as a kind of safety precaution which will obviate his potential to *kill* her.

Though she acknowledges that Edward is genuinely giving her the choice to continue their relationship, recognising that he will respect whatever decision she may make, Bella ultimately exercises her autonomy and *chooses* to ignore his threats. Plotting to protect Edward and his family from a potential public disaster – in the event of her 'accidental' death – she intentionally lies to her friends and family about their weekend plans. This choice, I argue, shifts responsibility in the narrative from the potential assailant to the potential assailed. By providing Bella with enough details about his violent nature to make an informed and rational decision about their relationship, which Bella knowingly disregards, Edward is acquitted of any guilt. As such, the narrative's naturalisation of male violence is clearly bolstered by its employment of a discourse of choice as an *uncomplicated* marker of female empowerment.

The series also highlights the ease with which these narratives of personal responsibility can shift into feelings of self-blame and guilt with the potential to silence victims of gender-based violence. This is most clearly perceptible in Meyer's depiction of the fraught relationship between Bella and her best friend, Jacob. In spite of her repeated assertions that he should not expect more than a friendship, Jacob consistently pushes against the parameters of their relationship and espouses a troubling 'persistence pays off' motto. Refusing to accept that his love is unrequited, he assumes to know the truth of Bella's desires, anticipating that she will eventually acknowledge and accept her feelings for him. In attempting to provoke Bella into realising this 'truth', Jacob exploits his physical prowess, forcing her into a non-consensual kiss:

> He took my chin in his hand, holding it firmly so that I couldn't look away from his intent gaze. "N – " I started to object, but it was too late. His lips crushed mine, stopping my protest. He kissed me angrily, roughly, his other hand gripping tight around the back of my neck, making escape impossible. I shoved against his chest with all my strength, but he didn't even seem to notice. His mouth was soft, despite the anger, his lips moulding to mine in a warm, unfamiliar way. I grabbed at his face, trying to push it away, failing again. He seemed to notice this time, though, and it aggravated him. His lips forced mine open, and I could feel his hot breath in my mouth. Acting on instinct, I let my hands drop to my side, and shut down. I opened my eyes and didn't fight, didn't feel . . . just waited for him to stop.
>
> (*Eclipse*, 330)

Both Bella's verbal protestations and the physical cues she attempts to send Jacob clearly underscore her lack of consent. At the same time, the aggression behind this forceful assault cannot be understated; it is disturbingly depicted as angry, rough and motivated predominantly by Jacob's feelings of aggravation. However, by detailing a fleeting incident in which Bella, investigating the truth of the Cullens' ontology, flirted with Jacob for information, the narrative appears to hold her responsible for *his* actions. Though Bella expressly regrets her decision to feign romantic interest in her friend, his subsequent eagerness to pursue a relationship with her engenders a feeling of remorse, which underscores her belief in her own culpability. She accepts responsibility for Jacob's 'perseverance' by interpreting it as a defect in her ability to set clear and definite boundaries.

As Bella becomes increasing crippled by these feelings of guilt and shame, the narrative underscores how her absolute acceptance of personal responsibility for her actions simultaneously enables Jacob to manipulate and abuse her:

> I held very still – my eyes closed, my fingers curled into fists at my sides – as his hands caught my face and his lips found mine with an eagerness that was not far from violence. I could feel his anger as his mouth discovered my passive resistance. One hand moved to the nape of my neck, twisting into a fist around the roots of my hair. The other hand grabbed roughly at my shoulder, shaking me, then dragging me to him. His hand continued down my arm, finding my wrist and pulling my arm up around his neck. I left it there, my hand still tightly balled up, unsure how far I could go in my desperation to keep him alive. . . . "You can do better than this, Bella," he whispered huskily . . . "Are you sure you want me to come back? Or did you really want me to die?"
>
> (*Eclipse*, 525–6)

Once more, the narrative highlights how Bella has not given her consent to be kissed. Rather, Jacob exploits his supernatural strength to control and dominate Bella's body against her will. Still, this scene notably differs from its apparent counterpart in *New Moon*. Threatening to commit suicide by intentionally throwing a fight with a group of dangerous, new-born vampires, Jacob also exploits Bella's guilt. No longer content with Bella's passive resistance, Jacob *utilises* this guilt to elicit his desired response, implying that he will return from the impending battle alive only if she is able to convince him of her feelings for him.

Crucially, this scene offers an alternative and contradictory perspective on male violence. On the one hand, the narrative seems to endorse a discourse in which women are encouraged to accept, understand, tolerate or rationalise violence against them. As I have argued, this is facilitated by Meyer's reanimation of the familiar archetype of the Bryonic hero, by her employment of rhetorics of true love and by her recoding of male violence as 'sexy'. Meyer also supplements her endorsement of retro-sexist gender norms by exploiting discourses of choice as a marker of female empowerment. Her narrative suggests that it is Bella's empowered right to choose to remain in her relationship and thus that she must accept all responsibility for this decision.

On the other hand, by drawing attention to how Bella's feelings of personal responsibility make her susceptible to manipulation and male violence, this scene undermines the narrative's promotion of choice as unambiguously empowering. It underscores how Bella is quite literally silenced by the self-same ideologies that have purportedly sanctioned her empowerment. Forced to view her problems and experiences through a depoliticised, individual lens, Bella does not read Jacob's entitlement to her body as a symptom of hegemonic masculinity but as a deficiency in her ability to clearly define the parameters of their relationship.

Therefore, the narrative calls into question if these discourses of personal choice as empowerment and personal responsibility as agency – synchronous with neoliberal postfeminism – are actually disguising the reinstatement of oppressive gender roles and entrapping women within a perpetual state of victimhood.

Eager for Eternal Damnation

Bella's interactions with Edward's sister, Rosalie Cullen, further disrupt the novels' postfeminist promise of liberation through empowered choice:

> My life was perfect . . . I was thrilled to be me, to be Rosalie Hale. Pleased that men's eyes watched me every where I went, from the year I turned twelve. Delighted that my girlfriends sighed with envy when they touched my hair . . . I wanted to be loved, to be adored. I wanted to have a huge, flowery wedding, where everyone in town would watch me walk down the aisle on my father's arm and think I was the most beautiful thing they'd ever seen. Admiration was like air to me, Bella . . . I wanted a big house with elegant furnishings that someone else would clean and a modern kitchen that someone else would cook in. . . . And Royce King seemed to be everything I'd dreamed of. The fairy tale prince, come to make me a princess."
>
> (Eclipse, 153–6)

Here, as Rosalie narrates her violent history and rebirth as a vampire to Bella, it is clear that her aspirations in life were decidedly superficial: she prioritised material wealth, beauty and class status above all. Framing the narrative of her human life as a kind of fairytale, Rosalie figures herself as a princess who believed that marrying her prince charming would enable her to satisfy these bourgeois dreams. Though Rosalie's life is cruelly cut short by a gang of violent men – including her soon-to-be-husband, Royce – her transformation into a vampire appeared to allow her to achieve all of the things she wanted in life: wealth, via her integration into the Cullen family, and eternal beauty.

Yet Rosalie comes to realise the superficiality of those desires, how silly and shallow she'd been in her avarice. While vampirism ultimately saved her 'life', healing her critical wounds, it concurrently foreclosed her future potential for procreation. Resentful about her new ontology, Rosalie desperately yearns for her own offspring and maintains that she is eternally incomplete without a child. That resentment also fosters a long-standing animosity towards Bella. Expressly criticising Bella's decision to become a vampire, Rosalie admonishes her sister-in-law for electing to throw away something 'invaluable' – her chances of becoming pregnant.

This 'Rosalie' subplot can be interpreted as an allegory for the contradictory demands of femininity as espoused by neoliberal postfeminism. On the one hand, it emphasises how agency and empowerment are achieved via unbridled consumerism and conformity to normative beauty ideals. On the other hand, it highlights how that agency is somehow deficient without a 'deeper purpose' like maternity. In other words, the narrative implies that it is impossible for women to cultivate a 'fairytale' life, to achieve true happiness, without re-adopting traditional gender roles. Read in this way, this subplot articulates the self-same anxieties of early gothic romances, suggesting that modern women are still contending with worlds in which their options, or choices, are brutally limited. And so, by drawing attention to those limitations, the series undermines its own promotion of 'choice' as unequivocally empowering.

Meyer's depiction of her protagonist further troubles the narrative's exaltation of neoliberal and postfeminist ideologies. From the outset, Bella struggles to reconcile the near-impossible demands of her female subjectivity amidst a climate of neoliberal and postfeminist logic. For example, as her relationship with Edward intensifies, Bella's self-deprecations become intrinsically entangled with her deep-rooted fears about ageing. In the opening moments of *New Moon*, Bella dreams that she is greeted by her deceased grandmother, Marie. Confused by her grandmother's peculiar behaviour, she acknowledges that Marie's movements are mimicking her own. When Bella realises that the aged woman in the mirror is actually a reflection of a withered version of herself, she is overcome by abject terror. Thereafter, Bella expresses an unrelenting desire to remain forever 17 – a desire which typifies postfeminism's preoccupation with the temporal and its exaltation of youth.

Preoccupied with her physical appearance, Bella is wholly committed to satisfying feminine beauty ideals. She dies in order to obviate the ageing process – to remain forever youthful and beautiful. Yet as Bella's awareness of her mortality increases, so do her anxieties, insecurities and self-doubt: she becomes increasingly fixated on inspecting her body for obvious signs of ageing and begins to regulate her facial expressions to prevent creasing and wrinkles. As this depiction of Bella's self-monitoring practices suggests, her commitment to those ideals engenders feelings of mental anguish and distress. These feelings, I argue, alert the reader to the limitations of the kind of empowerment that is offered by neoliberal postfeminism, implying that those hegemonic ideals actually effectuate women's suffering.

The narrative also persistently draws attention to Bella's feelings of powerlessness. Underscoring her fragility from the outset, Bella's status as a 'victim' is established from the very beginning – in Meyer's preface to *Twilight*. As Bella stares into the eyes of a hunter preparing to launch an attack and kill her, she is figured as an animalised prey. Bella's vulnerability is *so* pronounced that it becomes a source of comedy in the narrative. Edward jokes that she makes the cowardly lion look like the terminator and that her proclivity towards danger threatens to devastate the crime statistics in her hometown. Though these hyperbolised descriptions of Bella's powerlessness are often played for comedic effect, much narrative space is devoted to establishing her innate defencelessness, her inability to protect herself from danger. The entire Cullen family, at one stage or another, are individually obliged to rescue her from a series of never-ending threats including, but not limited to, a truck skidding off the school path in her direction, her potential gang rape by a group of intimidating men in Port Angeles, a violent attack by a savage vampire James and the threats of the 'vampire mafia', the Volturi.

In stark contrast to Bella, the Cullen family embodies neoliberal and postfeminist ideals of subjectivity. They are markedly beautiful, miraculously ageless and monumentally wealthy. When first meeting them, Bella remarks how Rosalie and Alice epitomise feminine beauty ideals: their perfect figures are reminiscent of *Sports Illustrated* models and resemble, for her, the airbrushed, inhuman perfection in fashion magazines. Later, Bella's descriptions of the grandeur of the Cullen family home underscore their obvious affluence and higher class positioning. In painstaking detail, she gushes about its high beamed ceilings, its massive curving staircases and its modernist glass walls. The vampires also possess super-human strength and are virtually indestructible.

Evidently awestruck by them, Bella's glorified descriptions of the 'perfect' Cullens promote a similar response in the reader. Bolstered by Meyer's use of first-person narration encouraging identification with Bella's point of view, the reader is prompted to regard the Cullen family – and the hegemonic ideal of neoliberal and postfeminist culture they epitomise – as aspirational. And so vampirism is figured as an attractive solution to all of Bella's problems.

Initiated into the wealthy Cullen family and 'reborn' as an eternally beautiful vampire, she is able to elevate her class status and resolve her low self-esteem. At the same time, Bella's transformation offers her a strategy for survival within an evidently dangerous patriarchal hegemony. Endowed with supernatural strength, Vampire Bella is a skilled predator who is practically invulnerable to future attacks.

Predicated on her submission to a man, Bella's transformation has been denounced by critics as regressive. Jessica Taylor, for example, suggests that it continues a problematic but established pattern from the gothic romance: a female protagonist achieves a lifetime of security and an elevated social standing through marriage. This pattern, Taylor argues, promotes retro-sexist gender norms as empowering and pleasurable for the series' readers. Yet I propose that Bella's primary motivation for becoming a vampire undermines this straightforward reading of Meyer's saga, drawing attention to the limitations of those norms. While Bella overtly acknowledges the allure of eternal beauty and wealth, it is specifically the *power* that vampirism conveys which she truly covets. More than anything, she wants to be "fierce and deadly . . . someone no one would dare mess with" (*Breaking Dawn*, 3).

In attempting to persuade Edward to turn her into a vampire, Bella makes clear her discomfort with the inequity between them. Recognising her own passivity, she argues:

> But it just seems logical . . . a man and woman have to be somewhat equal . . . as in, one of them can't always be swooping in and saving the other one. They have to save each other *equally* . . . I can't always be Lois Lane . . . I want to be Superman, too.
>
> (*Twilight*, 473)

Drawing on popular culture figures to highlight the imbalances underpinning her relationship, Bella demonstrates an awareness of how traditional gender norms, and her adherence to those norms, have actually sanctioned her subjugation and made her powerless. Portraying herself as a damsel in distress – a Lois Lane figure – she confesses to feeling vulnerable and impotent as a young woman under patriarchy. By contextualising Bella's desire for self-transformation in relation to those feelings, this scene disrupts the idea, promoted throughout the trilogy, that re-embracing retro-sexist gender roles is a sure pathway to self-gratification.

Bella also marks the Cullens' heightened capacity for self-actualisation as especially desirable throughout. Expressing her envy at the fluidity and grace of their movements, she frequently emphasises their marked command over their bodies and admires in particular their ability to control their lust for human blood. Epitomising the neoliberal ideal of entrepreneurial citizenship, the Cullens constantly strive to increase their market value: they study a multitude of different subjects, learn to play an array of instruments and regularly work to better their physical prowess via competitive hunting sessions and sports. In addition, the Cullens' supernatural faculties enable them to amplify their natural talents. As a result of his vampirism, Jasper's charisma from his human life is transformed into a psychic ability to manipulate the emotions of those around him. Likewise, Edward's natural gift for interpreting body language mutates into a capacity for mind reading. In short, as fully actualised subjects, these vampires have literally become the very best versions of themselves.

For Kelly Budruweit, the *Twilight* saga is particularly notable for this unusual reversal of the monstrous (272). As supernatural creatures who survive by drinking blood, the Cullens are certainly monsters. But they are notably not *monstrous*. Rather, as Budruweit observes, the series re-writes 'monstrosity' as a function of behaviour whilst marking the out-of-control body as abject for its readers (272). For example, the lawlessness of the Cullens' first antagonists – Victoria, James and Laurent – is written on their bodies. With wild, chaotic hair, restless eyes and frayed clothing that is covered with leaves and debris from the woods, these nomadic vampires are characterised by their lack of self-discipline and corporeal control. Similarly, the newborn vampire army – who arrive in Phoenix to hunt Bella in *Eclipse* – are framed as villainous precisely because of their inability to control both themselves and their desire for human blood.

However, Bella's adolescent female body is indisputably figured as the most ungovernable. Consumed by her corporeal discomfort, Bella's somatic limitations are continuously exaggerated. She is clumsy and uncoordinated and constantly injuring herself. Meyer's descriptions of Bella's physical appearance also emphasise her association with the monster. Troubling the stable boundaries of subjectivity, the translucent colour of her skin underscores her liminality and is notably reminiscent of the pallid complexion of the undead creature she will later become.

When Edward briefly ends their relationship in *New Moon*, the narrative further emphasises the indeterminacy of Bella's subjectivity. As demonstrated by Meyer's inclusion of a number of blank pages, Bella literally loses her ability to narrate – to write herself into existence. Later, she recognises the monstrous image of herself on a cinema screen in a dead, emotionless zombie. While ironically, Bella had once dreamed of becoming a mythical monster, a vampire, the fact that she comes to identify with a *zombie* is revealing: her identification with this creature, characterised by its lack of self-possession, crystallises her monstrosity as emblematic of the out-of-control female body as trouble incarnate.

In the moments before her re-birth, Bella's innate monstrosity is reinforced by Jacob. With colourless, transparent skin resembling that of a corpse, he describes her as hideous – "thing-from-the-swamp scary" (*Breaking Dawn*, 71). Likewise, Alice loses her psychic ability to predict her sister-in-law's future; in a liminal space between human and vampire, it is as if she doesn't exist. Ultimately, it is only in/through un-death that Bella resolves her indeterminate subjectivity and becomes empowered. As a vampire, she finally conquers her vulnerability and gains mastery over her own body. No longer clumsy and uncoordinated, the Cullens admire the marked grace of Bella's 'upgraded' physique. Impressed by her ability to govern her newfound blood lust, they theorise that self-control *must* be Bella's vampiric superpower. Thus, like the Cullens, Bella's transformation clearly enables her to self-actualise and become the very best version of herself.

Celia Jameson and Julia Dane frame Bella's transformation in the penultimate moments of the series as a kind of premature happy ending reminiscent of a prototypical romance. They maintain that Bella gains physical perfection, mastery over ageing, an enhanced sex life and the absolute and unconditional love of her partner – all without any real sacrifice. But, like Taylor, Jameson and Dane ignore the complexity of Meyer's narrative and its multiple points of disjuncture which gesture towards a more troubling reality.

For example, the post-coital scene in *Breaking Dawn* is particularly notable:

> I would have been happy to lie here forever, to never disturb this moment . . . Slowly, sinking through the many layers of bliss that clouded my head, came the realisation of a different atmosphere outside my own glowing sphere of happiness . . . "Look at yourself, Bella. Then tell me I'm not a monster." . . . Under the dusting of feathers, large purplish bruises were beginning to blossom across the pale skin of my arm. My eyes followed the trail they made up to my shoulder, and then down across my ribs. I pulled my hand free to poke at a discolouration on my left forearm, watching it fade where I touched and then reappear. It throbbed a little. "Don't ruin this," I told him. "I. Am. Happy. . . . I think for a first time, not knowing what to expect, we did amazing. With a little practice –"

> His expression was suddenly so livid that I broke off mid-sentence. "Assumed? Did you expect this, Bella? Were you anticipating that I would hurt you?"
>
> (*Breaking Dawn*, 33–6)

On the one hand, Bella's feelings of elation and euphoria suggest that she has finally been able to satisfy her sexual desire. What's more, she has been able to do so on her own terms – as a human and not as a vampire. Yet Bella does not emerge from her first sexual experience unscathed. Instead, she awakens to find her entire torso covered in painful, throbbing bruises. In line with the popular romance formula, Bella interprets Edward's brutality as a demonstration of his wild passion for her; the novel's descriptions of her viciously damaged body cannot be understated and are profoundly discomforting for the reader. Highlighting how Bella actually anticipated and welcomed her suffering as a masochistic form of self-harm, these descriptions underscore the harsh realities of neoliberal patriarchy, suggesting that women must accept or anticipate pain and suffering as a necessary consequence of achieving their desires.

This troubling sentiment is notably perceptible in Meyer's saga as early as *New Moon*. Devastated by the loss of Edward, Bella enters into a liminal state of non-existence in his absence. Her father describes her as an embodiment of the living dead – as a grotesque, animated corpse. Figured as an abject, zombie-like creature, she is marked as the antithesis of neoliberal ideals of self-possession and self-governance. Having lost the will to live without her true love, Bella becomes increasingly reckless. She begins to repeatedly and actively endanger her own life. These acts of self-harm enable her to conjure a hallucination of Edward, whose regulatory voice begins to merge with her own consciousness. The spectre of 'Edward' encourages Bella towards self-preservation; he instructs her to threaten a potential attacker, to stay still and not move, to beg for her life and to run in the opposite direction when confronted by a lone vampire. As a result, Bella starts to self-regulate. Yet evidently, she can do so by engaging in activities which patently cause her pain and often threaten her life. Thus, with Bella's self-actualisation predicated, long before she dies and becomes a vampire, on her submission to victimhood, the narrative reiterates the idea that suffering is a necessary prerequisite of her neoliberal subjectivity.

Still, the saga constantly stresses the pleasure and power Bella achieves by embracing the hegemonic ideals of neoliberal postfeminism. In a scene wholly reminiscent of a makeover-show reveal, the Cullen family gather together to witness Bella's 'awakening' from death and physical transformation. Vampire Bella has flawless, glistening skin, deep amber eyes and an extraordinarily toned and slender body. Like Rosalie and Alice, she epitomises idealised standards of feminine beauty. In contrast to her 'mirror moment' in *New Moon* – which engendered feelings of anxiety about her physical appearance – Bella is clearly riveted by her reflection post-transformation, overwhelmed with pleasure gazing at her newly created beauty.

Bella's transformation into the 'ideal' woman also notably coincides with her new maternal status. Having fallen pregnant as a result of her first sexual experience, Bella, who had never imagined herself a mother, is suddenly desperate for a child. She asserts that she needs her baby like she needs "air to breathe . . . not a choice but a necessity" (*Breaking Dawn*, 132). While Edward and his doctor father are concerned that she will not be able to carry her hybrid child to term and organise a swift abortion, Bella is willing to sacrifice her life. In one of the few instances where she successfully defies Edward, she makes a pact with Rosalie to protect her foetus – even at her own expense. That she suddenly develops this willpower and tenacity during pregnancy is significant, suggesting that women's re-adoption of traditional gender roles will fortify their agency and bolster their empowerment.

In fitting with the neoliberal rhetoric of changing who you are by transforming your outward appearance, Bella's makeover into a vampire is both a physical *and* a social transformation. Reared in a working-class family, Bella's financial struggles are underscored throughout. She works three days a week at a local sporting goods store to contribute to her inadequate college fund and drives a dilapidated truck that is older than her father. But by 'securing' a Cullen, Bella assumes wealth and social standing. As Taylor observes, she adopts a new social identity "marked by consumer capitalism (complete with prestige cars, the details of which are painstakingly laid out for the readers) and unlimited cash flow" (42).

Bella's physical transfiguration also changes how the other characters see her in the series. Post-transformation, she is refigured as elite and urbane. For example, when her search for Alice's lawyer, J. Jenks, leads her to an address in a ghettoised area, Bella is depicted as starkly contrasting her surroundings. Dressed in cashmere and driving an exclusive and expensive vehicle, Jenks's doorman acknowledges that she is not their usual client. Underscoring the postfeminist construction of identity through consumption and appearance, Bella's newfound beauty is presented as a marker of her elevated class. The doorman assumes that anyone who looks as perfect as Bella – like a "supermodel with a banging body" – must be a priority client of the highest importance (*Breaking Dawn*, 572).

By repeatedly emphasising her pleasure at her heightened beauty – whilst fetishising her newly affluent lifestyle and elevated class status – Jameson and Dane argue that Bella's transformation satisfies the basic requirements of a prototypical romantic happy ending. Her 'rebirth', they maintain, is presented as narratively gratifying and pleasurable for the reader. Moreover, Bella's obvious contentment clearly endorses neoliberal and postfeminist ideals of subjectivity as aspirational for women and girls, implying that true happiness can be achieved by embracing and embodying these hegemonic ideals.

Following this logic, Bella's transformation can certainly be interpreted as a utopian happy ending. Vampirism allows her to satisfy neoliberal and postfeminist ideals of subjectivity and to resolve her feelings of powerlessness. As a vampire, she is able to eradicate the vulnerability that had been a limiting feature of her humanity – to live without caution or fear. At the same time, we must acknowledge how Bella's transformation is an obvious impossibility, a resolution to her problems that exists only in the realm of fantasy. And so, Meyer's young readers are confronted with a discomforting truth: that they can never actually live up to these unrealistic ideals of the self in the world as it currently is.

Perhaps more pertinently, Jameson and Dane appear to ignore the peculiarity of offering death, and an excruciatingly painful physical transformation, as a pleasurable 'happy ending' for the series' readers. In order to become a vampire, Bella must suffer and survive what can only be described as intense torture. In graphic descriptions, she narrates her body being ripped apart by vampire venom:

> The pain was bewildering. Exactly that – I was bewildered. I couldn't understand, couldn't make sense of what was happening. My body tried to reject the pain, and I was sucked again and again into a blackness that cut out whole seconds or maybe even minutes of the agony, making it that much harder to keep up with reality . . . it felt like I was being sawed in half, hit by a bus, punched by a prize fighter, trampled by bulls, and submerged in acid, all at the same time. Reality was feeling my body twist and flip when I couldn't possibly move because of the pain. Reality was knowing there was something so much more important than all this torture, and not being able to remember

what it was . . . I wanted to raise my arms and claw my chest open and rip the heart from it – anything to get rid of this torture.

(*Breaking Dawn*, 141–3)

Employing a neoliberal and postfeminist rhetoric of personal choice, Bella is unequivocally committed to this transformation, believing, in spite of her agony, that it will ultimately be worthwhile. Nevertheless, these visceral descriptions disrupt any straightforward interpretation of that transformation as gratifying – a supernatural twist on the prototypical happy ending, engendering readerly pleasure. Rather, those descriptions emphasise how pain, both physical and emotional, is a necessary component of the journey Bella must undertake to become a 'better' or more socially approved version of herself. This raises an important question: if suffering is a constituent part of forging a feminine subjectivity in the postmillennial period, how empowered can women truly be?

As we have seen, feminist rhetoric is perceptible throughout the *Twilight* series. Influenced by her mother, a 'figurehead' of sorts for second-wave feminism, Bella formulates her life in feminist terms: she understands the importance of female independence and is motivated to become a vampire by her feelings of vulnerability as a young woman under neoliberal patriarchy. Likewise, Bella is uncomfortable with the asymmetries of power in her relationship. Interpreting Edward's 'protectiveness' as a kind of domination, she longs for equality between them. Yet, reflecting pervasive postfeminist discourses, feminism is ultimately superseded as an obstacle to Bella's pursuit of pleasure, dismissed as a hindrance to her happiness. Perhaps more pertinently, that feminist rhetoric is also corrupted in the narrative, integrated into the hegemonic ideology and exploited to support dominant systems of power. As I demonstrated, fundamental feminist notions like female empowerment and free choice, perverted by those hegemonic ideologies, were used to entrap Bella within a perpetual state of victimhood, privatising her suffering and silencing her critical voice.

Though the narrative sporadically gestures towards the insidious consequences of that perversion, demonstrating how it makes Bella more susceptible to gender-based violence, its malignancy is ultimately obscured, subsumed within a romantic happy ending. Nevertheless, those discomforting moments, embedded into the fiction, illuminate the discrepancies between expectations raised by dominant ideological formations – specifically that women are empowered, agentic and free – and Bella's lived reality. These discrepancies, as we will see, become more clearly discernible in the *Fifty Shades of Grey* series (James, 2011–2012), perhaps indicating an important shift in the cultural landscape, a growing sense of disillusionment with neoliberal postfeminism.

Reference List

Angel. Directed by Whedon, Josh, Mutant Enemy Productions, 1999–2004. The WB.
Austen, Jane. *Pride and Prejudice*. T. Egerton, 1813.
Bealer, Tracy L. "Of Monsters and Men: Toxic Masculinity and the Twenty-First Century Vampire in the Twilight Saga." *Bringing Light to Twilight: Perspectives on a Pop Culture Phenomenon*, edited by Giselle Liza Anatol, Palgrave Macmillan, 2011, pp. 139–153.
Bram Stoker's Dracula. Directed by Francis Ford Coppola, Columbia Pictures, 1992.
Breaking Dawn, Part 1. Directed by Bill Condon, Summit Entertainment, 2011.
Breaking Dawn, Part 2. Directed Bill Condon, Summit Entertainment, 2012.
Breaking Wind. Directed by Craig Moss, Lionsgate Home Entertainment, 2012.
Bronte, Charlotte. *Jane Eyre*. Smith, Elder & Company, 1847.

Bronte, Emily. *Wuthering Heights*. Thomas Cautley Newby, 1847.
Budruweit, Kelly. "Twilight's Heteronormative Reversal of the Monstrous: Utopia and the Gothic Design." *Journal of the Fantastic in the Arts*, vol. 27, no. 2, 2016, pp. 270–289. link.gale.com/apps/doc/A531844506/AONE?u=nuim&sid=AONE&xid=82ab2f1.
Buffy the Vampire Slayer. Directed by Whedon, Joss, Mutant Enemy Productions, 1997–2003. The WB.
Click, Melissa, et al. *Bitten by Twilight: Youth Culture, Media, & The Vampire Franchise*. Peter Lang, 2010.
Crawford, Joseph. *The Twilight of the Gothic: Vampire Fiction and the Rise of the Paranormal Romance*. University of Wales Press, 2014.
Day, Sara K. "Pure Passion: The Twilight Saga, 'Abstinence Porn,' and Adolescent Women's Fiction." *Children's Literature Association Quarterly*, vol. 39, no. 1, 2014, pp. 28–48. doi: 10.1353/chq.2014.0014.
Eclipse. Directed by David Slade, Summit Entertainment, 2010.
Gill, Rosalind. *Gender and the Media*. Polity Press, 2007.
Herter, Lori. *Confession*. Berkley Publishing Group, 1992.
Herter, Lori. *Eternity*. Berkley Publishing Group, 1993.
Herter, Lori. *Obsession*. Berkley Publishing Group, 1991.
Herter, Lori. *Possession*. Berkley Publishing Group, 1992.
James, E.L. *Fifty Shades Darker*. Vintage Books, 2012.
James, E.L. *Fifty Shades Freed*. Vintage Books, 2012.
James, E.L. *Fifty Shades of Grey*. Vintage Books, 2011.
Jameson, Celia and Julia Dane. "Bite Me! The Twilight Saga, a Fantasy Space of Self-Transformation as Self-Realisation." *The Journal of Communication Inquiry*, vol. 38, no. 3, 2014, pp. 243–258. doi: 10.1177/0196859914535953
McRobbie, Angela. *The Aftermath of Feminism: Gender, Culture and Social Change*. Sage Publications, 2008.
Mead, Richelle. *Vampire Academy*. Razorbill, 2007.
Meyer, Stephenie. *Breaking Dawn*. Atom, 2008.
Meyer, Stephenie. *Eclipse*. Atom, 2007.
Meyer, Stephenie. "Frequently Asked Questions: Breaking Dawn." *StephenieMeyer*, 2010, www.stepheniemeyer.com/the-books/breaking-dawn/frequently-asked-questions-breaking-dawn/.
Meyer, Stephenie. *New Moon*. Little, Brown Company, 2006.
Meyer, Stephenie. *Twilight*. Atom, 2005.
Modleski, Tania. *Loving with a Vengeance: Mass Produced Fantasies For Women*. The Shoe String Press, 1982.
Murphy, Colette. "Someday My Vampire Will Come? Society's (and the Media's) Lovesick Infatuation with Prince-Like Vampires." *Theorizing Twilight: Critical Essays on What's at Stake in a Post-Vampire World*, edited by Maggie Parke and Natalie Wilson, McFarland & Company, 2011, pp. 56–70
New Moon. Directed by Chris Weitz, Summit Entertainment, 2009.
Nosferatu. Directed by F.W. Murnau, Prana Film, 1922.
Owen, Susan A. "Vampires, Postmodernity and Postfeminist: Buffy the Vampire Slayer." *Journal of Popular Film and Television*, vol. 27, no. 2, 2010, pp. 24–31. doi: 10.1080/01956059909602801
Peterson, Anne Helen. "That Teenage Feeling: Twilight, Fantasy and Feminist Readers." *Feminist Media Studies*, vol. 12, no. 1, 2011, pp. 51–67. doi: 10.1080/14680777.2011.558348.
Plec, Julia and Kevin Williamson. *The Vampire Diaries*, Outerbanks Entertainment, 2009–2017. The CW.
Radway, Janice. *Reading the Romance: Women, Patriarchy and Popular Literature*. University of North Carolina Press, 1984.
Rice, Anne. *Interview with the Vampire*. Little Brown, 1976.
Shakespeare, William. *Romeo and Juliet*. 1597.
Stoker, Bram. *Dracula*. Archibald Constable and Company, 1897.

Taylor, Anthea. "'The Urge towards Love Is an Urge Towards (un)Death': Romance, Masochistic Desire and Postfeminism in the Twilight Novels." *International Journal of Cultural Studies*, vol. 15, no. 1, 2011, pp. 31–46. doi: 10.1177/1367877911399204

Taylor, Jessica. "Romance and the Female Gaze: Obscuring Gendered Violence in the Twilight Saga." *Feminist Media Studies*, vol. 14, no. 3, 2012, pp. 388–402. doi: 10.1080/14680777.2012.740493.

Twilight. Directed by Catherine Hardwicke, Summit Entertainment, 2008.

Vampires Suck. Directed by Jason Friedburg and Aaron Seltzer, Twentieth Century Fox, 2010.

Vampyr. Directed by Carl Dreyer, Carl Theodore Dreyer Filmproduktion, 1932.

Wood, Julia T. "The Normalization of Violence in Heterosexual Romantic Relationships: Women's Narratives of Love and Violence." *Journal of Social and Personal Relationships*, vol. 18, no. 2, 2001, pp. 239–261. doi: 10.1177/0265407501182005.

2 *Fifty Shades* of Neoliberalism

'Feminists for Orgasms?'

In 'Reading the BDSM Romance: Reader Responses to *Fifty Shades*', Clarissa Smith and Ruth Deller calculate that approximately 1,000 stories about *Fifty Shades of Grey* and its 'effects' circulated in the British mainstream press during the summer of 2012 alone (2013, 933). Variously derided by critics in the media as "mommy porn" (Barnett, 2012) and "abominably written trash" (Kilpatrick, 2012), *Fifty Shades* was nonetheless an overwhelming financial success, becoming the fastest selling paperback of all time. Originally conceived as *Twilight* fan-fiction by E.L. James, the pseudonym of Erika Leonard, the series comprises three novels: *Fifty Shades of Grey* (2011), *Fifty Shades Darker* (2012) and *Fifty Shades Freed* (2012). Since their initial publication, these novels have dominated best-seller lists and sold more than 125 million copies worldwide. The series's film adaptations – *Fifty Shades of Grey* (Sam Taylor-Johnson, 2015), *Fifty Shades Darker* (James Foley, 2017) and *Fifty Shades Freed* (James Foley, 2018) – have been equally lucrative. Current figures suggest a gross profit of 1.325 billion dollars for the franchise as a whole.

Underscoring its influence, Lynn Comella notes how the series quickly became a merchandising sensation. Recognising its commercial potential, retailers exploited the *Fifty Shades* 'brand' to add value to their products (564). In 2012, for example, UK retailers specialising in sex toys and lingerie – such as Naughty 'n' Nice and Simply Pleasure – displayed selections of 'light bondage' products alongside copies of the series on their websites. Meanwhile, in-store official collections capitalised on the trilogy's recognisable memorabilia. These collections included a pair of stainless steel handcuffs, floggers, blindfolds, feather ticklers and silver pleasure beads – all engraved with the *Fifty Shades of Grey* logo that enabled a substantial increase in price.

Inspiring a series of accessible how-to 'manuals' or beginners guides to BDSM – such as sex educator Tristan Taormino's *Fifty Shades of Kink* (2012) and M. Alan's *Fifty Shades of Grey Decoded: A Man's Playbook* (2012) – the *Fifty Shades* phenomenon is often credited with mainstreaming 'kink'. The series also generated readerly appetite for erotica, spawning a new subgenre of women's fiction centred on sadomasochist relationships termed "chick-whip" (Alex Dymock, 882). But in spite of its seemingly progressive depiction of sexuality, the series is ironically conventional. Structured like a classic romance narrative, it conforms to a recognisable Harlequin plot: a female protagonist ostensibly tames a wild, dangerous hero, and narrative closure is found in marriage and motherhood.

In accordance with this popular romance formula, the series chronicles the love affair between inexperienced and naive virgin Anastasia Steele – a 21-year-old literature student – and Christian Grey, a mercurial and wealthy entrepreneur in his late 20s whose practice of

BDSM is linked to a dark past. Like a prototypical Harlequin romance, the narrative's central tension is the resolution of the differences between these lovers whose romantic ideals are not aligned. While Anastasia longs for a traditional and committed romantic relationship – what the novels term 'hearts and flowers' – Christian explicitly does not 'do' romance or 'vanilla' sex. He requires Anastasia's consent to be his submissive to continue any form of relationship with her. Despite these differences, Anastasia and Christian are unable to break away from each other and are committed to navigating a successful romance. Framed as a series of negotiations, they attempt – in true Harlequin fashion – to find an appropriate middle ground.

Yet in contrast to the generic expectations of the popular romance, Anastasia and Christian consummate their relationship long before any commitments to each other are made or any feelings of love have been declared. Instead of adhering to a classic pattern – by framing sex solely as an expression of romantic love – the novels foreground sexual pleasure as an independent pursuit, freed from emotions. Consequentially, as Lisa Downing observes, critical responses to the *Fifty Shades* trilogy predictably turned to the question of what the series's popularity might reveal about female desire in the twenty-first century (95). The critics focused on asking: why has this representation of a submissive or even masochistic kind of female sexuality become so popular during a time in which women in the Western world are less dependent and subjugated than ever before?

In perhaps the most widely disparaged of such responses, *Newsweek's* Katie Roiphe highlighted the growth in representations of female fantasies of sexual submission in contemporary popular culture. Citing Lena Dunham's acclaimed series *Girls* (2012–17) as one primary example, she argued that the popularity of the *Fifty Shades* series confirmed that fantasies of sexual submission are inevitable for women who have been socialised in a culture in which male sexuality is linked to domination and conditioned to believe that their sexual power comes solely from being an object of male desire. Alarmingly, Roiphe also proposed that

> there is something exhausting about the relentless responsibility of a contemporary woman's life, about the pressure of economic participation, about all that strength and independence and desire and going out into the world. It may be that, for some, the more theatrical fantasies of sexual surrender offer a release, a vacation, an escape from the dreariness and hard work of equality.
>
> (2012)

In other words, she implied that popular interest in the *Fifty Shades* trilogy was indicative of contemporary women's deep-rooted desire to 'unburden' themselves from the responsibilities of 'equality' by surrendering their agency to a dominant man.

Refutations of Roiphe's contentious claims were lobbed predominantly from the ranks of 'sex-positive' feminists – including cultural critic Shira Tarrant and journalist Dana Goldstein – who contended that the series's depiction of sadomasochism could instead be understood as an expression of female sexual desire and agency (cited in Downing, 94). In contrast to Roiphe, these critics maintained that a woman being able to achieve sexual satisfaction on her own terms was in fact a feminist political act. Praising the series for inspiring sexual fantasies in readers who might previously have been reluctant to engage with any erotic fiction, they argued that *Fifty Shades* permitted a greater number of sexual possibilities for women. They also suggested that the series helped raise the subject of female sexuality in popular culture as a legitimate topic for wider public discussion and debate.

Catherine Roach furthered this celebration of the series as a site of feminist possibility, suggesting that the increasing popularity of contemporary women's erotica indicated an important moment of counter-resistance. Popular erotica, she argued, has the potential to disrupt a long-standing history of presenting romantic love as a prerequisite for women's sexual gratification. By foregrounding representations of female sexual pleasure that are separate from or not contingent on 'romance', Roach suggested that the subgenre could facilitate a reclamation of pornography – a genre which has historically privileged male sexual pleasure – and rehabilitate its definition in a feminist direction (2016, 79).

Evidently influenced by Tania Modleski's seminal work, Francesca Tripodi proposed that the appeal of *Fifty Shades* was rooted in fantasy. The series, she suggested, provided female readers a space for navigating the changing role and status of women in society – all amidst the familiar security of the romance genre's formulaic narrative. Rejecting Roiphe's reading of the novels as a semi-pornographic fantasy of female submission, Tripodi argued that James's readers did not fantasise about conceding agency. Rather, they used the series to guide them through a complicated postfeminist milieu, allowing them to rework their sexual attitudes and practices in response to an increasingly sexualised cultural environment (94).

Conversely, 'sex-negative' responses to the series posited that its appeal could be best understood in terms of women's oppression under patriarchy. Arguing that sadomasochism problematically recreates systemic patterns of heterosexual male dominance, popular feminist bloggers – including 'Maya' of Feministing – disparaged the series for romanticising BDSM and promoting female subjugation. They maintained that female readers who took pleasure in the series were, as women living in a patriarchal culture, experiencing a type of 'Stockholm-syndrome', attempting to "convert their oppression into a source of pleasure and illusory choice" (cited in Downing, 94).

As Smith's and Deller's research revealed, reader responses to the series were equally polarised and often contradictory (940). Some of the readers in their focus groups responded positively to the trilogy. They saw the novels as a way of spicing up their sex lives while praising James for facilitating discussions of female sexuality in the public arena. Others were disturbed by the series's representation of sexuality. Discomforted by its portrayal of BDSM, these readers criticised the novels' eroticisation of male domination.

Some feminist critics, however, were critical of the sex-positive/sex-negative discourse surrounding the series. Margot Weiss, for example, was dubious about the paring down of politics to sexual choice, noting that

> as an anthropologist and a queer studies scholar who has learned more than a little from the philosopher Michel Foucault, I am wary of the claim that embracing our inner sexual desires is a sure path to liberation.
>
> (2012)

Similarly, Downing rebutted both sides of this debate. Challenging sex-positive responses to the series, she was sceptical of the assumption that "by proliferating more and varied forms of sexual expression, practices and orgasms, a 'positive' and progressive – indeed feminist – agenda was being served" (95). At the same time, although Downing acknowledged the politically vital point that BDSM exists within, and is thus shaped by, patriarchal culture, she reproved sex-negative critics and refused to reduce ethically practiced 'kink' to female oppression.

Like Weiss and Downing, I am reluctant to account for the popularity of the *Fifty Shades* series by positing a totalising hypothesis about its readers. Instead, I believe that these bifurcated responses fail to address some of the texts' more troubling attributes. As we will see, the trilogy fetishes and glamorises a problematic neoliberal and postfeminist ideal of feminine subjectivity. But moments of 'affective dissonance', ubiquitous throughout the series, simultaneously undermine or even subvert this valorised ideal, alerting the reader to its limitations, oppressiveness and contradictions. More pertinently, this affective dissonance gestures towards a troubling reality: that these hegemonic ideologies are sanctioning and facilitating gender-based violence.

Following Rachel Greenwald Smith, this chapter will examine two types of affect or 'literary feeling'. The first, what Greenwald terms 'personal feelings', is anchored primarily in representations of characters and their individual emotions. These kinds of affects are "codified and thus easier to define" (2015, 19). Focusing specifically on Anastasia's 'personal feelings', I will track recurring gaps in her narration, which affectively express her discontent with gendered ideals. These gaps, I propose, rupture the narrative's endorsement of neoliberal and postfeminist ideologies as unambiguously empowering, opening up a space for critique.

The second type of 'literary feeling', Greenwald contends, is less immediately palpable and codifiable. These are 'impersonal feelings' – affects that are not generated through the representation of an individual character's emotions but by the aesthetics of the text (17). As will be demonstrated, the series's attempted amalgamation of two seemingly disparate genres begets an unusually deflated or affectless tone. This aesthetic, I believe, has an alienating effect on the readers, engendering 'impersonal feelings' which disrupt their identification with or acceptance of the hegemonic ideal of neoliberal postfeminism. By mapping and explicating these tonal shifts or discrepancies in the affective register, I will advocate for the series's subversive potential, arguing that affective dissonances can be interpreted as aesthetic forms of resistance to oppressive systems.

Affective Dissonance

In spite of the proliferation of discourses regarding neoliberalism, the term continues to be a contested concept. As Rosalind Gill, Christina Scharff and Ana Sofia Elias note, its meaning is "contingent, slippery and often remains undefined" (2017, 23). Most scholars, however, have come to agree that neoliberalism involves the extension of market principles into all areas of life. With every human endeavour and activity recast in entrepreneurial terms, the neoliberal subject must conduct their life as an enterprise. Encouraged to continually work upon themselves to increase their 'market value', they are bound by specific ideological rules which emphasise ambition, self-regulation and personal responsibility.

According to Gill, Scharff and Elias, this incitement towards self-optimisation necessitates 'aesthetic labour' – the heightened monitoring and management of one's physical appearance (5). As the primary pathway to self-actualisation, to becoming a 'self', aesthetic labour is a key part of creating and maintaining one's subjectivity in contemporary culture. But it has also effectuated new standards of feminine beauty, whereby women must persistently assess and modify their bodies, engaging in regimental programmes of self-management. All the while, discourses circulated by popular media reassure these women that this bodywork is not punishing or oppressive. Instead, it is framed as empowering and pleasurable, a positive act of self-indulgence and holistic self-care.

This discursive promotion of aesthetic labour is largely driven by consumer culture, suggesting that most needs and desires can be satisfied through commodity consumption. As a result, modern women's entitlement to guilt-free consumerism has become a mark of their indubitable empowerment, demonstrating their liberation. Troubling those rhetoric of 'girl power', however, Angela McRobbie suggests that the emergence of 'commodity feminism' has catalysed the advancement of new technologies of the self, which subtly enable the re-entrenchment of oppressive gender norms. These technologies, she argues, motivate women to prioritise self-gratification by re-adopting traditionally feminine roles, remoulding themselves in line with the expectations of idealised femininity. As such, McRobbie contends that these technologies secure anew the consent of women to existing social and political arrangements, re-vitalising patriarchal relations of power and domination for the postmillennial period (541).

Feminist critic Rachel Wood is similarly critical of commodity feminism, positing that it has significantly altered how women express their sexuality. In contrast to traditional discourses of a heterosexual femininity constituted through passivity, contemporary women have been transformed into active sexual agents in pursuit of their own auto-erotic pleasure. While these women are sexually savvy, embodying neoliberal rhetoric of agency, choice and self-determination, their sexuality has become harnessed to notions of consumerism, fashion and beauty – blurring the boundaries between them. Tasked with enhancing their 'sexiness' or 'attractiveness', neoliberal and postfeminist discourses, disseminated in the popular media, encourage women to work on their bodies in preparation for sex. According to Wood, this type of bodywork includes "getting fully groomed, getting a manicure, pedicure, full bikini wax, buying new lingerie and even hitting the gym in order to tighten their muscles" (2017, 320). Crucially, however, these discourses do not frame bodywork as arduous or objectifying, a way of satisfying the desires of men. Rather, as Wood observes, bodywork is promoted as an act of self-care, facilitating modern women's sexual fulfilment.

Stressing the contradictory nature of those discourses, Rosalind Gill suggests that women have a complex relationship with these notions about female sexuality. This is best encapsulated in what she terms the 'agency pendulum'. At one extreme of the pendulum, women who mobilise their newfound agency to choose self-sexualisation are actively engaged in their own sexual liberation. These women, Gill argues, interpret their bodywork as empowering and pleasurable – a pathway to sexual gratification. At the same time, they acknowledge the limitations of their self-sexualisation, perplexed by a confusing paradox: that behaviour which might have traditionally been critiqued as objectifying is now an expression of their free choice and agency. At this extreme of the pendulum, these women interpret their empowerment as alarmingly illusory, merely "a cynical rhetoric, wrapping sexual objectification in a shiny, feisty, postfeminist packaging that obscures the continued underlying sexism" in our culture (2003, 736).

While Gill is perturbed by the incongruity of these discourses, offering no solution for resolving them, she also stresses that those technologies of the self-encouraging and promoting bodywork are underpinned by particular affective investments. These affective investments, she suggests, are responsible for engendering a set of 'feelings rules' which necessitate the repudiation of negative emotions, demanding perpetual positivity and interminable self-confidence. For Gill, this affective regulation of femininity facilitates the oppression of women. It ensures that they individualise structural issues, transforming themselves and their inner psychic lives, rather than critiquing dominant systems of power for fostering their discontent. In other words, these 'feelings rules' support and fortify an inegalitarian status quo.

Following Gill's logic, Amy Shields Dobson and Akane Kanai recognise how neoliberal postfeminism is shaped by affective politics. They advocate for an examination of spaces where *affective dissonances* are expressed – where there is a discrepancy between expectations raised by dominant ideological formations and individual emotional responses to such formations. These affective dissonances, they propose, can be politically disruptive. Rupturing "the shiny veneer of girl-powered mythologies," they have the potential to undermine the feelings rules of neoliberal and postfeminist culture, moving us towards affective disinvestment in those hegemonic ideologies (775).

The *Fifty Shades* series notably opens with an insight into Anastasia Steele's regulatory processes. As she attempts to tame her hair into "submission" and recites an "*I must not sleep with my hair wet*" mantra to herself in the mirror, her wayward body is marked as unmanageable, chaotic and devoid of the neoliberal markers of self-governance (7). Although played to comedic effect, Anastasia's clumsiness during her first encounter with Christian Grey further underscores her corporeal recalcitrance. Tripping into his office and blaming her "two left feet," she admits that she is "all gawky and uncoordinated, barely able to get from A to B without falling flat on my face" (33).

In contrast, the novels foreground Christian's self-governance from the outset. Anastasia enviously remarks on how comfortable and at ease he is with his body as he moves gracefully through his office. Christian's regimental management of his life as if it is a stock portfolio emphasises his propensity for self-regulation. As he explains to Anastasia in the interview she conducts with him for her student publication:

> My belief is to achieve success in any scheme one has to make oneself master of that scheme . . . I work hard, very hard to do that. . . . The harder I work the more luck I seem to have. . . . I don't have a philosophy as such. Maybe a guiding principle – Carnegie's: "A man who acquires the ability to take full possession of his own mind may take possession of anything else to which he is justly entitled." "So you want to possess things?" "I want to deserve to possess them, but yes, bottom line, I do." "You sound like the ultimate consumer."
>
> (*Fifty Shades of Grey*, 10–12)

With a guiding principle centred on self-possession, Christian maintains that he is solely responsible for his own well-being and success. Committed to self-improvement, he consistently 'invests' in himself, believing that his entitlement to unbridled consumerism is contingent on this self-optimisation. Ambitious, competitive, driven and unwaveringly self-possessed, he is figured as the ideal neoliberal citizen.

While they are immediately attracted to each other, Christian is reluctant to pursue a relationship with Anastasia because their romantic ideals are misaligned. Yet, following a series of 'accidental' encounters, they realise that they are unwilling to relinquish this romantic attachment. And so Christian presents Anastasia with a 'relationship contract', allowing them to negotiate the 'terms and conditions' of their romance. This contract is initially presented as a necessary step for a dominant and his submissive to expressly outline their sexual limits. But, as we will see, its terms extend far beyond the bedroom, functioning instead as a blueprint for Anastasia to self-optimise.

Steeped in entrepreneurial language, the contract outlines how to be a good neoliberal citizen through self-improvement and self-care, highlighting for Anastasia the technologies of the self required to self-actualise. In signing the relationship contract, she must agree to ensure she achieves a minimum of seven hours sleep each night when she is not with the dominant; eat regularly and from a prescribed list of foods to maintain her health and well-being; partake in sessions with a personal trainer provided by the dominant; not drink to excess, smoke, take recreational drugs or put herself in any unnecessary danger; keep herself clean and shaved and/or waxed at all times; attend a beauty salon chosen by the dominant and undergo whatever treatments the dominant sees fit; and conduct herself in a respectful and modest manner at all times (*Fifty Shades of* Grey, 76). Though Anastasia is initially overwhelmed by these requirements, the contract has an immediate panopticon effect on her. She voluntarily begins to exercise and intensify her grooming regimes *before* she has even agreed to its terms and conditions. All the while, by emphasising how Anastasia can *choose* to sign this contract – to accept or reject its terms – the novels reinforce the idea that those self-regulations are expressions of free choice and agency.

These regulatory practices are promoted as empowering, pleasurable and a pathway to success in the novels. For instance, Anastasia's and Christian's self-governance is inextricably linked with their achievement of an affluent and glamorous lifestyle. Christian's personal success, which he accredits specifically to his capacity for self-management, manifests through, and morally legitimises, his accumulation of 'things' – fast cars, helicopters and multiple properties. Similarly, Anastasia's celebrated transformation and 'self-actualisation' in the later novels is accompanied by excessive descriptions of her expensive designer clothing – from her "Christian Louboutin Shoes . . . a steal at $3296" to her "$540 dollar Neiman Marcus Corset" which makes her feel like a "1930's movie star" (*Fifty Shades Darker*, 286).

The series also persistently endorses bodywork as a primary route to sexual pleasure. As stipulated in their relationship contract, Anastasia must exercise *at least* four times a week with a personal trainer. Though she is perturbed by this requirement, attempting to negotiate a better 'deal', Christian stresses to Anastasia that bodywork is not solely for his pleasure but also for her own by emphasising how it is a necessary stepping stone to her achievement of sexual gratification. This training, he maintains, will facilitate her sexual fulfilment, empowering her to optimise her endurance levels and allowing her to improve her sexual skills. That Anastasia's compliance with those requirements coincides with the heightening of her sexual pleasure – as demonstrated by the sheer volume of orgasms she has in the course of the narrative – arguably affirms for the series's readers the advantageousness of bodywork.

While Anastasia ultimately converts to Christian's point of view, enjoying the privileges with which she is rewarded for her submission to this conception of herself, her narrative is nonetheless populated with moments of frustration, dissatisfaction and disappointment. These kinds of emotions or affective gaps are notably discordant with the novels' promotion of neoliberal postfeminism, undermining its ideals as empowering and pleasurable. This becomes particularly apparent when Anastasia disputes that the fundamental purpose of Christian's contract is to facilitate her sexual gratification:

> Holy fuck. I can't bring myself to even consider the food list. I swallow hard, my mouth dry, and read it again. My head is buzzing. How can I possibly agree to all of this? And apparently it's for my benefit, *to explore my sensuality, my limits – safely* – oh, please! I scoff angrily.
>
> (*Fifty Shades of Grey*, 165)

Dubious about these 'personal benefits', Anastasia is discomforted by the overwhelming number of prerequisites she must satisfy to participate in a relationship with Christian. This dysphoria, I propose, affectively emphasises to the reader the limitations of Christian's neoliberal contract and the 'boundless' personal pleasure offered by it.

Crucially, however, the contract has a double function and can be interpreted as an allegory for the 'compromises' contemporary women must make to get what they want. The contract's repetition of the word 'submissive' supports this allegorical reading. While on the surface, 'submissive' is merely part of the lexicon of BDSM culture, it also has a symbolic resonance. Mirroring the wider cultural regulations habitually imposed on women, Anastasia's 'submission' to a very specific set of contractual rules is the only way she can satisfy her desires. And so, by affectively conveying her frustration with the contract and its rules, the novel underscores the limitations of Anastasia's empowerment as a subject under neoliberal postfeminism, emphasising how her agency is inhibited by these pernicious restrictions.

Still, the novels consistently stress the pleasure and empowerment Anastasia gains from submitting to the relationship contract. In stark contrast to the self-deprecating descriptions of her body which introduce us to the character in *Fifty Shades of Grey*, Anastasia's mirror moments in *Fifty Shades Darker* are revealing:

> I have entered an alternative universe. The young woman staring back at me looks worthy of a red carpet. Her strapless, floor-length, silver satin gown is simply stunning. Maybe I'll write Caroline Acton myself. It's fitted, and flatters what few curves I have. My hair falls in soft waves around my face, spilling over my shoulders to my breasts. I tuck one side behind my ear, revealing my second-chance earrings. I have kept makeup to a minimum, a natural look. Eyeliner, mascara, a little pink blush, and pale pink lipstick.
>
> (129)

Unable to tame her hair in the opening scenes of first novel, Anastasia is wholly transformed. No longer a signifier of abject or chaotic femininity, her beauty is now consummately and reassuringly feminine, demonstrative of what McRobbie describes as the "spectacularly feminine . . . the perfectible self" (2008, 60). More pertinently, Anastasia's glowing assessment of her makeover implies that pleasure can be derived from transforming the body in line with normative beauty ideals.

But as Anastasia assesses her transformation in the mirror, she admits that she cannot recognise herself in its reflection. Instead, she opts to evaluate the image before her as if it is a beautiful celebrity on the pages of a glossy magazine – a celebrity with an identity wholly separate to her own. Thus, while Christian's neoliberal contract enabled her to seamlessly reproduce normative beauty standards, to experience a state of confidence, Anastasia's affective orientation is once more disconnected from her material reality. As signalled by her shift from first- to third-person narration, she evidently feels alienated from, and cannot fully assimilate, this feeling of self-assurance. In other words, the narrative implies that Anastasia's newfound self-confidence is a performative facade. This undermines any straightforward interpretation of her transformation as empowering and pleasurable. By extension, it troubles those contemporary discourses, synonymous with neoliberal postfeminism, which suggest that satisfying normative beauty standards will cultivate feelings of happiness and content.

Nevertheless, Anastasia's physical transformation significantly impacts how she is perceived by others. Through aesthetic labour, she is able to project a new identity beyond that of the clumsy, awkward student to whom we were originally introduced. This is particularly apparent when, in *Fifty Shades Darker*, she bumps into a former colleague who comments on her "worldly . . . sophisticated" new demeanour. Observing how Anastasia exudes confidence, the colleague connects her newfound self-assurance to her updated physical appearance, inquiring "what's happened? . . . you changed your hair? . . . clothes?" (305). Anastasia's physical transformation also coincides with an elevation in her position of power in the narrative. Post-transformation, she not only becomes 'Mrs Grey', the wife of the world's wealthiest entrepreneur, but is quickly promoted from intern to editor-in-chief of SIP (within a short span of two months).

By connecting Anastasia's bodily regulations to her achievement of a 'successful' – and socially visible – kind of femininity, the narrative seems to endorse aesthetic labour as pleasurable and empowering for the reader. The more Anastasia submits to these gendered beauty standards, the more recognition she gains within the novels. But it is only by adopting normative standards of feminine beauty that Anastasia is able to self-actualise and satisfy her desires. This, I propose, reiterates that there are limitations to her empowerment. It implies that 'submission' to those feminine ideals is Anastasia's only recourse for agency in a system within which she is essentially powerless.

James's inclusion of a key trope from the gothic genre, the doppelgänger or double, further supports this interpretation of Anastasia's disempowerment. In *Fifty Shades Darker*, Anastasia is confronted by one of Christian's ex-submissives and notes their uncanny resemblances:

> "Miss Steele?" I turn expectantly, and an ashen young woman approaches me cautiously. She looks like a ghost – so pale and strangely blank. . . . Her voice is eerily soft. Like me, she has dark hair that starkly contrasts with her fair skin. Her eyes are brown, like bourbon, but flat. . . . On closer inspection, she looks odd, dishevelled, and uncared for. Her clothes are two sizes too big, including her designer trench coat. "I'm sorry – who are you" "Me? I'm nobody."
>
> (80)

Yet there is one key difference between these women. Influenced by the relationship contract, Anastasia has gained mastery over her own body and is persistently depicted as well-groomed and glamorous. In contrast, the stranger's unkempt appearance is indicative of a lack of bodily governance. This lack is notably conflated with her unstable subjective identity. As underscored by the pallor of her skin, she is framed as a spectre or ghost, a creature who is not fully formed. The stranger's shrunken physique also emphasises her depleting corporeality and therefore her abject liminality. Later that night, when Anastasia dreams of Leila, the ghost girl, she nightmarishly realises that they are one and the same. Foregrounding their mutual struggles with identity, she exclaims, "I'm nobody . . . are you nobody too?" (*Fifty Shades Darker*, 81). Read in this way, the gothic double represents Anastasia's deepest fears about failing to self-actualise. As she confesses to Christian: "I'm so scared I'll end up like Leila . . . a shadow . . . nobody" (*Fifty Shades Darker*, 324).

Although the narrative concludes with Anastasia's self-actualisation – she eventually becomes the 'best' version of herself – this episode is particularly notable. Through the depiction of Lelia, it implies that there are dire consequences for those women who cannot self-optimise and adhere to normative standards of feminine beauty: they are abjected. That Leila attempts to commit suicide further reinforces this reading of her powerlessness. As a woman who cannot satisfy ideals of femininity, she sees no other option than to take her own life. Thus, this episode reiterates that there are limitations to the kind of empowerment offered by contemporary gender ideologies. If women must satisfy these restrictive ideals to self-actualise, how empowered can they truly be?

In spite of these glaring limitations, the series presents *one* key obstacle to Anastasia's pursuit of pleasure and empowerment: the nagging 'subconscious' voice of feminism in her head. While the Subconscious is, implicitly, a branch of Anastasia's consciousness, she is deployed by James as a *character* who is partly independent from her 'creator'. This 'character' is committed to some loosely defined feminist principles and consistently gestures towards the gendered and political implications of Anastasia's actions. For example, expressing discomfort at Anastasia receiving clothing, laptops and underwear in 'exchange' for sex with Christian, the Subconscious highlights the imbalance of power between them, stressing the similarities between their 'arrangement' and an escort service. The Subconscious also implies that Christian's wealth obscures and glamorises the more insidious undertones of what she terms his 'slave contract'. This contact, she argues, facilitates Anastasia's subjugation in line with retro-sexist gender norms, allowing Christian to manipulate and control her.

Though Anastasia often acknowledges that these admonishments have merit and are worthy of further consideration, the Subconscious is depicted as an increasingly censorious presence in the narrative. "Snarky" and "judgemental," she frequently exploits a feminist lexicon to berate Anastasia, castigating her for succumbing to Christian's sexual advances and criticising her inability to regulate her erotic desires (*Fifty Shades of Grey*, 252). This condemnatory depiction of feminism and its rhetoric affirms Diane Negra's and Yvonne Tasker's theorisations of postfeminism (Tasker and Negra, 2007). Postfeminist culture, they argue, commodifies feminism and redeploys women as agentic consumers (2). Producing buzzwords and slogans to express visions of energetic personal empowerment, it incorporates and naturalises aspects of feminism. At the same time, its rhetoric paradoxically 'others' feminism, marking it as extreme and perpetually at odds with the essence of women's 'authentic' desires.

Figured as a prerequisite to their self-gratification, postfeminist discourses encourage women to supersede or dissociate themselves from the burdens of second-wave feminism, motivating them to re-adopt traditional feminine practices and stereotypes without apology. But this prioritisation of personal freedoms and pleasures over feminism comes with a price: it has fostered a culture of post-critique which detracts from a collective we-feminism needed for continuing dialogue and social change. In other words, as Negra and Tasker forewarn, postfeminism's detachment from the social and the systemic risks bolstering the obfuscation of disparities of power in the postmillennial period.

James's series makes manifest this tension between feminism and the pursuit of pleasure by providing the Subconscious with a 'foil': the Inner Goddess. Like the Subconscious, the Inner Goddess is a subdivision of Anastasia's consciousness, similarly independent. Yet the guiding principles of these 'characters' are framed antithetically. While the Subconscious appears to be motivated by second-wave feminist rhetoric, encouraging Anastasia towards independence from Christian, the Inner Goddess is an enthusiastic consumer, active in her pursuit of pleasure. Throughout the course of the narrative, she motivates Anastasia to ignore the Subconscious and prioritise self-gratification. For example, when Christian gifts Anastasia a convertible for her graduation, the Subconscious "cringes in disgust," reiterating her belief that these lavish exchanges fortify the imbalance of power in their relationship. In contrast, the Inner Goddess refuses to feel ashamed. Dismissing the criticisms levelled at her by the 'parsimonious' Subconscious, she "drools with delight," metaphorically "tackling her to the floor" to silence these admonishments (*Fifty Shades of Grey*, 232).

In privileging Anastasia's entitlement to pleasure, the fulfilment of her individual desires, the Inner Goddess epitomises the shift from second-wave feminism to postfeminism. She also reproduces a distinctively postfeminist rhetoric by presenting 'feminism' as an impediment to Anastasia's self-gratification:

> *You can't seriously be considering this.* . . . My subconscious sounds sane and rational, not her usual snarky self. My inner goddess is jumping up and down, clapping her hands like a five-year old. *Please, let's do this . . . otherwise we'll end up alone with lots of cats and your classic novels to keep you company.*
>
> (*Fifty Shades of Grey*, 176)

Here, the Subconscious is aghast at Anastasia's serious consideration of Christian's dominant–submissive contract, concerned that it is oppressive and subjugating. Conversely, the Inner Goddess is excited by its pleasurable possibilities, warning Anastasia that emotional isolation is a consequence of female independence. In other words, the Inner Goddess figures the Subconscious, and her feminist rhetoric, as the limit Anastasia must transgress to experience unbridled personal pleasure. Read in this way, the dichotomisation of these two voices functions as a comic allegory of modern women's complex and often fraught relationship with feminism.

Anastasia eventually supplants the voice of feminism with the Inner Goddess, embracing her postfeminist principles. This allows her to satisfy her narcissistic pursuit of pleasure, becoming rich, powerful, normatively beautiful and sexually fulfilled. More pertinently, this shift is presented as narratively satisfying for the reader, framing the repudiation of feminism as a necessary but innocuous condition of achieving one's desires. Still, moments of affective dissonance in Anastasia's narration gesture towards the more insidious political consequences of commodity feminism, underscoring how the prioritisation of pleasure, often at the expense of collective social justice, can entrap women within perpetual victimhood.

This is most clearly discernible when Anastasia attempts to unravel her contradictory reactions to Christian's use of spanking as a punishment method:

> Dear Mr. Grey, You wanted to know why I felt confused after you – which euphemism should we apply – spanked, punished, beat, assaulted me. Well, during the whole alarming process, I felt demeaned, debased and abused. And much to my mortification, you're right, I was aroused . . . all things sexual are new to me – I only wish I was more experienced and therefore more prepared. I was shocked to feel aroused. . . . But I felt very uncomfortable, guilty even, feeling that way. It doesn't sit well with me, and I'm confused as a result.
>
> (*Fifty Shades of Grey*, 292)

Though she confesses that she was aroused during the spanking, Anastasia also articulates her discomfort. She frames this experience as a violent assault which has left her feeling guilty, confused and dismayed. In his response, however, Christian challenges the validity of those feelings:

> Do you really feel like this or do you think you ought to feel like this? Two very different things. . . . Don't waste your energy on guilt, feelings of wrongdoing, etc. . . . You need to free your mind and listen to your body.
>
> (*Fifty Shades of Grey*, 293)

Echoing the Inner Goddess, he encourages Anastasia to ignore the political or gendered implications of her actions, prioritising her individual desires. By extension, he implies that Anastasia's feminist consciousness – her feelings of responsibility or obligation to disrupt traditional and regressive gender dichotomies – is a deterrent to her pursuit of pleasure. In presenting his argument, Christian also reproduces an alarming myth about female victims of sexual assault, implying that bodily arousal is indicative of enjoyment and therefore consent.

Anastasia's feelings of distress and shame are notably at odds with the confident and pleasurable subjectivities often associated with neoliberal postfeminism. These feelings emphasise the discrepancy between Anastasia's expectations of her relationship – as something that should be reciprocal and fulfilling – and her lived experience of intimacy. This,

I propose, creates an affective gap which confronts the reader with a disturbing possibility: that Anastasia's pursuit of pleasure inadvertently sanctions her subjugation and masks the disparities of power in her relationship.

As we have seen, the postfeminist promotion of pleasure over politics can easily be used to invalidate any potential challenge to hegemonic structures of power. Christian clearly exploits these discourses to control and manipulate Anastasia. At the same time, by internalising these discourses, Anastasia becomes more susceptible to Christian's abuse. Reflecting these postfeminist discourses, Anastasia can only satisfy her pursuit of pleasure by suppressing the subconscious voice of feminism and withholding her critique of patriarchy, illustrating to the reader how it is precisely feminist concerns which are silenced by those hegemonic ideologies.

Consent Is a *Grey* Area

Contemporary discourses surrounding sexual violence and consent persistently emphasise the importance of personal responsibility and choice. As Mellisa Burkett and Karine Hamilton observe, these discourses commonly promote a 'just-say-no' rhetoric, typified by a risk avoidance approach, which encourages young women to properly communicate their willingness or unwillingness to engage in sexual relations with men (816). Underpinned by the idea that all sexual choices can be freely chosen, this approach to consent strongly correlates with the neoliberal notion of active citizenship. It presupposes that all individuals are autonomous, rationally calculating and free, capable of transcending any socio-structural barriers inhibiting their individual freedoms and choices.

Reflecting these pervasive discourses, the *Fifty Shades* series frames consent as something easily negotiated between autonomous and agentic individuals. Christian's relationship contract stipulates very clearly the importance of consent. It necessitates a verbal discussion about sexual limits prior to any and all sexual activities and includes a 'safe-word' clause in the event that consent is retracted during 'play'. Christian also directs Anastasia to make an informed and rational decision about their relationship. While he is an experienced 'dominant', with a thorough knowledge of BDSM practices, Anastasia has never had a sexual experience. Discomforted by this disparity, he gives her a "school assignment," motivating her to investigate all of the sexual activities listed in his contract and providing her with a laptop to facilitate this research. By encouraging her to expand her sexual knowledge, Christian ensures that Anastasia can fastidiously consent to a BDSM relationship. This figures Anastasia as an active and individual agent, capable of assuming personal responsibility for her choices.

Later, Christian stresses to Anastasia the consequences of neglecting these personal responsibilities:

> For the record, you stood beside me knowing what I was going to do. You didn't at any time ask me to stop – you didn't use either safeword. You are an adult – you have choices.
>
> (*Fifty Shades of Grey*, 295)

After an upsetting sexual encounter earlier that day, Anastasia emails her lover to confess her discomfort. But Christian admonishes Anastasia for her imprudence, arguing that she is responsible for asserting or retracting consent. According to Christian, Anastasia is obliged to make her discomfort clear during or prior to 'play' – by either saying 'no' or using her safe word. If not, he will automatically assume she has consented to their activity. In other words, Christian reiterates how the responsibility for consent is located firmly within the individual.

A series of analogous subplots further clarifies the trilogy's stance on consent. These subplots are centred on overbearing men who misinterpret Anastasia's friendliness for desire and are thus vilified. For example, Jose – Anastasia's closest male companion – ignores her verbal protestations when he drunkenly attempts to kiss her without permission. The next day, Jose is mortified by his deplorable actions and pleads for Anastasia's forgiveness. This guilt and embarrassment, however, marks his behaviour as improper, stressing to the reader the importance of *express* consent.

Likewise, Anastasia's overbearing boss is characterised by his inability to follow the correct procedure for acquiring consent. Jack Hyde, whose name appears to be a thinly veiled reference to Robert Louis Stevenson's *The Strange Case of Dr Jekyll and Mr Hyde* (1886), is a commissioning editor at SIP who interviews Anastasia for an internship. Upon meeting him, Anastasia remarks on how similar he is to Christian Grey – constructing an overt parallel between them:

> "Ana Steele, I'm Jack Hyde, the acquisitions editor here at SIP, and I'm very pleased to meet you." We shake hands, and his dark expression is unreadable, though friendly enough, I think. He says my name softly and cocks his head to one side, like someone I know – it's unnerving. Doing my best to ignore the irrational wariness he inspires, I launch into my carefully prepared speech . . . "You have a very impressive GPA. What extracurricular activities did you indulge in at WSU?" Indulge? I blink at him. What an odd choice of word.
>
> (*Fifty Shades of Grey*, 379)

Recalling her first encounter with Christian, Anastasia is comparably unsettled by Jack. James recycles the phrase 'dark expression', often used as a descriptor for Christian, to stress their similarity. Hyde's use of double entendres, his confusingly suggestive play on words, also mirrors Christian's lascivious deployment of ambiguous sexual innuendos.

But Anastasia has starkly contrasting *emotional* responses to these seemingly homogenous men. While she is immediately attracted to Christian, welcoming his sexual advances, Jack's interminable flirtatiousness repulses her. Perturbed by his repeated invasion of her privacy, she admits that her "skin crawls at his proximity" (*Fifty Shades Darker*, 266). Though Anastasia informs Jack of her commitment to Christian, he persists with his pursuit, continually inviting her to private dinners and drinks and affectionately referring to her as 'honey' throughout. Nevertheless, Jack's behaviour is coded as repugnant for the reader. Words like unsettling, dangerous, delusional and maniac are frequently used to describe him. When Jack attempts to seduce Anastasia, cornering her in his office and demanding she acquiesce to his sexual demands, the series crystallises its 'unimpeachable' code of sexual ethics. Refusing to heed Anastasia's warning to "back off," Hyde is vilified and reframed as the series's primary antagonist (*Fifty Shades Darker*, 267).

However, affective dissonances in Anastasia's narration trouble this neoliberal model of consent and the assumption that it is unequivocally benign:

> This is it; our relationship hangs in the balance, right here, right now. Do I let him do this or do I say no, and then that's it? Because I know it will be over if I say no. . . . And then his hand is no longer there . . . and he hits me – hard. Ow! My eyes spring open in response to the pain, and I try to rise, but his hand moves between my shoulder blades,

keeping me down. . . . He hits me again and again, quickly in succession. Holy fuck it hurts. I make no sound, my face screwed up against the pain. I try to wiggle away from the blows – spurred on by dateline spiking and coursing through my body. . . . From somewhere deep inside, I want to beg him to stop. But I don't. . . . I cry out . . . my body is singing, singing from his merciless assault.

(*Fifty Shades of Grey*, 275)

Here, Anastasia acknowledges that Christian will terminate their relationship if she does not acquiesce to his sexual demands. Recognising that punishment is an exigent component of his erotic desire, she figures herself as responsible for attending to her partner's sexual needs. These feelings of obligation, around which she frames this 'play' scenario, are regulatory in nature. Her feelings motivate her to alter her behaviour – thus obfuscating any straightforward interpretation of her participation as consensual.

While Anastasia's actions are presented as freely chosen in the excerpt – she does not *expressly* retract her consent or articulate her discomfort to Christian – her affective disorientation further undermines the reader's understanding of this encounter as reciprocal or mutually beneficial. In attempting to describe her emotional response to this event, Anastasia draws on a very specific lexicon most commonly associated with assault, stifling her urge to beg Christian to stop hurting her. This highlights a discrepancy between the expectations raised by dominant ideological formations – namely, that all sexual choices are freely chosen by rational, autonomous and agentic individuals – and her lived reality (which *feels* like abuse).

The visceral descriptions of Anastasia's agony are similarly troubling. Her face becomes literally contorted with pain, while James's use of onomatopoeic sounds, 'ow', accentuates her discomfort and distress. These descriptions, I propose, in conjunction with Anastasia's affective dissonance, engender an emotional response in the reader that is notably discordant with the 'feelings rules' of neoliberal postfeminism. In identifying with Anastasia – as the first-person narrator and the series's central point of identification – the reader is motivated to share in her pain, to *feel* her suffering. This emotional response, I argue, takes the reader 'out of the fiction', providing them with enough critical distance to recognise the insidious effects of the neoliberal model of consent and consider if those approaches might be sanctioning gendered violence.

Alarmingly, the series also illustrates how this incitement towards personal responsibility can exacerbate discourses of victim blaming. As I have demonstrated, Christian persistently emphasises Anastasia's individual responsibility for consent. More pertinently, he maintains that her constant discomfort about their unstable relationship does not reflect the disparity of power between them or indicate any kind of emotional abuse or manipulation on his part. Rather, Christian consistently blames Anastasia for her own discontent, framing her unhappiness as evidence of poor self-confidence or low self-esteem. Following neoliberal logics, Anastasia's 'discomfort' is figured as a character deficiency. Christian repeatedly implores her to seek help from a therapist for her "real self-esteem issues" (*Fifty Shades of Grey*, 400). Thus, rather than addressing the imbalance of power in their relationship, the narrative shifts its focus towards Anastasia's internal obstacles, what she can change about herself. This obscures the very real emotional *and* physical impact of Christian's abhorrent and abusive behaviour. Simultaneously, it demonstrates the ease with which discourses of personal responsibility can be co-opted to support an inegalitarian status quo, sanctioning male violence.

The series has been widely disparaged for its purported promotion of an abusive relationship. Literary critics, for example, argued that *Fifty Shades* continued a long-standing pattern from the romance genre of conflating officious male behaviour with intimacy and love. Dionne Van Reenan was especially critical of the series, stressing that James's redeployment of key romantic tropes eroticised Christian's abuse of Anastasia, obfuscating the readers' interpretation of his behaviour as problematic (227). Christian's mercurial tendencies are certainly fetishised from the outset. While he is cold, arrogant and temperamental, he is also exceptionally attractive and alluring – a quintessential romantic hero. Likewise, Anastasia is depicted as a prototypical romantic heroine, apathetic towards the opposite sex. And so, perhaps predictably, meeting Christian piques her sexual desire for the very first time. Underscoring the potency of his appeal, she confesses her attraction and exclaims that "no one should be this good-looking" (*Fifty Shades of Grey*, 10).

During their initial encounter in the opening scenes of *Fifty Shades of Grey*, Christian is oddly cruel to Anastasia, reprimanding her lack of professionalism. Teasing and mocking her, his condescending tone has an infantilising effect that makes her feel like "an errant child" (13). As she becomes increasingly disarmed by his capriciousness, Anastasia adjusts her body language, attempting to look taller and more intimidating by squaring her shoulders. Nevertheless, some of the descriptions of Anastasia's bodily responses to Christian blur the lines between discomfort and arousal. The quickening of her heartbeat and the flushing of her face could be interpreted as either titillation or fear. Later, when Anastasia reflects on this destabilising experience, she clarifies her feelings for the reader, admitting that no man has ever had this kind of *erotic* effect on her.

This eroticisation of Christian's despotism continues throughout James's series. Baffled by his volatility and unpredictable mood swings, Anastasia drunkenly contacts Christian to berate him during a night-out with friends. Concerned by her level of intoxication, Christian arrives unannounced at her local bar, casually admits to tracking her phone without permission and insists she return with him to his hotel room to sober herself. While Anastasia is initially perturbed by these "stalker tendencies," she confesses:

> I feel safe. Protected. He cares enough to come and rescue me from some mistakenly perceived danger. He's not a dark knight at all but a white knight in shining, dazzling armour – a classic romantic hero – Sir Gawain or Sir Lancelot.
>
> (*Fifty Shades of Grey*, 68–9)

By figuring Christian as Anastasia's saviour, her 'white knight', the narrative overtly contextualises his behaviour within a traditional romance narrative and obscures its insidious undertones. That Anastasia interprets 'stalking' as a pleasurable affirmation of Christian's adoration is also particularly notable, romanticising this troubling behaviour and reframing it as benign.

Over the course of the narrative, Christian's authoritarianism escalates, and Anastasia begins to withhold information on her whereabouts. She even admits to fearing the repercussions of 'disobeying' her lover's demands. Although these responses seem to indicate her discomfort with being persistently surveilled, 'stalking' ultimately becomes a recurring joke between them. Anastasia playfully suggests that the Police's "Every Breath You Take" should be Christian's stalker anthem. Yet by converting 'stalking' into a comedic device, a source of humour for the reader, the malignancy of Christian's behaviour is once again obfuscated, concealing his pernicious desire to control and dominate Anastasia.

The series is also shaped like a prototypical beauty-and-the-beast narrative, synonymous with the romance genre. Derived from Gabrielle-Suzanne Barbot de Villeneuve's seminal fairy tale *Beauty and the Beast* (1740), these narratives are usually centred on a young heroine's attempts to transform an aggressive and troubled male hero through her adoration and devotion. Popularised in classic romances like Emily Bronte's *Wuthering Heights* (1847) and Margaret Mitchell's *Gone with the Wind* (1936), these types of narratives have been extensively critiqued for promoting a dangerous idea: that persevering with an abusive relationship is a sure pathway to ever-lasting love.

Reproducing this popular formula, Christian is figured as 'damaged', his proclivity for BDSM linked to the abuse he experienced as a child. As such, Anastasia functions as his saviour in the narrative. Through the transformative power of her love, she heals his wounds and initiates him into a happy, domestic hereto-normality. While Anastasia successfully 'tames' the 'beast', this is not an easy task for her. Rather, in the process of trying to mend Christian, she is forced to endure both mental and physical hardship, spending most of the series clearly upset or distressed by his abuse. Nevertheless, like Bella Swan – the protagonist of Meyer's *Twilight* (2005–2008) series – Anastasia is rewarded for her perseverance. By the narrative's conclusion, she satisfies her pursuit of pleasure and achieves long-term happiness through maternity and matrimony.

Much critical attention has been devoted to James's revitalisation of these familiar tropes and their pernicious effects. But scholars have failed to address the unusual structure of this purportedly prototypical 'romance'. For the most part, the trilogy follows Anastasia and Christian as they work on and attempt to settle the terms of their relationship. While Christian is a sadomasochist who requires his partners to be totally obedient and submissive, both in and out of the bedroom, Anastasia longs for a more conventional relationship. Viewing male domination as regressive and outdated, she pushes for a settlement of their differences through mutual concession – a compromise. Anastasia will agree to submit to being dominated during all sexual activities, if, in exchange, Christian adheres to her more traditional requirements of their relationship: they will go on dates and sleep in the same bed, and she will be able to introduce him to her friends as her boyfriend.

However, these attempts to find balance in their relationship are oddly framed as a series of contractual negotiations. As the driving force of the plot, the narrative is structured around the vacillations in these negotiations – which are explored in exhaustive detail. Although Anastasia and Christian recognise that the relationship contract is legally unenforceable, they approach these negotiations solemnly, as market entities who require consolidation through a 'merger and acquisitions' process. In attempting to mediate their differences, the lovers cover all the basic components required to maintain a healthy and successful relationship: frankly outlining their sexual history and sexual health, discussing contraceptive options, identifying the days of the week they will or will not see each other and defining clearly their 'hard and soft limits' for sexual activity. In short, their relationship is refigured as a project, an investment between the two parties which may or may not repay their interest or their efforts.

Thus, James combines two seemingly disparate elements in her series: a contractual negotiation, which relies on cold data and 'rational' actors, with the 'warmth' of a quintessential romance. In other words, the way she has structured her series, with its affectless focus on the mechanics of the neoliberal couple, seems at odds with the typical affects of a romance novel. This unusual combination, I propose, creates an affective gap in the narrative, which has an alienating effect on the reader, disrupting their suspension of disbelief. These formal aesthetics prevent the reader from 'feeling' their way into James's characters and deny them the customary affective responses often elicited from the reading of romance. This allows them to secure enough critical distance from the text to reconsider the banality of the kind of romance it promotes. And so, the unusual structure of the series, and its alienating effects, potentially expose the more insidious aspects of heterosexual relationships, thereby forcing the reader to challenge the dynamics of power underpinning heterosexuality.

This 'against-the-grain' reading of the series is most apparent in the parallels between Christian's relationship contract and a marriage 'contract'. Reluctant to agree to the terms of his contract, Anastasia debates the validity of female submission in an email exchange with Christian. While he facetiously provides her with a dictionary definition of 'submissive', illuminating his expectations about their relationship, Anastasia is mocking. Modern women, she tells him, would never agree to that kind of retrograde obedience:

> Sir, please note the date of origin: 1580–1590. I would respectfully remind Sir that the year is 2011. We have come a long way since then. May I offer a definition for *you* to consider for our meeting: compromise [kom-pr*uh*-mahyz] – noun 1. a settlement of differences by mutual concessions.
>
> (*Fifty Shades of Grey*, 209)

Instead, she appears to contextualise her response in relation to the achievements of the feminist movement, implying that gender inequity is a thing of the past. From this perspective, the dominant–submissive contract is marked as regressive, problematic and dated for the reader.

Nonetheless, the series continually draws attention to the similarities between this contract and the contractual manifestation of heterosexuality in marriage. For example, Anastasia expressly observes how their use of language is practically indistinguishable:

> Serve and obey in all things. All things! I shake my head in disbelief. Actually, don't the marriage vows use those words . . . obey? This throws me. Do couple still say that?
>
> (*Fifty Shades of Grey*, 175)

She notes how both contracts come with a set of terms and conditions which necessitate female obedience and passivity. While James's series does not persist with this critique of the institution of marriage, the political implications of the parallel it inadvertently constructs are impossible to ignore. It underscores how the self-same disparities of power which facilitate female subjugation in a dominant–submissive relationship are sanitised and normalised when re-situated within the context of a heterosexual romance.

Still, James's narrative consistently privileges heteronormativity, promoting 'coupledom' as a site of possibility and pleasure. As a "quivering mass of female hormones," Anastasia is clearly motivated by her sexual urges and desires, active in her pursuit of erotic pleasure. Yet it is only within the familiar boundaries of a committed and monogamous, heterosexual 'partnership' that she is able to satisfy her sexual appetite. In spite of her initial trepidations, Anastasia eventually learns how to assimilate the 'spirit' of the BDSM into a traditional relationship with Christian, initiating 'play' scenarios which replicate her sexual fantasies and elevate her pleasure. Thus, the novels figure heteronormativity as a pathway to sexual gratification for Anastasia – domesticating 'kink' in the process.

Crucially, this exaltation of heteronormativity effectively disguises the regulative power dynamics in Christian and Anastasia's relationship, facilitating the subtle re-entrenchment of pernicious gender norms. This becomes particularly apparent in one of the series's more insidious scenes. Whilst on their honeymoon, Anastasia discovers Christian's box of "insurance policies," a collection of pornographic images of his ex-submissives, preserved as a form of leverage against them (*Fifty Shades Freed*, 71). Inspired by this discovery, Anastasia purchases a camera, puts on her most expensive and seductive lingerie and encourages Christian to take her picture:

> Christian swallows and runs a hand through his hair.... "For me, photos like those have usually been an insurance policy, Ana ... I've objectified women for so long." "And you think taking pictures of me is ... um, objectifying me? Well, it was supposed to be fun, but apparently it's a symbol of women's oppression." His eyes darken, and his expression changes to predatory. "You want to be oppressed?" he murmurs silkily. "Not oppressed. No," I murmur back. "I could oppress you big time, Mrs. Grey."
>
> (*Fifty Shades Freed*, 73)

In attempting to arouse his scopophilic gaze, Anastasia figures herself as Christian's object, stressing that pleasing him gives her pleasure. But Christian is hesitant and careful in his response to this proposal, wanting to ensure that Anastasia feels no sense of obligation to partake in a pornographic photoshoot to satisfy his sexual fantasies. On the one hand, this episode emphasises Anastasia's sexual agency, underscoring how she actively and enthusiastically chooses to 'oppress' herself for her *own* sexual gratification. Anastasia does not interpret this self-objectification as a kind of entrapment within a subordinating patriarchal web. Rather, she understands it as both empowering and pleasurable, bolstering her self-gratification.

On the other hand, by highlighting how Anastasia adapts herself to become the reflection of Christian's desire, the series highlights the limitations of her purported empowerment. In opting to self-objectify, Anastasia adopts a traditionally subordinate role as a passive, eroticised object of the male gaze. This clearly upholds hetero-patriarchal ideologies which privilege male domination and necessitate female submission. Thus, the series once more calls into question the benevolence of contemporary gendered power dynamics, forcing us to consider if the kind of sexual liberation which is being offered to women as a substitute for feminism is – as Gill has suggested – merely a new "mechanism of objectification in an even more pernicious guise" (106).

When contextualised within Christian and Anastasia's earliest discussion of sexual objectification, this episode becomes particularly illuminating. Having just received a copy of Thomas Hardy's *Tess of the D'Urbervilles: A Pure Woman Faithfully Presented* (1891), Anastasia queries Christian's very peculiar choice of gift:

> "Why did you give me *Tess of the D'Urbervilles* specifically?" I ask. Christian stares at me for a moment. I think he's surprised by my question. "Well, you said you liked Thomas Hardy." "Is that the only reason?" "It seemed appropriate. I could hold you to some impossibly high ideal like Angel Clare or debase you completely like Alec d'Urberville," he murmurs and his eyes flash dark and dangerous. "If there are only two choices, I'll take the debasement," I whisper, gazing at him. He gasps. "Anastasia, stop biting your lip, please. It's very distracting."
>
> (*Fifty Shades of Grey*, 95)

Here, Christian interprets Hardy's narrative to identify two potential outcomes of his relationship: he will either sexually objectify Anastasia or abstain from all sexual activity in order to 'preserve' her virtuous character. While Christian invokes the language of individualism – framing the two pathways for relationship progression as specific to his evolving romance – these options might also function as an allegory of contemporary female sexuality. Thus, by underscoring how these bifurcated options are both restrictive and constraining, the narrative highlights the limitations of Anastasia's purported agency, undermining neoliberal and postfeminist discourses of female empowerment in the process. That Anastasia is forced to 'choose' sexual objectification to satisfy her sexual urges is also particularly revealing. When read as an allegory, it implies that sexual subordination – 'debasement' – is perhaps a necessary condition of contemporary women's sexual liberation.

As we have seen, both *Fifty Shades of Grey* and the *Twilight* series fetishise and romanticise the hegemonic ideal of neoliberal postfeminism. They do this, predominantly, by reanimating key tropes from the romance genre – specifically the modern gothic romance and the Harlequin romance. At the same time, affects like discontent, vulnerability, unhappiness, fear, anxiety and pain, ubiquitous in the trilogies, simultaneously undermine their promotion of those ideologies as empowering and pleasurable for women. But I propose that there is a revealing distinction between the *perceptibly* of those affects in these novels, perhaps signalling a shift in the ideological landscape during the mid-2010s.

Like Anastasia, Bella seems to experience affective dissonances whereby she *feels* the discrepancies between the expectations raised by dominant ideological formations and her lived reality. In contrast to those neoliberal and postfeminist discourses reassuring women that equality has been achieved, Bella recognises the asymmetries of power in her relationship, drawing on recognisable figures from popular culture to demonstrate that imbalance. She is also clearly motivated to become a vampire by her *feelings* of vulnerability as a young woman under neoliberal patriarchy, understanding that the threat of male violence is an unavoidable and constant presence in her life. Yet these affective gaps in her narration – Bella's 'personal feelings' – are sporadic at best, scattered unpredictably throughout the narrative. Instead, those aforementioned affects, discordant with the feelings rules of neoliberal postfeminism, are largely atypical in *Twilight*, 'impersonal feelings' which are elicited in the reader by the copious descriptions of Bella's body in pain.

While Bella interprets her suffering as a worthwhile pursuit, a necessary condition for achieving her desires, those visceral descriptions are arguably jarring for the series's readers, engendering feelings of discomfort and unease in them. These affects, I argued, confronted the reader with the possibility that suffering is a constituent part of forging feminine subjectivity in the post-millennial period. Nevertheless, those affects were often indiscernible or difficult to detect. Concealed within the fiction, they were sublimated by the dominant affect of sentimentality synonymous with the romance genre.

In this chapter, I contended that James's trilogy also effectuated 'impersonal feelings' in the reader. It did this by amalgamating two seemingly disparate genres – the cold, neoliberal contract with the warmth of the popular romance – thus creating a lacuna in the affective register. These impersonal feelings, I suggested, were aesthetic forms of resistance to dominant systems of power. Yet, unlike *Twilight*, affective dissonances in Anastasia's narration are ubiquitous in the *Fifty Shades* series. As I have demonstrated, Anastasia struggles to reconcile her 'personal feelings' of inadequacy, self-consciousness and dissatisfaction with the image of herself as an empowered, self-assured woman perpetuated by neoliberal and postfeminist discourses. In this way, her disillusionment with those hegemonic ideologies feels more tangible than Bella's, constantly bubbling beneath the surface of her narration.

This tangibility, I propose, indicates an important moment of counter-resistance, whereby the *tone* of women's fiction begins to mutate. As we will see in Chapters 3 and 4, dissonant affects like rage and malaise become dominant, permeating throughout domestic noir. These affects not only undermine the 'feelings rules' of neoliberal and postfeminist culture but also directly dispute their benignity, confronting the reader with their pernicious effects.

And so, while Anastasia's affective dissonance is neatly resolved by the series's conclusion, subsumed within a prototypical romantic happy ending, the palpability of her disaffection suggests a growing frustration with those hegemonic ideologies – a frustration which might catalyse a feminist challenge to the status quo.

Reference List

Alan, M. *Fifty Shades of Grey Decoded: A Man's Playbook*. Self-Published, 2012.
Barnett, Laura. "Mommy Porn? *Fifty Shades of Grey* by EL James: Review." *The Telegraph*, 13 Apr. 2012, www.telegraph.co.uk/culture/books/bookreviews/9201010/Mommy-porn-Fifty-Shades-of-Grey-by-EL-James-review.html.
Bronte, Emily. *Wuthering Heights*. Thomas Cautley Newby, 1847.
Burkett, Melissa and Karine Hamilton. "Postfeminist Sexual Agency: Young Women's Negotiations of Sexual Consent." *Sexualities*, vol. 15, no. 7, 2012, pp. 815–833. doi: 10.1177/1363460712454076.
Comella, Lynn. "Fifty Shades of Erotic Stimulus." *Feminist Media Studies*, vol. 13, no. 3, 2013, pp. 563–566. doi: 10.1080/14680777.2013.786269.
de Villeneuve, Gabrielle-Suzanne Barbot. *Beauty and the Beast*. 1740.
Deller, Ruth A. and Clarissa Smith. "Reading the BDSM Romance: Reader Responses to Fifty Shades." *Sexualities*, vol. 16, no. 8, 2013, pp. 932–950. doi: 10.1177/1363460713508882.
Dobson, Amy Shields and Akane Kanai. "From 'Can-Do' Girls to Insecure and Angry: Affective Dissonances in Young Women's Post-Recessional Media." *Feminist Media Studies*, vol. 19, no. 6, 2019, pp. 771–786. doi: 10.1080/14680777.2018.1546206.
Downing, Lisa. "Safewording! Kinkphobia and Gender Normativity in *Fifty Shades of Grey*." *Psychology and Sexuality*, vol. 4, no. 1, 2013, pp. 92–102. doi: 10.1080/19419899.2012.740067.
Fifty Shades Darker. Directed by James Foley, Universal Pictures, 2017.
Fifty Shades Freed. Directed by James Foley, Universal Pictures, 2018.
Fifty Shades of Grey. Directed by Sam Taylor-Johnson, Universal Pictures, 2015.
Gill, Rosalind, et al. *Aesthetic Labour: Rethinking Beauty Politics in Neoliberalism*. Palgrave Macmillan, 2017.
Gill, Rosalind, et al. "From Sexual Objectification to Sexual Subjectification: The Resexualisation of Women's Bodies in the Media." *Feminist Media Studies*, vol. 3, no. 1, 2003, pp. 100–106. doi: 0.1080/1468077032000080158.
Gill, Rosalind, et al. "Media, Empowerment and the 'Sexualisation of Culture' Debates." *Sex Roles*, vol. 66, no. 11, 2012, pp. 736–745. doi: 10.1007/s11199-011-0107-1.
Girls. Dunham, Lena, Apatow Productions. HBO, 2012–2017.
James, E.L. *Fifty Shades Freed*. Vintage Books, 2012.
James, E.L. *Fifty Shades of Darker*. Vintage Books, 2012.
James, E.L. *Fifty Shades of Grey*. Vintage Books, 2011.
Hardy, Thomas. *Tess of the d'Urbervilles: A Pure Woman Faithfully Presented*. McIlvaine & Company, 1891.
Kilpatrick, Chris. "Forget Fifty Shades of Grey . . . Try Reading the Bible Instead." *Belfast Telegraph*, 22 Aug. 2012, www.belfasttelegraph.co.uk/news/northern-ireland/forget-fifty-shades-of-grey-try-reading-bible-instead-28783749.html.
McRobbie, Angela. *The Aftermath of Feminism: Gender, Culture and Social Change*. Sage Publications, 2008.
McRobbie, Angela. "Young Women and Consumer Culture." *Journal of Cultural Studies*, vol. 22, no. 5, 2008, pp. 531–550. *EBSCOhost*, doi: 10.1080/09502380802245803
Meyer, Stephenie. *Breaking Dawn*. Atom, 2008.
Meyer, Stephenie. *Eclipse*. Atom, 2007.
Meyer, Stephenie. *New Moon*. Little, Brown Company, 2006.
Meyer, Stephenie. *Twilight*. Atom, 2005.

Mitchell, Margaret. *Gone with the Wind*. Macmillan Publishers, 1936.

Roach, Catherine M. *Happily Ever After: The Romance Story in Popular Culture*. Indiana University Press, 2016.

Roiphe, Katie. "Working Women's Fantasies." *Newsweek*, 16 Apr. 2012, www.newsweek.com/working-womens-fantasies-63915.

Smith, Rachel Greenwald. *Affect and American Literature in the Age of Neoliberalism*. Cambridge University Press, 2015.

Stevenson, Robert Louis. *The Strange Case of Dr Jekyll and Mr Hyde*. Longmans, Green & Company, 1886.

Taormino, Tristan. *50 Shades of Kink: An Introduction to BDSM*. Cleis Press, 2012.

Tasker, Yvonne and Diane Negra. *Interrogating Postfeminism: Gender and the Politics of Popular Culture*. Duke University Press, 2007.

Tripodi, Francesca. "Fifty Shades of Consent?" *Feminist Media Studies*, vol. 27, no. 1, 2017, pp. 93–107. doi: 10.1080/14680777.2017.1261846.

Van Reenan, Dionne. "Is This Really What Women Want? An Analysis of Fifty Shades of Grey and Modern Feminist Thought." *South African Journal of Philosophy*, vol. 33, no. 2, 2014, pp. 223–233. doi: 10.1080/02580136.2014.925730.

Weiss, Margot. "BDSM and Feminism: Notes on an Impasse." *Tenured Radical Blog*, 23 May 2012, www.works.bepress.com/mdweiss/11/.

Wood, Rachel. "Look Good, Feel Good: Sexiness and Sexual Pleasure in Neoliberalism." *Aesthetic Labour: Rethinking Beauty Politics in Neoliberalism*, edited by Rosalind Gill, Christina Scharff and Ana Sofia Elis, Palgrave Macmillan, 2017, pp. 317–330.

3 Happily Never After

'Vagina-Dentata Dames'?

In *Dead Blondes and Bad Mothers: Monstrosity, Patriarchy and the Fear of Female Power* (2019), Sady Doyle emphasises how myths about female monstrosity have a long-standing history in Western culture. From the Furies who tore men apart with razor-sharp claws to the Irish fae who enchanted mortal men and drained the souls from their bodies, these myths, Doyle argues, are ubiquitous and continue to inform contemporary reiterations of the monstrous feminine (xii). As constructed within and by a patriarchal and phallocentric ideology, these myths are often centred on the 'problem' of sexual difference. Across the history of Western culture, femininity has been positioned as the Other against which the masculine Self is defined. From Aristotle, who concluded that every woman was a mutilated male, to Sigmund Freud, who modernised the reduction of women to grotesque walking wounds, arguing that male children were traumatised for life by the knowledge that their mothers were maimed and incomplete without a penis, women have been marked as monstrous as a result of their perceived castration.

Building on this idea that a woman's 'lack' perpetually threatens to trigger male castration anxiety, Barbara Creed surmised that Freud's theory inadvertently engendered another, perhaps more frightening, phantasy of the monstrous feminine – that of a woman as a castrator. In contrast to Freud, who argued that women only terrify when represented as man's castrated Other, Creed posited that women have been persistently figured as monsters in Western culture precisely because they are *not* castrated (1993, 7). Instead, they are potent and physically whole without a penis. It is this fear of female power – in conjunction with a woman's sexual difference or otherness – which Creed suggests provokes the utmost anxiety in the male subject.

Evolving in tandem with myths about the dangers of feminine difference, the 'castrating' female monster has taken on many forms in contemporary popular culture. However, she is invariably depicted as a frighteningly powerful manifestation of ungovernable femininity. Giving rise to what Doyle describes as "countless, bluntly anatomical nightmares" of femininity in excess, she is defined by an unruliness or lawlessness which is often written on her body (xii). Refusing to adhere to the expectations of her gender, she deviates from traditional feminine norms. This deviation further heightens the threat she poses to the stability of the symbolic order.

In possessing the power to subvert or overthrow patriarchal systems that rely on her subordination, the prototypical female monster embodies, in Julia Kristeva's terms, the 'abject'. The abject, for Kristeva, is "radically excluded . . . yet, from its place of banishment, does not cease challenging its master" (1982, 7). As both the necessary 'not-me' against which the subject defines itself and an unthinkable yet unrelenting threat to subjectivity, the abject must exist on the borders of society. From this periphery, it provokes terror and disgust in the subject, troubling the unstable boundaries of their subject-hood.

Steven Jay Schneider's study of 'psychopathic' villains in horror and thriller genres affirms this idea that a woman's monstrosity is usually associated with her lack of self-governance or her refusal to adhere to patriarchal regulations. Highlighting how representations of monstrosity are specifically gendered, Schneider argues that the psycho-pathologies of fictional male psycho-killers starkly contrast with those of female villains. Male psycho-killers, he observes, tend to be depicted as either arational – demonstrating a robotic, inhuman nature – or hyper-rational – verbose and witty, with carefully considered and meticulously executed crimes (2006, 240). Conversely, Schneider maintains that female psycho-killers are almost always depicted as *irrational*. The spontaneous and messy acts of violence committed by these monstrous women can usually be interpreted as crimes of either passion or obsession. Motivated predominantly by their ungovernable emotions, these women are often capricious and erratic. Their primary modes of self-expression frequently occur through "involuntary rages and hysterical bodily performances" (244).

For Schneider, one of the most potent contemporary manifestations of the monstrous feminine is the female psycho-killer of neo-noir cinema. Notable examples of this archetype include S*ingle White Female*'s Hedra Carlson (Barbet Schroeder, 1992) and *Basic Instinct*'s Catherine Tramell (Paul Verhoeven, 1992). These women, Schneider argues, gave nightmarish expression to the inversion of patriarchy's normative femininity whereby "passivity became possessiveness, vulnerability was replaced by viciousness and maternal love was transformed into a maniacal, passionate hate" (244). Overtly sexual and ferociously ambitious, they threatened to upend traditional gender norms in the early 1990s. But it was Glenn Close's performance as an unhinged seductress in Adrian Lyne's Fatal Attraction (1987) which propelled this female villain to new heights of popularity – solidifying her enduring position within wider popular culture.

Staging a dichotomy between Close's Alex Forest and her opposite – the homemaking wife – *Fatal Attraction* encapsulated what Susan Faludi has since described as a postfeminist 'backlash' against second-wave feminism (1991, 4). This 'backlash' coincided with the re-entrenchment of conservatism in the USA and the UK – advanced by Ronald Reagan and Margaret Thatcher – and framed feminism as a source of unhappiness for women (4). Indeed, throughout the 1980s, copious narratives circulated in the popular media maintaining that women were more miserable than ever before, despite their newfound agency. Positing that feminism was responsible for these woes, these narratives suggested that women were undergoing a crisis of identity and longed to return to more traditional roles as wives and mothers.

Distributed during this time in which fears about women's liberation were rapidly escalating, *Fatal Attraction* underscored what could happen when feminism went 'too far'. As an unmarried, independent, sexually liberated, career woman, Alex is figured as the embodiment of feminism – as a prototype of the modern woman. However, when she enters into a weekend affair with a married man, Alex begins to covet the connubial pleasures that might be found in the domestic sphere – pleasures which her career aspirations have seemingly denied her. Determined not to be ignored, Alex demands that her increasingly distant and disdainful lover is held accountable for his actions. She insists that he leave his wife and commit to a new relationship with her. Though he repeatedly rebuffs her advances and adamantly rejects her offer, Alex refuses to yield. Opting to harass him into submission, she repeatedly calls his work and home, kidnaps his daughter from school and even falsifies a pregnancy to entrap him.

Embodying all that threatens the dominant social order, Alex is a quintessential female monster. Refusing to obey the unwritten rules which support patriarchal systems of power, she lives out her sexuality and emotions aggressively and excessively. Nevertheless, as Doyle stresses, this monster – "the thing that exists outside of our acceptable roles and definitions" – must be suppressed or the patriarchal system will collapse (xx). Thus, *Fatal Attraction* concludes with the violent death of its antagonist. Forcefully denigrating notions of female independence and unfettered sexuality, the narrative culminates in the punishment of Alex as a vengeful and hysterical madwoman. She is ultimately murdered by her lover's unwaveringly forgiving 'good wife'. Reinforcing the troubling notion that an uncontrollable or agentic woman is both deadly and dangerous, the film's vilification of Alex – alongside its exaltation of the subservient wife – advocates traditional gender roles. In its narrative, patriarchal order can only be restored via the destruction of a monstrous, recalcitrant woman. What's more, the audience is positioned to actively enjoy this conclusion; Alex's death is presented as both narratively pleasurable and righteous for the viewer.

While Alex came to be seen by moviegoers and journalists alike as an embodiment of evil – the most hated woman in America – the protagonist of Gillian Flynn's *Gone Girl* (2012) was similarly reviled. Amy Elliot Dunne has since been dubbed the "most disturbing female villain of all time" (Katey Rich, 2015). Following the disintegration of a tumultuous marriage, *Gone Girl*'s narrative vacillates between the contradictory viewpoints of Amy and her husband Nick. Structured as a series of confessional diary entries, Amy's delineation of her marital woes is used to elucidate the events which have led up to her disappearance on the morning of her fifth wedding anniversary. Plagued by her suspicion that her husband might kill her, Amy's recollections of Nick's violent outbursts and volatile temperament become progressively more incriminating, casting a shadow of suspicion over the unemployed journalist-turned-bar owner and community college professor whose own narrative is populated with troubling inconsistencies. But the reader eventually discovers that Amy falsified these diary entries. Tired of trying to adhere to a performance of the 'Cool Girl' – a contemporary ideal of femininity – she devised a plan of action: she faked her own disappearance in a revenge plot against a philandering spouse who cast her aside in favour of a considerably younger woman.

Almost immediately upon her novel's release, copious reviews and think-pieces surfaced in which the charge of virulent misogyny was levelled against Flynn, criticising her characterisation of Amy as the monstrous architect of Nick's downfall. Amy's falsification of two charges of rape was particularly reviled in the popular media. Eva Wiseman of *The Observer* argued that this plot confirmed a pervasive narrative: that women are "scheming harridans" – misandrists who use their sexuality as a weapon to control and destroy the virtuous men in their lives (2013). *Vanity Fair*'s Richard Lawson was similarly critical of Flynn's protagonist. Figuring her as a two-dimensional, sociopathic villainess, Lawson maintained that Amy acutely encapsulated and actively perpetuated the most persistent fears of the Men's Rights Association (2014).

While these damning interpretations of Flynn's protagonist continued to circulate in popular culture, literary critics – including Jacqueline Rose – were equally reproving. Highlighting the exploitative quality of *Gone Girl*'s 'big reveal', Rose argued that the sinister effect of the narrative's shocking twist should not be understated. This twist, she suggested, facilitated the perpetuation of a thousand reductive myths about 'monstrous' female behaviour and simultaneously threatened to discredit the real-world victims of intimate partner violence (2015).

Like Amy, the protagonist of Paula Hawkins's *The Girl on the Train* (2015) was disparaged by critics in the popular media and dismissed as a sexist reanimation of the monstrous feminine. Hawkins's novel centres predominantly on Rachel Watson – a recently divorced woman who is struggling with alcoholism. In attempting to preserve the facade of employment after she has lost her job due to her drinking, she makes a daily commute on the train. From the window of her new sanctuary, Rachel becomes a voyeur fixated on the inhabitants of 15 Blenheim Road – Scott and Megan Hipwell. At the same time, Rachel gazes from the train to the neighbouring house at number 23. This, we discover, is her cherished former home, now inhabited by her ex-husband Tom, his new wife Anna and their baby. When she witnesses what she believes to be an act of violence against Megan – who, she discovers, has subsequently disappeared – Rachel is struck with dread. She maintains that she saw something important but cannot articulate the memory. As Rachel attempts to unravel this mystery, her investigation begins to point her in a disturbing direction, forcing her to finally address a repressed trauma.

Writing for the *New York Times*, Jean Hanff Korelitz's critique of Rachel encapsulated the popular sentiment: Rachel was so dislikable that she provoked a misogynist response in the reader, who was encouraged to collude in her abjection (2015). Comparing her to the archetypical clueless 'ditz' of the classic slasher film, Korelitz was especially critical of Rachel's self-destructive and often illogical behaviour. Solidifying her monstrosity, she maintained that Rachel's lack of self-control and bodily governance precluded her from becoming a truly affirmative or aspirational heroine for modern women; a depressed, unemployed, self-pitying drunk, she was too 'difficult' a character to root for.

Both Amy and Rachel have been widely denigrated as reductive reiterations of the archetypical female monster. However, I posit an alternative reading of their monstrosity. *Gone Girl* and *The Girl on the Train* offer readers a different kind of female monster – one modified for, and reflective of, the neoliberal, postfeminist age. Where traditional castrating female monsters incited fear by refusing to be subjugated within the dominant patriarchal system, what makes Amy monstrous is her superhuman dedication to being normatively feminine. Through this subversion of Amy's motivations, Flynn highlights the punishing nature of contemporary gender ideologies and their potential to pathologise women. In other words, she redeploys this archetype not to rehearse an archaic misogynistic conception of femininity but to critique a dominant modern conception of a woman figured as the purportedly 'empowered' subject of neoliberal postfeminism. As will be demonstrated, Amy's attempts to resolve the contradictory demands of her feminine identity make her a monster. But these attempts also notably entrap her within the role of a perpetual victim. By underscoring this connection, Flynn further heightens her critique of oppressive gender ideologies whilst drawing attention to the quotidian reality of gender-based violence in contemporary culture.

In contrast to Amy, Rachel's monstrosity is framed as a direct consequence of her *inability* to adhere to contemporary gender norms. At a cursory glance, this depiction of Rachel as an embodiment of 'failed' femininity appears to affirm popular myths about female monstrosity. However, Hawkins finds a way to trouble this straightforward interpretation of her protagonist. While Rachel's unsuccessful attempts to satisfy neoliberal and postfeminist ideals of femininity have made her a monster, Hawkins underscores how these efforts have simultaneously stripped her of agency and facilitated her subjugation; disturbingly enabling her ex-husband to manipulate, control and abuse her. Thus, as with Flynn, Hawkins refuses to depoliticise her female monster. Instead, she deploys the archetype of the female monster to emphasise the connection between retro-sexist gender norms and the increasing number of acts of violence against women.

The Cool Girl

In *Chick Lit: The New Woman's Fiction* (2006), Suzanne Ferriss and Mallory Young suggest that 'chick culture' can be defined as a "group of mostly American and British popular culture media forms focused primarily on twenty-to-thirty-something middle-class women" (1). Popularised in literature by figures such as Carrie Bradshaw – protagonist of Candace Bushnell's *Sex and the City* (1997) – and Bridget Jones – heroine of Helen Fielding's *Bridget Jones's Diary* (1996) – the stereotypical protagonist of chick lit is "single, lives and works in an urban centre, is surrounded by a network of friends, and is struggling to find a fulfilling job and a meaningful relationship" (Ferris & Young, 2).

In tandem with its prototypical single-girl-in-the-city format, these narratives tend to attach a specific catalogue of features to their heroines; they are often active, sexual agents who usually possess one or several flaws, a lack of self-esteem and an obsession with their weight, their looks, or a man. While the heroines of chick lit are rarely depicted as perfect, they habitually strive for some form of self-improvement – physical, mental, romantic or financial. This commitment to self-improvement is often rewarded. Having worked to rectify their 'flaws', the female protagonists of chick lit are recompensed, and their narratives usually culminate with the happy ending of a stable, heterosexual relationship though notably, marriage as such is not a generic necessity.

Flynn's novel explicitly evokes these generic conventions in Amy's diary. 'Diary Amy' aligns with the quintessential heroine of chick lit. As a fledgling writer of personality quizzes for a women's magazine, she is dissatisfied with her career. Committed to self-improvement, she is using her journal to hone her skills – "to become a genuine, talented writer" (Flynn, 10). Set in New York City, these journal entries include recurring references to a contemporary, urban, cosmopolitan and affluent lifestyle. In line with chick lit's seemingly liberated attitudes towards female sexuality, Diary Amy is also uninhibited in her expressions of desire; she proudly attests to having had 11 sexual partners and asserts that she "likes to be fucked properly!" (Flynn, 12).

In her adoption of a first-person confessional style narrative – exemplified by the diary format – Flynn's novel reanimates the prototypical *voice* of the chick lit heroine. Consequentially, Diary Amy is made very familiar by bearing a striking resemblance to Fielding's seminal protagonist. Neither superwoman nor role model, Diary Amy is as ordinary and relatable as Bridget. Her confiding, chatty and casual narrative voice is nearly indistinguishable from a conversation with our best girlfriends. Immediately establishing this intimacy with the reader, Diary Amy's journal opens with a giddy, juvenile declaration of love: "I met a boy! I met a boy, a great, gorgeous dude, a funny, cool-ass guy" (Flynn 12).

Diary Amy's pervasive humour, irony and self-deprecation entices the reader to identify and empathise with her:

> So I know I am right not to settle, but it doesn't make me feel better as my friends pair off and I stay home on Friday night with a bottle of wine and make myself an extravagant meal and tell myself, This is *perfect*, as if I'm the one dating me.
>
> (Flynn, 28)

While Amy confesses that she feels lonely as the sole single woman amidst her group of married friends, she is clearly comfortable with mocking herself and her 'abhorrent' single status. Still, by underscoring her fears about 'singledom' – and highlighting her awareness of the cultural expectations placed on single women – she is framed sympathetically for the reader.

Plagued by her fear of becoming a spinster-at-thirty, Diary Amy is as committed to her search for 'Mr Right' as Bridget. This sanguine faith in true love, however, is often rattled by her awareness that her 'quest' is time sensitive. In line with the contemporary promulgation of matrimonial panic, her dwindling optimism is explicitly linked with her maturation. As she quickly approaches 40, her singleness presents itself as a problem in need of rectification. This becomes particularly apparent when Diary Amy attends a launch party for the most recent edition of *Amazing Amy* – a successful series of children's books written by her parents. In this novel, the eponymous heroine finally settles down and marries 'Able Andy'. Confronted with her own singleness, Diary Amy is pressed to shamefully acknowledge her single status by a series of interviewers who wonder how it feels to see that her literary counterpart has ultimately 'beat her down the aisle':

> '*I'm happily single right now, no Able Andy in my life!*'
> '*Yes, I am single. No Able Andy in my life right now.*'
> '*Yes, I am single.*'
> '*Yes, my parents are definitely soul mates.*'
> '*Yes, I would like that for myself one day.*'
> '*Yep, single, motherfucker.*'
>
> (Flynn, 27)

As her responses to these interview questions become increasingly fraught, the narrative underscores not only her agitation and embarrassment but the continued naturalisation and celebration of heterosexual romance in contemporary culture.

Perturbed by her feelings of insufficiency as an unmarried 30-something woman, Diary Amy is acutely aware of the contradictory demands of contemporary femininity. She struggles to reconcile the 'responsibilities' of second-wave feminism with the need to regulate her behaviour to attain a 'successfully' feminine subjectivity. This postfeminist paradox permeates the chick lit genre. As McRobbie observes, Bridget Jones is overtly indebted to feminism but isn't quite sure that it is what she wants – that it is what makes her happy (2008, 12). Likewise, Diary Amy willingly forfeits her "Independent Young Feminist card" in order to prioritise her pursuit of romance and the finding of a suitable husband (Flynn, 36).

In a reaffirmation of postfeminist ideologies, the pressures of feminist responsibility are figured as a burden hindering Diary Amy's pursuit of happiness. She wants nothing more than to enjoy all sorts of traditional feminine pleasures without apology. Though she is explicitly aware that she has adopted a rather retro – or retro-sexist – traditional wife role, Diary Amy repeatedly underscores her contentment. As a "happy busy bumblebee of martial enthusiasm" – who balances Nick's check book, trims his hair and spends her days thinking of sweet things to do for him – she exclaims that she is entirely satisfied (Flynn, 36). In the ultimate display of her embrace of the traditional, Diary Amy also confesses that she enjoys being Nick's object – his possession. After a series of tentative sexual encounters with 'repugnantly' nervous men, she explicitly derives pleasure from her lover's overtly territorial and dominating behaviour.

Just as Bridget Jones is fully aware that her ideas about relationships – and how to successfully achieve one – are the result of years of consuming a popular media which figures pleasing your man as a source of empowerment, Diary Amy similarly monitors and modifies her behaviour in order to appear more palatable to the opposite sex. While she admits that the personality quizzes she constructs contain only "zippy stereotypes of femininity," they increasingly bleed into her everyday life as a series of multiple-choice questions which allow her to carefully control her responses to differing events (Flynn, 10).

Having accidentally bumped into Nick on Seventh Avenue – several months after their first romantic encounter – Diary Amy employs a personality quiz to determine her behaviour:

A) 'Do I know you?' (manipulative, challenging)
B) 'Oh, wow, I'm so happy to see you!' (eager, doormat like)
C) 'Go fuck yourself.' (aggressive, bitter)
D) 'Well, you certainly take your time about it, don't you Nick?' (light, playful, laid back).
Answer: D
And now we're together.

(Flynn, 24)

Diary Amy chooses her answer on how she believes that she will be perceived by Nick and not her authentic emotional response. In contrast to the laid-back version of herself she chooses to perform, her precise counting of the time it has taken Nick to contact her – eight months, two weeks and a couple of days – alongside her overt confession that she was irritated by his behaviour indicate the true feelings she is compelled to repress. It is only by censoring these 'unpalatable' emotions that Diary Amy is able to get what she wants – a committed relationship.

Diary Amy links this urge to censor her emotions and behaviour to her deep-rooted fear of being marked as unappealing or unattractive. Highlighting the restrictive limitations of her gender, she invalidates affective responses – such as irritation or displeasure – in trepidation of becoming "some pert-mouthed, strident angry-girl . . . the shrew with hair curlers and the rolling pin" (Flynn 148). When Diary Amy's performance as this 'unchallenging', easy-going woman begins to falter, she discredits her own emotions on the basis of her sex as if to suggest that 'girlishness' is some kind of disease that must be remedied; she asserts: "I am being a girl . . . I was doing the awful chick talk-cry: *mwaha-waah-gwwahh-and-waa-waa-*. . . . I'm feeling like some shrill fishwife or a foolish doormat" (Flynn, 51). But in line with a neoliberal and postfeminist version of femininity, Diary Amy continually underscores her behavioural modifications as freely chosen – however traditional, old-fashioned or inegalitarian they may be, she voluntarily invokes a strict adherence to rules and repeatedly rejects her own needs in favour of prioritising Nick.

Ultimately, these idyllic journal entries are revealed to be carefully calculated fabrications; Narrator Amy has manufactured a false narrative in order to implicate her philandering husband in her staged disappearance. In the process, the novel's reanimation of the quintessential chick lit heroine is also exposed as a parodical homage to the contemporary ideals of femininity Narrator Amy so vehemently detests. Through this exposition, Flynn's objective becomes clearly discernible: she has deployed this familiar literary archetype as a means of enacting a pointed critique of contemporary gender ideologies.

With her infamous 'Cool Girl' speech, Narrator Amy cynically figures contemporary femininity as a masquerade. Calculated and controlled in line with neoliberal and postfeminist ideologies, it is a gendered performance that is entirely artificial. Highlighting the oppressive nature of this feminine ideal, Rosalind Gill, Christina Scharff and Ana Elias argue that neoliberal and postfeminist ideologies are responsible for amplifying the demands of idealised femininity and warranting heightened levels of gender performativity for women. On the one hand, Gill, Scharff and Elias underscore how these ideologies have compounded traditional standards of beauty. Incited to enact a clinical gaze on the self, contemporary women must engage in intense surveillance of their external appearance via constant monitoring and self-discipline (2017, 32). On the other hand, these increasingly unattainable standards of beauty have been extended into the arena of subjectivity. Encouraged to invest equal amounts of her energy into working on both her body and her psychic disposition, the female subject must endeavour to maintain a culturally appropriate level of attractiveness whilst continually remodelling her interior life. With a focus on her positive mental attitude, she must work to repudiate all traces of self-doubt.

Forced to repeatedly assess herself against exacting but ill-defined benchmarks, this female subject must strive for perfection in *all* areas; she must pursue her goals with an inexorable seriousness whilst adhering to unattainable beauty ideals. Constructing a carefully monitored life plan – facilitated by modern technologies – this female subject is motivated to track her calorie intake, daily steps, ovulation patterns and sleep cycle. Simultaneously, her actions must feel freely chosen – as evidence of her irrefutable empowerment.

Responsible for the formation of a new disciplinary regime, this incitement towards 'perfection' is a practical mode of self-governance equating successful femininity with the illusion of self-control. However, as Gill maintains, the contemporary female subject is endowed with an 'agency' that is severely limited. Invited to become a particular kind of self, she has been granted mastery over her own body and behaviour, but only on condition that she construct herself as a subject closely resembling the heterosexual male fantasy (2003, 103).

Narrator Amy explicitly highlights the illusory nature of this contemporary ideal of femininity, recognising the 'Cool Girl' as a culturally constructed fantasy:

> Cool Girl is a hot, brilliant, funny woman who adores football, poker, dirty jokes and burping who plays video games, drinks cheap beer, loves threesomes and anal sex. . . . Men actually think this girl exists. Maybe they're fooled because so many women are willing to pretend to be this girl. Pretty soon Cool Girl became the standard girl . . . she wasn't just a dream girl one in a million. Every girl was supposed to be this girl and if you weren't there was something wrong with *you*. . . . If you let a man cancel plans or decline to do things for you, you *lose*. You don't get what you want. Sure, he may be happy, he may say you're *the coolest girl ever*, but he's saying it because *he got his way*. He's calling you a Cool Girl to fool you! That's what men do: they try to make it sound like you are the Cool Girl so you will bow to their wishes.
>
> (Flynn, 210–12)

As she begins to question her conformity to this ideal, Narrator Amy registers that the 'agency' she achieved as the embodied subject of neoliberal postfeminism is alarmingly limited. As the 'Cool Girl', Narrator Amy has been able to experience new forms of sexual, social and economic assertiveness. But these novel liberations are conspicuously conditional, predicated on a retreat from the challenge to male domination. In a scathing dismissal of the superficiality of popular discourses of female empowerment, Narrator Amy highlights how 'Cool Girls' – the women who actively perform an idealised version of femininity – are characterised by an 'agreeability' which ensures both their silence and their subjugation. Through this disassemblage of contemporary gender norms, she underscores how female 'likability' is a thinly veiled code of conduct, dictating a woman's behaviour in line with a heterosexual male fantasy which essentially fortifies hegemonic masculinity.

Still, Narrator Amy registers the power of the 'Cool Girl' as a desirable contemporary commodity. Having spent her life assiduously performing a 'Cool Girl' act, she fluidly morphed between different versions of the feminine ideal: 'Preppy Eighties Girl', 'Ultimate

Frisbee Granola girl', 'Blushing Ingenue', 'Witty Hepburnian Sophisticate', 'Brainy Iconic Girl' and 'Boho Babe'. Affirming Gill's assertion that it is the performance of a very narrow and prescribed version of femininity which is encouraged and rewarded in contemporary culture, these superficial alterations of Narrator Amy's 'public persona' are ultimately always in line with "what's *au courant*" (Flynn, 210). In short, the narrative emphasises that in order to achieve 'successful' femininity, you can only ever be some variation of the 'Cool Girl'.

Exhibiting an acute awareness of her own commodification as a female subject, Narrator Amy confesses that she has never really felt like a person but a product. In spite of this knowledge, she diligently adheres to an idealised version of femininity as promoted by neoliberal postfeminism. She continues to internalise a market logic. Consistently endeavouring to be the very best version of herself, she tries to be "brilliant, creative, kind, thoughtful, witty and happy" at all times (Flynn, 211). Enrolled in an intense regime of the perfect, Narrator Amy accepts that she must endlessly work on herself to increase her market value. As an entrepreneurial subject, she must "cook French cuisine and speak fluent Spanish and garden and knit and run marathons and day-trade stocks and fly a plane and look like a runway model doing it" (Flynn, 42).

These tenets of neoliberalism – self-surveillance, personal transformation, self-discipline and individualism – have evidently been instilled in Amy by her parents, Rand and Marybeth Elliot. Embracing the neoliberal mantra that anything is achievable if you're willing to work hard enough and "put your mind to it", the Elliots firmly believe that every trait "should be considered, judged, categorised" (Flynn, 57, 175). Developing a didactic book series which centres on Amy's ideal alter-ego, 'Amazing Amy', they have treated their daughter's existence as an investment and have reaped the financial rewards accordingly. As their 'bread and butter', the primary source of their wealth, the *Amazing Amy* series has allowed them to live lavishly in the upper echelons of New York City.

Moulded into "the walking ideal . . . Amazing Amy in the flesh," Narrator Amy has been conditioned by the Elliots to view her body as a "beautiful, perfect economy . . . every feature calibrated, everything in balance" (Flynn, 237). But she repeatedly projects her internalised methods of bodily and behavioural governance outwards – preserving and perpetuating troubling discourses of misogyny in the process. Though she reluctantly agrees to relocate from Manhattan to the suburbs of Carthage, Missouri, Narrator Amy is horrified by the women who populate her new home-town. With the narrative of their lives built upon their list of shortcomings – "the unappreciative boyfriend, the extra ten pounds, the dismissive boss, the conniving sister, the straying husband" – she is disdainful of these women whose personas she believes are woven from a benign mediocrity (Flynn, 223).

Outwardly, Narrator Amy nods sympathetically along with these 'average' women. But she accounts for their 'failures' by underscoring their lack of bodily governance; she notes, "how foolish they are, these women, to let these things happen, how undisciplined" (Flynn, 223). For Narrator Amy, this failure to successfully self-market and self-manage is unforgivable. For instance, Shawna Kelly – the ageing 'cougar' pursuing Nick – is repudiated as a "desperate old slut", while Noelle Hawthorne is condemned as an attention seeker because "ugly girls can be such thunder stealers" (Flynn, 246, 254).

This contradiction, between Narrator Amy's incisive feminist diagnosis of 'Cool Girl' and her misogynistic judgement on other women, is revealing. As I have demonstrated, Narrator Amy is unable to break away from the dominant ideology, recognising that her adherence to those norms allows her to operate as a subject within the public sphere. Though Narrator Amy does not endorse these ideologies – and is clearly critical of the inegalitarian nature of gendered neoliberalism – she discursively exemplifies them. More pertinently, she repeatedly polices those women around her unable to attain her standards of self-discipline. That Amy, in spite of her awareness of the oppressive nature of contemporary gender norms, continues to project her internalised misogyny outwards might be interpreted as Flynn's acerbic indictment of contemporary feminism. It implies that it is impossible to become a truly feminist agent in the world as it currently is.

Making a (Neoliberal) Monster

As neoliberalism deepens its hold on contemporary culture – developing from a macro-political and economic rationality to a central organising ethic of society that shapes the way we live, think and feel – feminist critics have stressed that the punishing nature of the regulations it imposes on female behaviour has the potential to be pathologising. Noting the rapid proliferation of 'postfeminist disorders' – including bulimia, anorexia, depression and forms of addiction – McRobbie highlights how the expectation of today's young women to strive for perfection in all spheres is creating an unliveable pressure. In a constant battle to achieve and maintain impossible standards of feminine 'excellence', these women are doubly compromising their mental health (2008, 97).

For McRobbie, the insidious effects of a neoliberal postfeminist hegemony cannot be overstated: creating a contemporary terrain in which female suffering has become both normalised and quotidian. Flynn situates her protagonist's 'pathology' firmly within this terrain of female suffering. Although Narrator Amy has been critically denigrated as a 'psycho-bitch' – problematically affirming disturbing myths about women – Flynn refuses to depoliticise her female monster. On the contrary, by subverting this ubiquitous archetype, she presents Narrator Amy's 'pathology' as an *inevitable* consequence of trying to adhere to impossible ideals of femininity.

No longer the overtly emotional, out of control and irrational female monster of 1990s literature and film, Narrator Amy's internalisation of neoliberal and postfeminist ideologies has enabled her to develop an innate capacity for self-discipline, self-surveillance and self-control. Her discipline is exemplified by the elaborate scheme for wreaking revenge on her womanising husband, which she plans meticulously for a whole year. She skims small, unremarkable amounts of money from a joint bank account to accumulate her get-away funds, for instance, and composes 152 incriminating diary entries using different pens to ensure her journal looks authentic.

Having mastered the neoliberal ideal of bodily governance required to maintain her performance of the 'Cool Girl', Narrator Amy exploits her acquired skill. She gradually increases her weight to ensure that she will be less recognisable when she is 'on the lam'. Parodying the self-monitoring practices of contemporary femininity, she also constructs checklist after checklist of carefully considered items to support her crimes. Further, in the ultimate demonstration of her bodily governance, Narrator Amy skilfully self-mutilates with an eerily mechanical precision. As she slices her own wrist with a box cutter, she is careful not to spill too much blood nor to cut a vital vein or artery. Meanwhile, she is expertly able to control her emotional responses to her excruciating physical pain. She demonstrates an innate capacity for self-harm, which has perhaps been bolstered by the quotidian reality of female suffering in a neoliberal and postfeminist cultural climate.

In line with the expectations of her gender, Narrator Amy is also adept at disguising her true nature and becoming what other people expect her to be. Secretly befriending Noelle Hawthorne, she performs her 'Diary Amy' act to support the narrative she has constructed in her journal – thus further condemning Nick. Boasting of her ability to always take the "extra step that others don't," Narrator Amy is figured as a fully realised version of the controlled, self-determined and individualistic subject of neoliberalism taken to its frightening extreme (Flynn, 208). But her internalisation of those gendered neoliberal ideologies has made her a monster and, ironically, provided her with the optimal tools to successfully enact her disturbing plot for revenge. From this perspective, Flynn's novel stages a reclamation of the archetype of the female monster and a rehabilitation of her definition in a feminist direction. Refusing to wholly vilify Narrator Amy, the novel implies that her monstrous behaviour can be understood as a coherent response to the stifling constraints of contemporary femininity.

However, for critics including Rose, Flynn's absolution of Nick as the innocent victim of a vengeful woman ultimately undermines the subversive potential of her narrative and its critique of contemporary gender ideologies. Though Nick expressly desires to *murder* Amy by the novel's conclusion, Rose maintains that the reader is encouraged to identify with his fury – to believe that Amy is a deserving recipient of his homicidal rage. Rose contends that Narrator Amy is beyond reprieve. But I argue that Flynn's depiction of Nick steers the reader towards an alternative reading of her novel – as a critique of a contemporary iteration of hegemonic masculinity.

Flynn explicitly parallels Nick – as a benevolent 'good guy' – and his overtly misogynist father. As the authoritarian head of his household, Bill Dunne exhibits all the key signifiers of conventionally 'bad masculinity'. For example, his communications with his wife are purely transactional:

> *We're out of milk again. (I'll get some today.) I need this ironed properly. (I'll do that today.) How hard is it to buy milk? (Silence.) You forgot to call the plumber. (Sigh.) Goddammit, put on your coat, right now, and go out and get some goddam milk."*
>
> (Flynn, 56)

Enraged by even the most minute display of her insubordination, Bill's dictatorial expectations evidently align with traditional and regressive gender roles. While he works to support the family financially, he requires his wife to effectively and efficiently manage their domestic space.

In Nick's recollections of his childhood, he emphasises his father's hatred and abuse of women. Bill repeatedly and explicitly reiterated his fundamental conviction about their inherent inferiority. Disturbed by this rhetoric, Nick uses his father as a frame of reference for how to be a 'feminist'. He rejects all paternal influences and is determined to model himself on his openly liberal mother. Repeatedly emphasising how he is disgusted and ashamed of his father's misogyny, the reader is encouraged to empathise with Nick – to believe that he is a model of 'good masculinity'. Yet, Nick's narrative is also populated with troubling inconsistencies. Though he is committed to this idealised version of himself as a benign and unwaveringly respectful good guy, recurrent slippages in his narration highlight a deeply rooted misogyny.

The qualities Nick favours in his mistress, Andie, are certainly revealing. As Amy's antithesis, she is the 'Cool Girl' personified:

> Soon Andie became a physical counterpoint to all things Amy. She laughed with me and made me laugh, she didn't immediately contradict or second guess me. She never scowled at me. She was easy. It was all so fucking easy. . . . I had been happy all my life, and now I was not, and Andie was there, lingering after class, asking me questions that Amy never had, not lately. Making me feel like a worthwhile man, not the idiot who lost

his job, the dope who forgot to put the toilet down, the blunder who just could never get it quite right, whatever it was.

(Flynn, 138–9)

Nick's explicit exaltation of Andie's 'agreeability' – which he repeatedly contrasts with Amy's confronting and challenging behaviour – underscores his unconscious preference for passive, quiet and obedient women. His depiction of his lover is objectifying; she is the docile body against which he is able to construct a more laudable version of himself to support his ego.

While on the surface, Nick celebrates his wife's intellect – her brilliant, popping brain – he often lapses into appraising women solely in terms of their physical appearance: he identifies Detective Boney exclusively as 'the ugly woman' and is proud of his sister's ability to attract multiple suitors because of her unusual attractiveness. Nick also equates women's ageing with a decrease in their 'market' value. He juxtaposes Andie's soft, baby-like skin with Amy's repugnant daily moisturising routine and ruthlessly asserts that "pathetic" middle-aged women are "oblivious to their lack of appeal" (Flynn, 176).

Despite his critical awareness of his father's chauvinism, Nick evidently struggles to control his own misogynist thoughts. His rage and hatred for a particular kind of active and agentic woman are reiterated in a series of italicised asides: "*Ellen Abbott, you fucking cunt*"; "*Fucking Shawna crazy bitch whore*"; "*stupid bitch*"; "*bitch bitch bitch*" (Flynn, 153, 54, 47). As these asides become increasingly vitriolic, Nick's narrative voice is inextricably merged with the voice of his father to the point that they are virtually indistinguishable; he becomes similarly complicit in the same universal degradation of women as the inferior sex.

This doubling of the initially disparate voices of Nick and Bill Dunne functions as a clever device which highlights how misogyny has undergone a troubling transformation in the public sphere. With a nearly indiscernible shape that has enabled it to seamlessly permeate all aspects of our culture, contemporary iterations of misogyny now covertly exist in tandem with more overtly liberal attitudes towards gender norms. They have therefore become more difficult to identify and eradicate. By disrupting the dichotomy of 'good' and 'bad' masculinity, Flynn's Nick indicates to the reader that you do not have to be a *monster* – a wife killer, a violent father – to be a *misogynist* who is worthy of critique.

I would be remiss, however, not to acknowledge how critical responses to *Gone Girl* force us to consider the political risks attached to the use of misogynist tropes as a strategy for feminist ends. The case of Jennifer Dulos reiterates the dangerous implications this narrative strategy can have in the real world. Implicated in her disappearance and presumed murder, Jennifer's estranged husband offered an unusual and alarming defence in the summer of 2019: he suggested that the missing mother of five, in retaliation for his infidelity, had staged her own disappearance in a plot similar to that of the 2012 Gillian Flynn novel. Flynn's reanimation of the female monster exposes and critiques regulatory femininity in contemporary culture. But the case of Jennifer Dulos highlights how easily this 'strategy' can misfire and be assimilated into the misogynist imaginary of patriarchy.

Everyone Loves the Dead Girl

For Eva Burke, much of the vitriolic frustration Narrator Amy expresses throughout the course of *Gone Girl* hinges on a kind of paradoxical resentment: "she possesses enough self-awareness to question other people's conformity to gender and class norms, but her contempt for these norms seems to stem from disappointment at her own inability to internalise them" (2018, 78). Narrator Amy certainly exhibits an acute and critical awareness of the expectations of her gender. But I am inclined to disagree with Burke about the source of her disappointment. Having adeptly internalised these gendered norms, Narrator Amy's rage and resentment stem instead from her 'cruelly optimistic' attachment to the fantasy of 'the good life' endorsed by neoliberal and postfeminist ideologies.

According to Lauren Berlant, a relation of cruel optimism exists when something you desire is actually an obstacle to your flourishing. At the centre of this desire, Berlant explains, are 'conventional' fantasies of the good life. These fantasies include political equality, durable intimacy and upward mobility, all of which are synonymous with neoliberal and postfeminist discourses. While cruelly optimistic attachments to these fantasies of the good life are often inhibiting, Berlant argues that contemporary subjects remain unwaveringly invested in them; paradoxically, these attachments threaten the subject's well-being whilst facilitating their coherent sense of self (2011, 1).

As I have demonstrated, Narrator Amy certainly has an antagonistic relation to the dominant paradigm. In her 'Cool Girl' speech, she explicitly articulates her feelings of disenfranchisement as a female subject under neoliberal postfeminism. Her discontent is also reflected in the cultural landscape of the novel. As a post-recession narrative, *Gone Girl* is populated with images of American suburbia in decay. This is particularly evident in Diary Amy's descriptions of her new hometown:

> It's a rented house right along the Mississippi River, a house that screams Suburban Nouveau Riche, the kind of place Nick aspired to as a kid from his split-level, shag-carpet side of the town. The kind of house that is immediately familiar: a generically grand, unchallenging, new, new, new house. . . . Driving into our development occasionally makes me shiver, the sheer number of gaping dark houses – home that have never known inhabitants.
>
> (Flynn, 4)

Here, the artificiality of these houses – their contrived grandeur – functions as a metaphor for the artificiality of a neoliberal and postfeminist subjective identity characterised by material wealth and consumerism. That these grandiose houses are conspicuously desolate indicates that this subjective identity is nothing more than an empty facade. In short, these descriptions gesture towards the idea that the neoliberal and postfeminist incitement towards upward mobility is ultimately illusory – that it is impossible to satisfy.

Despite her evident feelings of disillusionment throughout, Narrator Amy is unable to relinquish her attachment to the fantasies of the good life – specifically, the fantasy of romantic reciprocity. When Narrator Amy enters her relationship with Nick, she consciously chooses to perform as the ideal 'Cool Girl', accepting a subordinating return to traditionalism as a prerequisite of their romance. At the same time, Narrator Amy explicitly rejects the idea of unconditional love. Having credulously invested in the fantasy of the good life, she wholeheartedly believed that she would be *compensated* for this sacrifice; she would be happy to continue to perform as the ideal 'Cool Girl' but only alongside a modern-day 'Prince Charming'.

The narrative repeatedly draws attention to both Nick's awareness of this obligation to perform the role of 'Prince Charming' and his struggle to contend with those expectations. From the outset, he operates as though he is a puppet whose mechanical behaviours are being controlled by omniscient outside forces. His eyes flip open at exactly 6 A.M. every morning with a "spooky ventriloquist dummy click of the lids", and he thinks to himself –

"*Showtime!*" (Flynn, 3). When his wife suddenly disappears, Nick's perfunctory 'routine' is thrown into disarray. As a result, he begins to figure himself as a flailing actor in a television series.

In order to affirm an idealised version of himself as the perfect, grieving husband – as a hero who has stuck by his wife though the horrible decline in her family's circumstances – Nick spends his interviews with the media searching for the 'correct' thing to say and trying to recall some TV-appropriate lines. To be received positively by his 'audience', he consciously attempts to regulate his own behaviour. Throughout the course of the narrative, he persistently instructs himself to behave felicitously – to "*act correctly, don't blow it, act the way a man acts when he hears this news . . . don't smile . . . do not smile. PAUSE. BREATHE. NO SMILE*" (52, 190, 181).

When Amy's disappearance forces Nick to nostalgically reflect on their relationship, his "romantic-movie kind of guy" exterior begins to disintegrate (Flynn, 198). He gradually acknowledges that he has never been able to perfect his performance of the ideal husband. A liar and a cheat, Nick is not the dashing and heroic lead of the narrative which his wife has followed with unassailable fidelity. It is this disparity between Narrator Amy's fantasy of the good life – a fantasy which guaranteed her romantic reciprocity – and her lived experience of this fantasy which has ultimately engendered her feelings of disappointment and anger. As such, her vehement rage appears to stem from her feelings of being betrayed by a system that has duped her.

Tired of being silenced and subordinated, Narrator Amy refuses to continue to perform a masquerade of femininity that requires an effort on her part for which she is not recompensed. Yearning for liberation from a narrative in which she can only ever be a version of the 'Cool Girl', she is determined to create her own story – one that will punish Nick for his complicity in her subjugation. Thus, Narrator Amy's plot for revenge might best be understood as her struggle to reclaim narrative agency. The structure of the novel itself reinforces the significance of this struggle, fluctuating, from chapter to chapter, between Nick's narrative voice and the voice of Narrator Amy.

Crucially, in an effort to exact her revenge and become the master of her own narrative, Narrator Amy exploits a well-known archetype of crime fiction; she recasts herself as Diary Amy – the ideal female victim of a violent crime. With a long-standing history of objectifying and eroticising dead or missing women, gratuitous depictions of gender-based violence remain a key feature of the CF genre. As Emma Miller notes, contemporary reiterations continue to reduce female victims to nothing more than "inert bodies to be looked at, dissected and penetrated both criminally and then in the pursuit of justice" (2018, 100).

Yet, this fetishisation of female victims is not exclusive to the literary terrain. Instead, as Kelly Oliver astutely encapsulates, depictions of the 'Dead Girl' ideal in the mainstream media have become so prevalent that they are verging on banal. Citing an episode of *America's Next Top Model* that aired in the fall of 2012, Oliver details a photoshoot during which beautiful young female models were posed as big-game trophies in a taxidermist's lair – their heads mounted on the walls – as just one striking example of the increasing eroticisation and commodification of the 'Dead Girl' in contemporary culture (2016).

With the surge in popularity of true crime narratives signalled by the abundance of podcasts – *Serial* (2014–present), *My Favourite Murder* (2016–present) and *Someone Knows Something* (2016–present) – and documentaries – *Making a Murderer* (2015), *The Staircase* (2004) and *The Jinx* (2015) – across the popular media, it is clear that the appetite for stories about women who have been mutilated, brutalised and murdered has risen alarmingly. Predominantly produced and circulated in the USA, these narratives are progressively becoming more readily available for worldwide consumption facilitated by globally accessible streaming sites such as Netflix and YouTube. Consequentially, the fetishisation of dead or missing women in popular narratives has become an even more potent cultural phenomenon.

Nowhere is this fetishisation more visible than in the figure of the 'Missing White Woman' or the 'Lost White Girl'. As encapsulated by the global interest in cases like those of Laci Peterson, Elizabeth Smart, Natalie Holloway and the host of others like them, the disappearances and murders of particular kinds of women – young, attractive, white women from middle- to upper-class backgrounds – have been increasingly made into media and cultural events; their stories have been narrativised and neatly packaged into marketable, glossy who-dun-its. In the process of this narrativisation, however, these women have been stripped of their individualising characteristics. Figured as virtuous, fairy-tale heroines, they are fetishised and deified in the popular medias. Words such as 'perfect', 'ideal' and 'angelic' are commonly used to describe them and their lives. Canonised as symbols of idealised femininity, this reification of the 'Dead Girl' in true crime is nonetheless essential: it reduces her to a fictional character in a juicy new mystery which ultimately obscures the reality of the violence she has endured.

Throughout the course of Flynn's novel, Narrator Amy demonstrates an unmistakable awareness that the 'Dead Girl' represents the ultimate ideal of femininity in the post-millennial period. Initially, her plan to cement her perfection in the media – to make herself the subject of widespread adoration – is contingent on her own suicide because, as she astutely asserts, "everyone loves the Dead Girl" (Flynn 222). Narrator Amy's idealisation of this cultural figure was evidently instilled in her from infancy – inherited from her parents. Haunted by the spectres of the children her mother had miscarried prior to her birth, she notes:

> I've always been jealous too, always – seven dead dancing princesses. They get to be perfect without even trying, without even facing one moment of existence, while I am stuck here on earth, and every day I must try, and every day is a chance to be less than perfect. It's an exhausting way to live.
>
> (Flynn, 209)

Here, Narrator Amy figures her own feelings of insufficiency as a direct consequence of trying – and failing – to match the un-tarnishable levels of perfection of her deceased sisters. In the ultimate glorification of the 'Dead Girl', she acknowledges that her parents will always view her as deficient in comparison to 'The Hopes'.

Armed with this awareness of the potency of the 'Dead Girl' ideal, Narrator Amy anticipates the marketability of her spurious 'Diary Amy' creation. Ensuring her fictitious journal is retrieved by the police and leaked to the media, she is empowered to exploit popular systems of discourse to her advantage. Performing as 'Diary Amy' – a loyal and subservient wife who yearns for a child of her own – Narrator Amy secures her spot on *Ellen Abbot*, the biggest cable crime-news show in the country. With a penchant for these missing women narratives, the eponymous Ellen Abbot is infamous for capitalising on the 'Dead Girl' and sensationalising her story. She seizes on a suspect – often the husband – with a virulence on which Narrator Amy's plot for revenge is reliant.

In order to ensure the "big-time, round-the-clock, frantic, never-ending *Ellen Abbott* coverage" required to permanently besmirch Nick's character in the media, Narrator Amy intentionally intensifies her own fetishisation (Flynn, 232). While she is aware that Diary Amy – as the ideal lost or dead girl – will be universally adored by the public, Narrator Amy decides that a pregnancy would inevitably heighten the potency of her creation. As a missing mother, she believes that Diary Amy's story would be simply irresistible for the media. In other words, Narrator Amy opts to utilise a privileged archetype of femininity as a means of crystallising her status as the ideal woman in the public sphere. Yet, by having Narrator Amy strategically adopt this maternal subjectivity to increase her 'popularity', the narrative underscores how it is a particular *kind* of dead or missing woman who has been reified as an ideal of passive femininity in contemporary culture – one that notably embodies traditional gender norms.

That Narrator Amy exploits her privilege as a white, attractive, middle- to upper-class, heteronormative woman in order to get what she wants has been a significant point of contention for critics. As Kendra Marston observes, by refusing to acknowledge or directly confront her protagonist's privilege, Flynn's narrative continues a pattern of exclusion which underpins neoliberal postfeminism (2018). It foregrounds a post-racial and post-class version of society in which one's skin colour or class status is not accepted as determining one's life chances.

While Marston's argument is certainly valid, I would posit an alternative reading of Flynn's novel. By making Narrator Amy's plot for revenge contingent on the potency of this Missing White Girl figure, Flynn is attempting to *highlight* the exclusionary nature of neoliberal postfeminism – to expose and critique the ways in which a certain kind of 'woman' is privileged in contemporary culture. Narrator Amy's revenge scheme is also contingent upon the de-personalisation of narratives of victimhood in the media. In line with neoliberal ideologies – which reject any systemic analysis of the increasing number of acts of violence committed against women – she is aware that her disappearance will be individualised, refigured as an isolated incident with Nick as 'the big, bad wolf'. Empowered by this knowledge, Narrator Amy constructs 'Diary Amy' in line with the expectations of the ideal lost or dead girl and 'Diary Nick' as a menacing monster – the guilty perpetrator of a violent crime.

Evidently, Narrator Amy is wholly familiar with the intricacies of popular discourses surrounding female victimhood. She understands the potency of the 'Dead Girl' ideal and recognises that female victims of gendered violence are habitually reduced to caricatures of idealised femininity in the media. It is this objective awareness which allows her to manipulate popular discourses to her advantage and tighten the noose around Nick's neck. But Narrator Amy's ability to exploit her own victimisation is only possible because this type of violence is so troublingly familiar. In this context, the plausibility of her masterplan exposes how these narratives of violence against women are so woven into the fabric of our contemporary culture that they have been taken for granted and normalised; they are frighteningly ubiquitous. This revelation forces the reader to consider if perhaps it is not coincidental that at a time in which women are being increasingly controlled and subjugated by neoliberal and postfeminist ideologies, we are seeing more and more of these narratives about missing or dead girls.

Nonetheless, Flynn's narrative simultaneously disrupts and subverts any straightforward interpretation of female victimisation. On the one hand, Narrator Amy's masquerade as the ideal lost or dead girl – the benevolent victim of gender-based violence – is irrefutably advantageous; she uses it as a tactic to get what she wants. By embracing her status as victim at the novel's conclusion, she permanently secures the attention of both her parents and her husband – attention which she has so desperately craved. This suggests that victimhood is a wholly agentic position for Narrator Amy.

On the other hand, the novel's bleak conclusion to its heroine's journey towards agency and empowerment is impossible to ignore. Nick offers his wife a 'get-out-of-jail-free card' in the guise of a new narrative which figures her as a tough, vibrant, independent woman who has killed her kidnapper and rid herself of her idiot cheat husband. But Narrator Amy rejects his proposal. Instead, she concludes her narrative with an ominous threat which underscores her inability to relinquish her toxic investment in the fantasy of the good life:

> Start with the facade. We will have a happy marriage if it kills him . . . I know Nick isn't in love with me yet, but he will be. I do have faith in that. Fake it until you make it, isn't that an expression? For now he acts like the old Nick, and I act like the old Amy. Back when we were happy.
>
> (Flynn, 380)

In a desperate attempt to reconstruct their image as an affluent and contented suburban couple, Narrator Amy pantomimes as Diary Amy whilst forcing Nick to perform the role of doting husband alongside her. Rather than offer a challenge to the patriarchal powers that bind her, she continues to internalise neoliberal and postfeminist gender norms.

In order to get what she wants – to reclaim her narrative control – Narrator Amy must re-adopt the *limiting* roles of a wife, mother and victim. As such, by the novel's conclusion, she is no closer to living an authentic existence. Though Flynn assures us that there *is* a 'Real Amy' – who is "so much better, more interesting and complicated and challenging" than 'Cool Amy' or 'Dead Amy' or 'Victim Amy' – her conclusion is unquestionably ambiguous (378). By having Narrator Amy re-embrace these restrictive gender norms, readers are left to wonder if there is, or can be, a 'Real Amy' beyond the performance.

'Well, If It Isn't Nancy Drew'

While 'Cool Girl' Amy masters the neoliberal tenets of self-control, self-regulation and discipline required to maintain a performance of the feminine ideal, Rachel's incapacity for self-governance is pathologised as a source of failure. Buckling under the pressures of the expectations of her gender, her masquerade of femininity has been increasingly corroded and is unsustainable. Consumed by a debilitating unhappiness, Rachel's narrative is populated with recollections of the dissolution of her marriage:

> There was a time when I had willpower, when I could run 10k before breakfast and subsist for weeks on 1,300 calories a day. It was one of the things Tom loved about me, he said: my stubbornness, my strength. I remember an argument, right at the end, when things were about as bad as they could be; he lost his temper with me. "What happened to you, Rachel?" he asked me. "When did you become so weak?"
>
> (Hawkins, 79)

In these recollections, Rachel's waning self-discipline is figured as the catalyst for the disintegration of the relationship and a source of disgust for her ex-husband, Tom. While Rachel acknowledges that she might have been considered attractive in her youth, her excessive drinking has resulted in a drastic increase in her weight, which she believes has limited the potency of her sexual appeal:

> I am not the girl I used to be. I am no longer desirable, I'm off-putting in some way. It's not just that I've put on weight, or that my face is puffy from the drinking and the lack of sleep; it's as if people can see the damage written all over me, they can see it in my face, the way I hold myself, the way I move.
>
> (Hawkins, 10)

In accordance with neoliberal and postfeminist ideologies – which figure thinness as a corporeal expression of individual responsibility and self-control – Rachel's weight gain becomes indicative of a complementary disfunction in her character. To the wider public in the social world of the novel, she is repugnant and damaged – the embodiment of failed femininity.

The reader is encouraged to adopt a moralising and individualist interpretation of Rachel, holding her accountable for these 'failures'. Hawkins's recurrent use of abject imagery to describe Rachel's body certainly emphasises her inherent 'otherness' and 'monstrosity'. Throughout the course of the narrative, we see her in "piss-soaked knickers" and in puddles of her own vomit, bleeding from open wounds (Hawkins, 42). Arguably, these images are meant to invoke feelings of disgust in the reader who is persuaded to collude in the degradation of Rachel as utterly repellent – a source of revulsion. The reader's abject response to Rachel is also mirrored by the nameless characters on the train who try not to get too close to her and actively avoid her gaze.

Following the loss of her marriage, her home and finally her job, Rachel no longer assumes a fixed place. Even in the rented apartment that she shares with a friend, she feels like a guest who has overstayed her welcome. Instead, Rachel lingers in peripheries and operates on the borders of society. She spends most of her days in transit and observing people from the window of a train. This innate liminality – as exemplified by the transience of the train itself – further underscores Rachel's abjection for the reader and frames her as a menacing outsider and frightening 'other'. However, Kendra Marston posits an alternative reading of representations of female melancholia in popular culture. Noting the prevalence of narratives centred on a disempowered female protagonist searching for alternative forms of agency, Marston argues that contemporary cultural texts are increasingly utilising women's melancholia as a vehicle to explore the excesses of late capitalism and the failures of neoliberal postfeminism. These texts, she observes, frame women "as victims of governmental forms and associated corporate structures that have promised members of socially empowered groups happiness and fulfilment yet have inevitably failed to deliver" (21). Thus, according to Marston, representations of women's melancholia can be used as a tool to signify malaise and dissatisfaction with the status quo.

In line with Marston's assertions, Hawkins frames her protagonist's melancholy as a direct response to the impossible demands of contemporary ideals of femininity. Overtly acknowledging the inegalitarian nature of these ideals, Rachel is critical of how women are still appraised on the basis of their physical appearance and their traditional roles as wives and mothers. Still, Rachel continues to view these ideals as aspirational. For example, her desire to become a mother is all-consuming. She repeatedly fantasises about what it might be like to rear a child – to dress it, to feed it, to nurture it. Reproducing prevalent postfeminist discourses on gender – which have re-established maternity as an essential part of femininity – Rachel foregrounds motherhood as her 'raisin d'être'. In contrast to Tom, who was certainly eager to have a child, she figures maternity as a necessity and as indispensable for any woman.

When Rachel's attempts to conceive via in-vitro fertilisation are unsuccessful, she is overcome with profound sadness:

> No doctor has been able to explain to me why I can't get pregnant. I'm young enough, fit enough, I wasn't drinking heavily when we were trying. . . . It just didn't happen. . . . The thing about being barren is that you're not allowed to get away from it. Not when you're in your thirties. I was asked about it all the time. . . . failure cloaked me like a mantle, it overwhelmed me, dragged me under and I gave up hope. At the time, I resented the fact

> that it was always seen as my fault, that I was the one letting the side down.... I'm not beautiful, and I can't have kids, so what does that make me? Worthless.
>
> (Hawkins, 77–9)

Despite the assurances of her doctors that it is not her fault, Rachel's unexplained infertility appears to provoke a perverse self-blaming mechanism. As a woman who has been unable to fulfil her 'biological destiny', she believes that she is a failure. Infertile, 'unattractive' and quickly approaching middle age, Rachel is deemed redundant by her culture. Unable to satisfy the restrictive limitations of her gender, she is rendered disposable and excluded as a subject from the neoliberal milieu – she is abjected. Yet, by presenting Rachel's melancholy as a ramification of gendered ideals of femininity, perhaps Hawkins's narrative is attempting to describe the impact of neoliberal postfeminism in affective terms, highlighting how the desire to satisfy these contemporary ideals of femininity induces feelings of despondency and dejection in women.

As Rachel's self-governance continues to plummet, she begins to lose authority over her own narrative voice. She confesses, "I have lost control over everything, even the places in my head" (Hawkins, 9). Unable to determine whether her elusive fragments of memory are based in reality, Rachel's alcohol-induced blackouts affect her ability to narrativise her own experience. Specifically, her attempts to recall the night of Saturday 13th of July – the night of Megan Hipwell's disappearance – are inhibited by this binge drinking. While Rachel indicates that she remembers being on the train, she admits that her recollections have been obfuscated by alcohol and are subsumed by a gulf of blackness – a void.

As Rachel tries to make sense of a narrative which continues to evade her, her cerebral timelines become increasingly disjointed and disrupted; she can't tell whether a memory belongs to Saturday night or to another time. Rachel's repeated use of tentative language to present these recollections further undermines her narrative authority:

> I couldn't bear to have other images in my head, yet more memories that I can't trust, memories that merge and morph and shift, fooling me into believing that what is, is not, telling me to look one way when really I should be looking another way.
>
> (Hawkins, 228)

Continually questioning the authenticity of her memories, she figures her own evocations as untrustworthy. While she *knows* that something terrible has happened, she is unable to unequivocally determine whether her recollections are real.

Hesitant in her speculations about what she has or has not seen, Rachel consistently allows her narrative to be controlled and dictated by the male characters in the text. Trusting in the fidelity of his recollections, she often unambiguously surrenders her narrative authority to Tom. Though she overtly acknowledges that his depiction of her seems uncharacteristic, she continually adopts his memories as her own. For instance, accepting Tom's version of the events which brought about the dissolution of their marriage, Rachel believes that she had attempted to attack him with a golf club during a violent, drunken episode. But this incident is later revealed to be a pure fabrication; Tom has exploited Rachel's alcoholism to manipulate the narrative to his advantage. When Rachel seeks out a nameless, male passenger from the train to corroborate her recollections of the night of Megan's disappearance, she also allows him to construct and place her within a narrative which does not feel entirely authentic. Though she confesses that "something feels off" about his recollections, she ultimately privileges his narrative above her own (Hawkins, 256).

Attempting to elucidate the anterograde forms of amnesia that often follow her episodes of excessive drinking, Rachel purchases a self-help book written by a doctor. But the doctor's postulations on the effects of the 'drunken blackout' only crystallise her loss of narrative authority. Surmising that a blackout forces the subject into a state in which their brain can no longer produce short-term memories, the doctor's theorisation exposes an uncomfortable truth: it underscores how Rachel's drinking quite literally alienates her from her ability to narrate.

As with Amy Elliot Dunne, Rachel also exhibits a cruelly optimistic attachment to fantasy narratives of the good life promoted by neoliberal and postfeminist ideologies. If, as Berlant suggests, cruelly optimistic attachments involve a sustaining inclination to return to the scene of fantasy which ignites a sense of possibility for the subject, then Rachel's repetitive compulsion to return to her old neighbourhood and home underscores her unwavering investment in these fantasies (3). From the window of the train, she engages in an obsessive surveillance of the upper middle classes whose lifestyles she figures as aspirational. This is particularly evident in her descriptions of Megan and Scott Hipwell.

Embodying gendered ideals of masculinity and femininity, Megan and Scott are notably attractive; Rachel emphasises their beauty by comparing them to popular celebrities. This comparison also suggests an affluent lifestyle and gestures towards their material wealth. Projecting a romanticised narrative of heteronormativity onto their bodies, Rachel figures Megan and Scott as the epitome of suburban, marital bliss. They are the picture of happiness and contentment. For Rachel, these fantasies of heteronormative bliss are always synonymous with her nostalgic remembrance of what she believes she has lost. Underscoring her innate attachment to the fantasies of the good life, her narrativising gaze re-constructs Megan and Scott as a successful iteration of her failed relationship with Tom – a relationship which she continues to crave and mourn.

However, as Gayle Greene argues, it is important to note that nostalgia and 'remembering' are antithetical. While 'remembering' involves the attempted recollection of facts, nostalgia is a kind of reductive 'forgetting' which edits unpleasant details from our memories in favour of a utopian or idealistic version of the past. For Greene, this distinction is crucial. Nostalgia, she contends, inhibits the subject's ability to move forward – to "transform disabling fictions to enabling fictions" (1991, 298). Signifying a desire for an imagined past which does not reflect reality, nostalgia, Greene maintains, can only ever be advantageous to those who have power and dangerous for those who do not. Thus, in Hawkins's novel, Rachel's nostalgic attachment to the fantasies of the good life – her romanticised idea of the 'home' she believes she has lost – is figured as both subjugating and highly dangerous. These fraudulent fantasies of marital contentment obfuscate the actual history of domestic abuse at the hands of her beloved ex-partner, Tom.

Though Rachel recalls her romantic relationship with glassy-eyed affection, penetrative bursts of the violence she has repressed continually make their way to the surface of her consciousness. As her past increasingly impedes on her present, she begins to remember a series of violent incidents that she cannot definitively dismiss as inauthentic: she recalls ducking to avoid a blow and is filled with visceral terror when she is struck by an image of herself lying on the ground, crying and bleeding. While the fragmentation of Rachel's memory had been figured as a consequence of her alcoholism from the outset, these violent recollections gesture towards an alternative reality. By contextualising the disruption of her memory in relation to this violence, it becomes clear that the novel's aesthetics are mimicking the prototypical aesthetics of trauma narratives. Rachel's disjointed and disrupted cerebral timelines – her inability to recall these painful and disturbing memories – are a consequence of the violence she has endured.

As Rachel struggles to regain authority over her own narrative, she remains incapable of articulating this trauma. Instead, she suffers it directly in her body:

> I kept thinking about that night. Every time I passed that hole in the wall I thought about it. One day I was standing there – it was evening and I was coming out of the bedroom and I just stopped, because I remembered. I was on the floor, my back to the wall, sobbing and sobbing, Tom standing over me, begging me to calm down, the golf club on the carpet next to my feet, and I felt it, I felt it. I was terrified. The memory doesn't fit with the reality, because I don't remember anger, raging fury. I remember fear.
>
> (Hawkins, 230)

Having plainly accepted his version of events, Rachel believes that she is responsible for damaging the wall in her home in the midst of attacking Tom. However, while she can't wholly recall the truth of what has happened to her, she can somehow *feel* it. In an attempt to repossess her lost narrative, she 'speaks' to herself through what Luce Irigaray has described as a distinctly feminine language of the body (1974, 143).

Further underscoring Rachel's struggle to recover her narrative agency and fidelity, Hawkins's expertly exploits a familiar literary archetype. In her presentation of Rachel as a divorced, middle-aged woman-turned-detective, she offers a cleverly subversive play on the prototypical female detective spinster. As with seminal characters such as Agatha Christie's Jane Marple and Anna Katherine Green's Amelia Butterworth – who were not taken seriously by the police due to their old age and spinster status – Rachel is ridiculed as an unmarried busybody. Failing to conform to the dictates of normative femininity has made her an object of derision. Like Marple and Butterworth, Rachel's attempts to insert herself into the official investigation of Megan's disappearance are also mocked. Her narrative is discredited by the lead detective who believes she has nothing of substance to offer to the inquiry.

Masters of observation, both Marple and Butterworth are renowned for making lists – be it physically or mentally – to support their theories. Similarly, Rachel's process of retrieving her lost memories – and thus of re-gaining narrative control – is supported by her repetitive assemblage of evidentiary lists to support her claims. For example, on the back of a receipt, Rachel probes some of the most likely possible explanations for the disappearance of Megan Hipwell:

1. She has run off with her boyfriend, who from here on in I will refer to as B.
2. B has harmed her.
3. Scott has harmed her.
4. She has simply left her husband and gone to live elsewhere.
5. Someone other than B or Scott has harmed her.

(Hawkins, 63)

In attempting to piece this mystery together – to make sense of everything – Rachel consults her journal entries and these copious notes as means of gleaning information. From this perspective, Hawkins's narrative verges on metafictional, making explicit Rachel's process of struggling to narrativise.

Intimate Terrorism

The structural arrangement of Hawkins's novel further bolsters her narrative's critique of neoliberal postfeminism. Rachel Watson, the eponymous girl on the train, is arguably the novel's protagonist. But her account of the 'present' is frequently interspersed with Megan

Hipwell's narrative from the past. Crucially, at the beginning of the novel, these women are figured in juxtaposition to each other. Epitomising 'failed' or abject femininity, Rachel is a divorced, childless, overweight, alcoholic who is consumed by her melancholy. In contrast, Megan is the embodiment of contemporary gender ideals. She is slim, blonde and beautiful and married to a handsome, affluent husband. Although the reader is initially encouraged to view these women as antithetical, the novel's arrangement disrupts this structure. Hawkins gradually draws the reader's attention to Megan's and Rachel's innate similarities as their life experiences have been practically indistinguishable. This is bolstered by the novel's reanimation of a classic literary trope from the gothic genre: the uncanny double.

As immortalised through characters such as Bertha Mason – in Charlotte Bronte's *Jane Eyre* (1847) – and Rebecca De Winter – the titular antagonist of Daphne du Maurier's *Rebecca* (1938) – the trope of the female double or doppelgänger is ubiquitous throughout the gothic genre. By presenting a notion of subjectivity as split, it also signals one of the genre's key themes: the question of identity and self-ownership. As a spectral projection of the self, the double enables the subject to become the object of their own gaze, affording them the opportunity to investigate their subjective identity. Self-conscious in her use of this gothic imagery, Hawkins figures 'Dead Girl' Megan as Rachel's uncanny double. Struggling to find an 'authentic' self amidst her fragmented memories, Rachel's subjectivity is destabilised from the outset. Similarly, Megan maintains that she is "playing at real life, instead of actually living it" (Hawkins, 20). As a self-proclaimed master of reinvention, Megan's behaviour is overtly performative. She consciously adopts a series of personas – a runway, a wife, a waitress, a gallery manager, a nanny – which she acknowledges are not reflective of her real self, "the self nobody knows" (Hawkins, 46).

While Rachel has struggled and failed to adhere to a masquerade of the ideal feminine, Megan recognises that her adept performance has actually enabled her subjugation:

> I want to run. I want to take a road trip, in a convertible, with the top down. I want to drive to the coast – any coast. I want to walk on a beach . . . I need to find something that I must do, something undeniable. I can't do this, I can't just be a wife. I don't understand how anyone does it – there is literally nothing to do but wait. Wait for a man to come home and love you.
>
> (Hawkins, 21–2)

Megan is overtly critical of contemporary gender norms and understands that those norms romanticise a version of traditionalism which has determined her passivity. Condemned to this unbearable stagnancy, Megan rejects her prescribed gender role – and by extension the fantasy of the good life – as restrictive and entirely unsatisfactory. Instead, she yearns for freedom and mobility, for an authentic kind of agency which she has hitherto been denied.

Unable to satisfy contemporary ideals of femininity, Rachel and Megan are abjected from the symbolic order and refused subjectivity. As women who have transgressed from the norm in contemporary culture, they are considered aberrant ontological and social anomalies. Underscoring their abjection, these women are figured as liminal, half-formed subjects. According to Anna, Tom's current wife, they have a spectral presence in her home. Framed as a kind of gothic 'haunting', she notes "everywhere I look now, I have to see not only Rachel, but Megan too . . . every time I close my eyes I see them sitting there at the kitchen table" (Hawkins, 199).

Tired of being silenced and subordinated by cultural discourses beyond her control, Megan fights to reclaim her narrative voice. For Megan, this need to speak her truth – "to say the words out loud" – becomes imperative (Hawkins, 163). Acknowledging that the loss of her agentic voice signals her annihilation, she fears that her words might stick in her throat and choke her in her sleep. While Megan feels increasingly 'suffocated' by this loss, Rachel starts to experience a disturbing, recurring nightmare in which she is buried alive. As Rachel imagines that she is being smothered by mud, her voice becomes similarly muted. Like Megan, she loses the capacity to speak.

Abounding with these motifs of verbal suppression, the novel tacitly merges Megan's and Rachel's battle for narrative agency. Yet the significance of this merging can only be appreciated when contextualised in relation to an alarming paradigm which pervades both the crime and true crime genres. Looking specifically at what she terms 'Dead Girl shows' – such as *True Detective* (2014–present) and *Twin Peaks* (1990–present) – Alice Bolin argues that dead or missing women are rarely figured as multi-faceted characters in these narratives. Instead, it is the discovery of their bodies – or the desire to solve the mystery of their disappearance – which often spawns a semi-sexual obsession for a typical investigator with a good-guy complex (2018, 78). Utilised as plot devices to further *someone else's* narrative, these women are ultimately silenced, muted within their own stories.

While the silencing of the 'Dead Girl' has become an increasingly quotidian facet of contemporary crime narratives, this pattern has notably transcended the 'Dead Girl' show. It is also appearing with a troubling frequency across true crime texts. We need only look at Sarah Koenig's acclaimed podcast *Serial* (2014–Present) to see how victim Hae Min Lee's narrative voice – as expressed through the initial inclusion of her journal entries – is de-prioritised, quickly removed to make way for the musings of her ex-boyfriend Adnan Syed (who has been convicted of her murder).

With true crime now reaching its apex of popularity, the marketability of the 'Dead Girl' narrative cannot be understated. Every week, a new docuseries centred on the 'Dead Girl' seems to materialise. Although our cultural fascination with this discursive figure is self-evident – we persistently reiterate her story – she continues to be de-politicised. Instead of acknowledging how the ubiquity of these stories might indicate the prevalence of gendered violence in contemporary culture, the 'Dead Girl' is repeatedly reduced to a singular anomaly, nothing more than the juicy new mystery of the week. But Hawkins's reanimation of the gothic double offers a challenge to this perpetual de-politicisation of gender-based violence in the popular media. By doubling the experiences of women who have been silenced by hegemonic ideologies, and have been victims of male violence in the process, Hawkins refuses the singularity of the 'Dead Girl' story. Rather, her narrative suggests that the silencing of women is not an isolated or unique experience but a growing epidemic.

Just as Rachel's nostalgic attachment to the fantasies of the good life enabled Tom to manipulate and control her, Megan's acquiescence to contemporary ideals of femininity normalised Scott's dominating behaviour. Persistently monitoring her email accounts and internet browser history, Scott tracks Megan's whereabouts and attempts to control her daily schedule. While Megan is perturbed by this repeated invasion of her privacy, she obediently performs the role of Scott's subservient wife. Rendered docile by the expectations of this gendered role, her discomfort is repudiated. Meanwhile, her husband's authoritarian behaviour is permitted to continue without critique.

As the novel reaches its denouement, Hawkins integrates yet another female voice into her narrative: Anna Watson. Like Rachel and Megan, Anna exhibits a sense of duty or responsibility to maintain her performance of the feminine ideal. In line with neoliberal and postfeminist ideologies – which ensure that 'disagreeable' female emotions like anger and sadness are repudiated or concealed – she repeatedly disguises her displeasure in the presence of her husband. For example, when Anna discovers what she believes to be Tom's burner phone, she begins to suspect foul play and fears that he may have actually been involved in Megan's murder. Anna is evidently distraught by this discovery, sobbing privately in her bedroom. But in order to please and placate Tom, Anna disguises her misgivings and chooses to re-emphasise her masquerade of femininity: she beautifies herself for her husband by styling her hair, carefully applying fresh makeup and putting on a seductive dress and high heels. Mirroring the experiences of Rachel and Megan, Anna's adherence to the expectations of this gendered role suppresses her critical voice, entrapping her in a dangerous situation and allowing Tom to evade justice.

In order to satisfy contemporary gender ideals and embody 'successful' femininity, Rachel, Megan and Anna must carefully control their emotions, appearing happy, 'positive' and confident. In conjunction with this 'mandatory optimism', these women are forced to conceal their 'unpalatable' responses to discomforting events, disguising their indignation. Through this sanguine performance of affability, their suffering is privatised, re-framed as an individual issue requiring self-adjustment. This suppression of those 'unpalatable' emotions, as part of their masquerade of femininity, permits the domineering men in their lives to control and abuse them. As evidenced in the novel, the sublimation of their 'negative' emotions facilitates their subordination and sanctions male domination. And so, by gradually exposing the uniformity of their experiences, the novel illustrates the pernicious effect of the hegemonic ideal of neoliberal and postfeminist culture. It demonstrates how Rachel's, Megan's and Anna's adherence to this ideal has made them more vulnerable to male abuse.

The style of the novel further troubles the effect of positivity synonymous with neoliberal postfeminism. Skilfully split between the complementary voices of three suffering women, the narrative emphasises how Rachel, Megan and Anna are disempowered by contemporary gender ideologies. Through her use of first-person narration, Hawkins encourages the reader to identify with these women. In the process, the reader is also forced to textually inhabit their experiences of suffering – to 'feel' or share their pain. By facilitating this affective response, Hawkins's narrative ruptures the thin veneer of the fantasies of the good life, exhorting the reader to reconsider the banality of these fantasies and their promise of happiness and equality.

In contrast to contemporary popular narratives in which female victims of male violence are reduced to stock characters, Hawkins also refuses to de-humanise her 'Dead Girl' and to write Megan off as 'just another' corpse amidst a long history of women who have been brutalised and murdered. As Rachel ardently asserts:

> Megan is not a mystery to be solved, she is not a figure who wanders into the tracking shot at the beginning of a film, beautiful, ethereal, insubstantial. She is not a cipher. She is real.
> (Hawkins, 106)

Here, Rachel explicitly addresses the dominant paradigms that surround representations of female victims in the popular media. While these women are appraised on the basis of their physical appearances, Rachel underscores their intangibility. She emphasises how these popular narratives strip women of their corporeality and reconstitute them as benign nonentities. Conversely, Hawkins gives depth and complexity to her female victim, refusing to exclude Megan's narrative voice from the pages of her novel. While *The Girl on the Train* begins and ends with her death, Megan's murder is not attenuated to a reductive framing device. Instead, her voice is a consistent presence in the narrative, and she continues her attempts to delineate her authentic truth throughout. In other words, Hawkins *refuses* to erase 'Dead Girl' Megan from her own story.

Hawkins furthers her commentary on the problematic representation of female victims in the popular media by including a subplot concerning the drowning of Megan's baby. In this subplot, Megan recounts her experience of losing her child. As a teenager desperate to escape a troubled home, she became involved with a significantly older man. When Megan fell pregnant, her lover deserted her. Isolated and struggling to fend for herself, she accidentally drowns her child by falling asleep with it in her arms in the bath. At first, this disturbing subplot seems odd and incongruous to the narrative – especially if we consider how crime plots are usually ruthless in their arrangement. Typically, in crime narratives, every detail is important even if its meaning only becomes apparent as the plot progresses. But the inclusion of this subplot feels utterly superfluous. It doesn't appear to have any bearing on Hawkins's overarching narrative.

This subplot could be discredited as a mere 'plot hole', a consequence of 'bad' writing. Worse yet, it might be read as an unnecessary way to heighten and exploit Megan's suffering for shock-value. However, this subplot could also function as a critique of how victims are often dichotomised into 'good' and 'bad' categories in the popular media. In what he terms the 'ideal victim', Nils Christie argues that the media has created a hierarchy of victimhood and identifies factors that are most likely to legitimise someone as a victim of a crime (1986, 22). This ideal victim is usually depicted as defenceless or blameless and thus deserving of sympathy. In contrast, Christie posits that victims who have 'mismanaged' their lives are often repudiated in the media as 'unworthy'. They are made responsible for their own victimisation as a result of their 'poor' life choices.

Motivated initially by her belief in Megan's 'goodness' – in the integrity of her character – Rachel is wholly committed to her investigation. But once she discovers that Megan was involved in the death of her child – information leaked by the media – Rachel is completely disgusted. In response, she opts to temporarily cease her detective-work. As the novel's primary protagonist and first-person narrator, the reader is arguably encouraged to identify with Rachel's condemnation of Megan and to share in her disgust. Made complicit in Rachel's degradation of her character, the reader is persuaded to individualise Megan's actions and remove them from their socio-political context. Her victimhood, we are led to believe, is a symptom of her 'mismanaged' life.

Later, Rachel reprimands herself – and by extension, the reader – for this vilification of Megan:

> It hits me like a wave, I can feel blood rushing to my face. I remember admitting it to myself. Thinking the thought and not dismissing it, embracing it . . . I forgot what I was supposed to be feeling. I ignored the fact that at the very best, Jess is nothing but a figment of my imagination, and at the worst, Jess is not nothing, she is Megan – she is dead, a body battered and left to rot. Worse than that: I didn't forget. I didn't care. I didn't care because I've started to believe what they're saying about her. Did I, for just the briefest of moments, think she got what was coming to her, too?
>
> (Hawkins, 217–8)

Encouraged by a media-driven narrative of Megan as 'bad mother', Rachel dismissed Megan as unworthy of empathy and somehow responsible for her own murder. Yet by emphasising how Rachel is ashamed of this behaviour as exemplified by her blushing face, the narrative implies that the reader should feel similarly embarrassed. Like Rachel, the reader should be disgusted that they have colluded in the abasement of Megan. The inclusion of this visceral description of Megan's decaying corpse is also particularly jarring, confronting the reader with the reality of the violence she has endured. Thus, contrary to popular discourses about female victims, Hawkins's narrative ultimately resists dehumanising Megan. Rather, it emphasises that *all* female victims of gendered violence are deserving of our consideration and our sympathy – regardless of their 'life choices'.

Rachel's retrieval of her lost memories – her repossession of her narrative authority – further affirms the novel's commitment to the potential for feminist solidarity. In a subversion of the traditional 'new-wife-versus-old-wife' trope – canonised in texts such du Maurier's *Rebecca* – Rachel returns to the home she once occupied with Tom to ensure that Anna will not be doomed to repeat her fate. Freshly aware of the violent ramifications of her own subjugation, her impulse is to share her story. While her version of events is initially discredited, Rachel's determination to excavate her memories and speak the truth of her victimisation ultimately empowers Anna to connect the proverbial dots. By articulating her trauma – and highlighting their shared experience – Rachel facilitates her rival's epiphany: Anna begins to appreciate that there will be dangerous consequences if she continues to ignore the reality of her situation with Tom. In emphasising the importance of this verbal connection – it is essentially Tom's undoing – the narrative functions as a call for collective forms of female action which have been eroded by individualising neoliberal and postfeminist ideologies.

As the novel reaches its denouement, Rachel realigns her priorities by committing to protecting Anna, whatever the cost. Arriving unannounced at her old home, she confronts Tom about his misdeeds and consequentially endures a violent beating. Blinded by this attack, she sightlessly searches in a familiar kitchen drawer to retrieve a corkscrew and launch her retaliation. Ironically, it is Rachel's intrinsic knowledge of the domestic space which allows her to secure this weapon and ultimately to regain her agency. Taking the law into their own hands in the face of male violence, Rachel and Anna come together to jam their (comically) phallic weapon into Tom's jugular – symbolically silencing him once and for all. In other words, the novel concludes with Rachel's and Anna's utter rejection of the fantasies of a good life as subjugating and ultimately hazardous for women.

Nevertheless, it is important to note that this 'empowering' image of 'sisterhood' upholds a troubling victim-perpetrator dichotomy. At the moment in which Rachel and Anna reject their victimisation, regaining control over their own narratives, they concurrently become murderers. As Rose asserts, "they enact a violence that is meant to belong to men alone" (4). Thus, as with *Gone Girl*, Hawkins's narrative forces us to question whether Rachel and Anna are any closer to living authentically as female subjects. Or, conversely, if these women can only 'exist' by adopting pre-determined subjectivities which crystallise problematic contemporary dichotomies.

Gone Girl and *The Girl on the Train* redeploy the archetype of the female monster to critique contemporary gender ideologies by reiterating how these ideologies pathologise women. At the same time, the novels emphasise the connection between the entrenchment of those ideologies and the quotidian reality of violence against women. Refusing to depoliticise this violence, the novels are actively critical of media constructions of female victims – specifically the 'Dead Girl' figure. These novels demonstrate how the reification of those victims by the media into caricatures of ideal femininity stifles any meaningful systemic discussion about gender-based violence. The novels are also critical of crime fiction as well as the newer 'true life' versions of crime narratives that are increasingly circulating in our culture.

Paradoxically, however, the 'success' of these novels hinges on Hawkins's and Flynn's ability to skilfully and satisfyingly utilise the very conventions they critique. By replicating the familiar aesthetics of crime fiction, these novels encourage readerly pleasure in the genre.

In addition, the commercial success of the novels – their attainment of a large readership – was reliant on reader appetite for these stories about dead or missing women. This unusual tension, between reproducing and subverting the problematic conventions of the crime genre, is particularly notable. On the one hand, these novels clearly satisfy the conditions of feminist crime fiction as defined by Adrienne E. Gavin. The central concern of feminist crime fiction, Gavin contends, is violence against women. In emphasising this violence, she argues, the subgenre functions as a kind of "gendered protest" (2010, 268). In fitting with Gavin's theory, both Flynn and Hawkins expertly exploit the conventions of the crime genre for distinctly feminist ends. As I have demonstrated, they use these conventions – and reader familiarity with them – to deliver their pointed critique about gender-based violence. On the other hand, critical responses to these novels force us to consider the limitations of this strategy. In other words, those critical responses illustrate the ease with which the lines between subversion and reiteration are blurred.

Still, the novels notably differ in *tone* from the earlier iterations of 'romance' in this study. As we saw in *Twilight* (Meyer, 2005–2008) and *Fifty Shades* (James, 2011–2012), affects like discomfort, sadness and distress were subsumed by dominant affects like positivity, happiness and confidence. In contrast, *Gone Girl* and *The Girl on the Train* are tonally bleak, offering only dark pictures of women's lives under neoliberal postfeminism. This tonal shift, I propose, signalled an important moment in 'women's fiction'. Influenced by those novels, a mass of duplicate narratives – produced by female authors for a largely female readership – suddenly emerged to challenge the shiny veneer of 'romance' in the postmillennial period. Like Flynn and Hawkins, these novelists amalgamated the conventions of crime fiction with key tropes and archetypes from 'romance'. In doing so, they crystallised the remoulding of the genre into something new – a space to foreground women's frustration and disaffection with the status quo.

Catalysing this shift, Flynn's and Hawkins's seminal novels profoundly altered the shape and tone of popular women's fiction. Yet I argue that the popularity of these novels indicated a critical moment of counter-resistance in our culture. Fatigued by the 'feelings rules' of neoliberal and postfeminist ideologies, women were clearly searching for ways to address their feelings of disillusionment and dissatisfaction, using fiction to try to reconcile the discrepancies between those ideologies and their lived reality. Thus, the reading of these novels might be interpreted as a kind of active resistance to, or explicit rejection of, neoliberal postfeminism, gesturing towards something crucial: that women were no longer content with being silenced and subjugated by those hegemonic gender ideologies.

Reference List

Basic Instinct. Directed by Paul Verhoeven, TriStar Pictures, 1992.
Berlant, Lauren. *Cruel Optimism*. Duke University Press, 2011.
Bolin, Alice. *Dead Girls: Essays on Surviving an American Obsession*. William Morrow Paperbacks, 2018.
Bronte, Charlotte. *Jane Eyre*. Smith, Elder & Company, 1847.
Burke, Eva. "From Cool Girl to Dead Girl: Gone Girl and the Allure of Female Victimhood." *Domestic Noir: The New Face of 21st Century Crime Writing*, edited by Laura Joyce and Henry Sutton, Palgrave Macmillan, 2018, pp. 71–87.
Bushnell, Candace. *Sex and the City*. Warner Books, 1997.
Christie, Nils. "The Ideal Victim." *From Crime Policy to Victim Policy: Reorienting the Justice System*, edited by Ezzat A. Fattah, Springer, 1986, pp. 17–30.
Creed, Barbara. *The Monstrous Feminine: Film, Feminism, Psychoanalysis*. Routledge, 1993.

Doyle, Sady. *Dead Blondes and Bad Mothers: Monstrosity, Patriarchy and the Fear of Female Power*. Melville House Printing, 2019.

Du Maurier, Daphne. *Rebecca*. Victor Gollancz, 1938.

Faludi, Susan. *Backlash: The Undeclared War Against American Women*. Crown Publishing Group, 1991.

Fatal Attraction. Directed by Adrian Lyne, Paramount Pictures, 1987.

Ferriss, Suzanne and Mallory Young. *Chick Lit: The New Woman's Fiction*. Routledge, 2006.

Fielding, Helen. *Bridget Jones's Diary*. Picador, 1996.

Flynn, Gillian. *Gone Girl*. Crown Publishing Group, 2012.

Gavin, Adrienne E. "Feminist Crime Fiction and Female Sleuths." *A Companion to Crime Fiction*, edited by Charles J. Rzepka and Lee Horsley, Wiley, 2010, pp. 258–269.

Gill, Rosalind, et al. *Aesthetic Labour: Rethinking Beauty Politics in Neoliberalism*. Palgrave Macmillan, 2017.

Gill, Rosalind, et al. "From Sexual Objectification to Sexual Subjectification: The Re-Sexualisation of Women's Bodies in the Media." *Feminist Media Studies*, vol. 3, no. 1, 2003, pp. 100–106. doi: 10.1080/1468077032000080158.

Greene, Gayle. "Feminist Fiction and the Uses of Memory." *Signs*, vol. 16, no. 2, 1991, pp. 290–322. www.jstor.org/stable/3174512.

Hawkins, Paula. *The Girl on the Train*. Doubleday, 2015.

Irigaray, Luce. *Speculum of the Other Woman*. Cornell University Press, 1974.

James, E.L. *Fifty Shades Darker*. Vintage Books, 2012.

James, E.L. *Fifty Shades Freed*. Vintage Books, 2012.

James, E.L. *Fifty Shades of Grey*. Vintage Books, 2011.

Korelitz, Jean Hanff. "The Girl on the Train by Paula Hawkins." *The New York Times*, 30 Jan. 2015, www.nytimes.com/2015/02/01/books/review/the-girl-on-the-train-by-paula-hawkins.html.

Kristeva, Julia. *Powers of Horror: An Essay on Abjection*. Columbia University Press, 1982.

Lawson, Richard. "Gone Girl, Fall's Most Anticipated Thriller, Doesn't Disappoint." *Vanity Fair*, 30 Sep. 2014, www.vanityfair.com/hollywood/2014/09/gone-girl-review.

Lynch, David and Mark Frost. *Twin Peaks*. Lynch/Frost Productions, 1990.

Making a Murderer. Directed by Laura Ricciardi and Moira Demos, Synthesis Films, 2015. Netflix.

Marston, Kendra. *Postfeminist Whiteness: Problematising Melancholic Burden in Contemporary Hollywood*. Edinburgh University Press, 2018.

McRobbie, Angela. *The Aftermath of Feminism: Gender, Culture and Social Change*. Sage Publications, 2008.

Meyer, Stephenie. *Breaking Dawn*. Atom, 2008.

Meyer, Stephenie. *Eclipse*. Atom, 2007.

Meyer, Stephenie. *New Moon*. Little, Brown Company, 2006.

Meyer, Stephenie. *Twilight*. Atom, 2005.

Miller, Emma. "'How Much Do You Want to Pay for This Beauty?': Domestic Noir and the Active Turn in Feminist Crime Fiction." *Domestic Noir: The New Face of 21st Century Crime Writing*, edited by Laura Joyce and Henry Sutton, Palgrave Macmillan, 2018, pp. 89–115.

My Favourite Murder. Exactly Right, 2016-present, www.myfavoritemurder.com/episodes.

Oliver, Kelly. *Hunting Girls: Sexual Violence from The Hunger Games to Campus Rape*. Columbia University Press, 2016.

Rich, Katey. "Why *Gone Girl*'s Amy Dunne Is the Most Disturbing Female Villain of All Time." *Vanity Fair*, 17 Mar. 2015, www.vanityfair.com/hollywood/2015/03/gone-girl-amy-psychopath.

Rose, Jacqueline. "Corkscrew in the Neck." *London Review of Books*, vol. 37, no. 17, 2015, www.lrb.co.uk/the-paper/v37/n17/jacqueline-rose/corkscrew-in-the-neck.

Schneider, Steven Jay. "The Madwomen in Our Movies: Female Psycho-Killers in American Horror Cinema." *Killing Women: The Visual Culture of Gender and Violence*, edited by Annette Burfoot and Susan Lord, Wilfrid Laurier University Press, 2006, pp. 237–251.

Serial. WBEZ, 2014-present, www.serialpodcast.org/season-one.

Single White Female. Directed by Barbet Schroder, Columbia Pictures, 1992.
Someone Knows Something. CBC Radio, 2016-present, www.cbc.ca/radio/sks.
The Jinx: The Life and Deaths of Robert Durst. Directed by Andrew Jarecki, HBO Documentary Films, 2015. HBO.
The Staircase. Directed by Jean-Xavier de Lestrade, Maha Productions, 2004. Netflix.
True Detective. Pizzolatto, Nic, Anonymous Content, 2014–present.
Wiseman, Eva. "The Truth about Women Crying Rape." *The Guardian*, 31 Mar. 2013, www.theguardian.com/lifeandstyle/2013/mar/31/truth-about-women-crying-rape.

4 Hell Hath No Fury

Female Rage and the Postfeminist Masquerade

In *Future Girl: Young Women in the Twenty-First Century* (2004), Anita Harris explicates how neoliberal and postfeminist ideologies have played a critical role in the remaking of feminine subjectivities in contemporary culture. In an expansion of traditional gender roles – in which women were limited to the subjective positions of wives and mothers – these new modes of femininity are inextricably bound up with success and striving for success in the public sphere. As Harris observes, young women are now celebrated for their determination to take charge of their lives, seize chances and achieve their goals (1).

Refigured as "top girls" who are "highly efficient assemblages of productivity," Angela McRobbie suggests that today's young women must evince an unwavering commitment to elaborate planning for success (2008, 59). In line with neoliberal and postfeminist ideologies, they are expected to be flexible, individualised, self-driven and self-made. With a renewed emphasis on self-optimisation, these 'top-girls' must internalise a competitive ethic as an inner drive which motivates them to meet a set of self-directed goals. Thus, as McRobbie proposes, competitive individualism has become a key mark of modern womanhood.

While this 'top girl' has been endowed with agency – and has been welcomed into the public sphere as an active citizen – McRobbie emphasises that there are insidious terms and conditions to her new-found freedom. Specifically, she suggests that a range of technologies of the self must be set in motion before this invitation to come forward as an active citizen can be issued at all. Foregrounding what she terms the 'postfeminist masquerade' – as one crucial way in which patriarchy has begun to relocate women within 'normative' gender hierarchies – McRobbie argues that neoliberal and postfeminist ideologies have redefined the parameters of idealised femininity and have thus intensified traditional feminine practices of self-maintenance. As a result, she suggests that no aspect of women's physical appearance can be left unattended; they must ritually monitor their bodies with a microscopic attention to detail and routinely engage in a kind of bodywork or aesthetic labour which is conveniently constitutive of 'normative' femininity. It is the submission to these harsh yet habitual self-monitoring practices which McRobbie identifies as the price women must pay for their entry into the dominant social order. Nonetheless, McRobbie stresses that this bodywork must *always* be presented as freely chosen – as irrefutable evidence of women's empowerment.

Building on McRobbie's argument, Rosalind Gill, Ana Elias and Christina Scharff posit that neoliberal postfeminism also has an affective or 'psychic' life. Predicated not only on her commitment to physical labour, a woman's success, they argue, is also simultaneously contingent on the regulation of her emotions to embrace qualities such as confidence, happiness and authenticity (2017, 5). In a collaborative article with Shani Orgad, Gill furthers

DOI: 10.4324/9781003322009-5

this theory by suggesting that the cultural favouring of 'positive' over 'negative' effects prohibits the expression of women's discontent – specifically, the promotion of 'good' feelings proscribes anger. Yet, as Gill and Orgad emphasise, casting women's anger as irrational or unreasonable has a long-standing history in Western civilisation (2019, 598). Maligned as a kind of hormonal hysteria or dismissed as evidence of a paranoid mental state, women's anger has been perpetually marked as dangerous, deviant and even monstrous.

Despite the emergence of the #MeToo movement in 2017, Gill and Orgad maintain that the pathologisation or vilification of female rage has only intensified in the contemporary popular media. Accrediting this intensification to the increased presence of neoliberal and postfeminist ideologies, they argue that women have been progressively compelled to hyper-regulate their own anger – to exercise the utmost restraint over any potentially 'disruptive' expression of their unpalatable emotions. Gill and Orgad also stress how women are obliged not only to mediate this anger but also to transform it into something more 'palatable' in order to operate successfully as subjects within the dominant social order. In short, Gill and Orgad contend that female anger or rage has been systematically outlawed by neoliberal postfeminism.

Following Gill and Orgad's logic, this incitement to minimise one's negative emotions arguably functions as a disciplinary mechanism through which the female subject is individually made responsible for her inability to resolve her social disadvantage. The heightened pressure on women to regulate their behaviour by repudiating any expression of discontent has also allowed for the discursive formation of a new ideal of femininity: the 'cool girl', a markedly confident and fun-loving woman, whose affective lexicon obviates negativity. In this context, the 'cool girl' appears to be a logical extension of the kind of idealised femininity which Angela McRobbie proposed was part of an emerging postfeminist masquerade. Though, as previously outlined, McRobbie focuses specifically on what she suggests is the reconstitution of the 'spectacularly feminine' – through women's heightened management of their bodies in line with narrow and normative ideals of female beauty – this regulation of women's affective responses to injustice also facilitates their subordination. It similarly diminishes the 'threat' that they pose to the dominant social order by allowing them to navigate the terrain of hegemonic masculinity without being positioned as aggressively feminine. In other words, by adopting this mask of affability, women can avert any patriarchal retribution.

In order to be counted as subjects, women must consistently monitor, regulate and discipline their own bodies, behaviour and emotions in line with the increasingly impossible demands of idealised femininity. Simultaneously, the discursive proliferation of 'feelings rules' embargo the expression of any kind of female discontent about the unliveable pressures of maintaining a feminine subjectivity. Ensuring that women submit to these intensified regimes of self-discipline as part of the 'postfeminist masquerade', neoliberal and postfeminist ideologies make the silencing of women's critical voices a condition for social status and economic power.

While contemporary women are obliged to perform a kind of benign affability, McRobbie argues that female anger persistently bubbles beneath the surface of the 'postfeminist masquerade'. But without a structural basis for expression, this anger is ultimately misdirected *away* from patriarchy. It is turned either inwards, against the self, or outwards towards other women. In what she terms 'postfeminist disorders', McRobbie notes an increase in the range of demarcated pathologies associated almost exclusively with young women such as binge drinking, anorexia, bulimia and cutting (96). Alarmingly, these overt symptoms of acute female suffering have been normalised in contemporary culture. As McRobbie emphasises, they have been figured as a constituent part of becoming a woman.

This reduction of female suffering to some kind of sociological banality has also undercut the need for any new feminist initiative, since it has depoliticised these 'feminine' pathologies by reconstituting them as autonomous issues which do not require a feminist intervention. With attention deflected away from a socio-political rationale for their genesis, these 'postfeminist disorders' have become naturalised. In the process, neoliberal and postfeminist ideologies have been permitted to evade social scrutiny. As such, McRobbie argues that the self-harming practices of today's young women might be best understood as expressions of their 'illegible rage' – as their corporeal responses to the inegalitarian nature of neoliberal postfeminism. The proliferation of these distinctly feminine disorders, McRobbie determines, is a refracted indictment of social forces in a culture within which expressions of female suffering have been both obscured and de-politicised.

In line with McRobbie's assertions, Susan Bordo firmly situates her analysis of young women's self-harming practices in their material conditions. Arguing for their re-politicisation, she suggests that the symptomatology of these feminine disorders should be recognised as a form of textuality (1993). For Bordo, the bodies of disordered women are graphic texts with potently symbolic meanings; they signify what socio-political conditions make it impossible to express linguistically. Bordo re-frames these 'gendered disorders' as a kind of mute or embodied protest – as an inchoate and often counterproductive remonstrance adopted by women who have been denied an effective language to articulate their distress.

Though McRobbie maintains that the proliferation of these 'gendered disorders' highlights how women have been forced to embody their rage – to literally experience it in their bodies – she also suggests that the proscription of female rage has triggered a second avenue of misdirection. Specifically, she argues that the neoliberal incitement towards competitive individualism and self-optimisation – in conjunction with the proscription of female rage – has fostered an outer-directed competition or antagonism between women; it has reanimated traditional modes of girls competing within the confines of normative femininity (2015, 6).

According to McRobbie, this idea that competitiveness is an inherent part of modern femininity is predominantly perpetuated by the popular media. While tabloid newspapers such as the Daily Mail frequently report on female celebrity 'frenemies', blockbuster movies including *Bride Wars* (Gary Winick, 2009) and *Mean Girls* (Mark Waters, 2004) centre on young women whose innately competitive impulses have begun to erode their friendships. Yet McRobbie stresses that there are real-world ramifications to these discursive constructions of femininity: their proliferation facilitates the misdirection of female rage towards other women whilst ensuring that any outright critique of the hegemonic power structures which have generated impossible ideals of femininity notably disappears.

For Alison Winch, the girlfriend gaze – a 'by-product' of neoliberal and postfeminist ideologies – is particularly effective at facilitating this competition between women. Extending Foucault's configuration of the panopticon, she argues that women have begun to regulate each other's bodies through affective networks of control which constitute a *gynaeopticon* (2013, 5). With its emphasis on peer-regulation and surveillance, this gynaeopticon encourages and promotes regimes of looking between women, establishing networks of mutual governance in which the body is a project to be perpetually worked upon. Though Winch posits that the gynaeopticon is a sociological phenomenon, she also highlights how it is naturalised by the popular media. The pernicious effects of peer regulation, she argues, are visible across a multitude of cultural texts including HBO's *Sex and the City* (1998–2004) and MTV's *The Hills* (2006–10).

The gynaeopticon, Winch argues, has become essential to the formation and production of feminine identities. It enables contemporary young women to establish and define the codes of normative femininity in the mirror of their girlfriend's gaze. While appearing as a form of relationship between women, Winch maintains that the gynaeopticon is actually a function of patriarchal domination; it makes women complicit in the regulation and policing of female bodies and behaviour. In this context, by ensuring that women seamlessly conduct themselves in line with the expectations of idealised femininity, the girlfriend gaze facilitates the perpetuation and obfuscation of hegemonic power structures.

While these regulatory 'girlfriendships' are promoted as supportive networks of female solidarity in the popular media, 'girlfriend culture' has paradoxically generated what Winch terms "affective girlfriendliness – a loving meanness" (Winch, 14). Discourses of cruelty have become a means through which women can fortify their interpersonal bonds. In conforming to the normative standards of the group, they achieve a sense of belonging which is then bolstered by the humiliation and denigration of others. Under the guise of benevolent encouragement, the savage disciplining of each other's bodies can be understood as evidence of a deep intimacy between women. Thus, women's rage about contemporary ideals of femininity is not only misdirected towards other women but also misinterpreted as intimacy and solidarity.

Gillian Flynn's *Sharp Objects* (2006) and Megan Abbott's *Dare Me* (2012) certainly engage with the theme of power struggles between women. Explicitly marketed as crime fiction, *Dare Me* examines the cut-throat world of competitive cheerleading. It explores the shifting power dynamics between 16-year-old Beth – the most popular girl in school – and narrator Addy – her self-proclaimed "forever-lieutenant" (Abbott, 7). Over the course of the novel, the relationship between these 'frenemies' becomes increasingly fraught because of Addy's idolisation of their enigmatic new cheerleading coach, Colette French. As Beth gradually acknowledges that her power over her 'second-in-command' has begun to waver, she plots to expose Coach French as a fraud who is engaging in an illicit extra-marital affair. When Colette's lover is found dead, Beth seizes the opportunity to take down her opponent. She actively investigates the death of Sargent Will Mosley in order to implicate her rival in his presumed murder. Thus, Addy becomes trapped in a complex, triangular web of competition between her volatile, life-long friend and her aspirational yet troubled new coach.

Flynn's *Sharp Objects*, which is structured like a prototypical murder mystery, explores the relationship between three generations of women: Camille, the novel's first-person narrator; her wealthy and controlling mother, Adora; and her estranged teenage half-sister, Amma. An ambitious but troubled journalist, Camille reluctantly returns to her hometown to report on and investigate the gruesome murders of two adolescent girls – Ann and Natalie. In pursuit of the truth, Camille is forced to confront her personal demons; she must address her fraught relationship with her family whilst attempting to resolve the trauma of her sister Marian's death years before. Interspersed with her recollections of the past, Camille's 'present' narrative is populated with references to her sister, who she acknowledges was a sickly child from infancy. Yet Camille has no real explanation for Marian's premature death, nor does she know what grave illness had plagued her throughout her short life. As she begins to unravel the mystery at the centre of her investigation, Camille simultaneously uncovers a dark family secret. While Amma is revealed to be the serial killer who has been terrorising Windgap all along, Adora – who suffers from an illness called Munchausen Syndrome by Proxy – is exposed as Marian's murderer. Several years prior to the timeline of the narrative, she had accidentally administered a fatal dose of poison to her daughter.

There is an important tension between contradictory narrative impulses in these novels. Both novels foreground female protagonists who attempt to become the 'top girl' by adopting the postfeminist masquerade and who neatly conform to neoliberal tenets of competitive individualism and self-optimisation. In this way, the novels endorse the hegemonic ideal of neoliberal and postfeminist culture. However, affirming those norms at the level of story and characterisation is undermined at the level of style and affect by copious descriptions of female bodies in pain. This tension underscores the limitations of the kind of empowerment that is offered to contemporary Western women as part of the postfeminist masquerade. Figuring their protagonist's suffering as a direct consequence of the silencing of their critical voices, these novels underscore how women's rage, when denied a structural basis for expression, becomes embodied, individualised as a personal issue and removed from its socio-political context. From this perspective, the novels highlight how the misdirection of female rage functions as a tool of patriarchy which facilitates the depoliticisation and individualisation of women's suffering – thus enabling hegemonic structures of power to remain intact and evade critique.

Moreover, both novels reanimate a key literary archetype of monstrous femininity – the mean girl – to underscore the political consequences of this misdirection of female rage. By exploiting and subverting this archetype, these novels highlight how neoliberal and postfeminist ideologies have penetrated the intimate relationships between women in contemporary culture. Troubling the notion of female solidarity, the novels force the reader to consider what kind of 'sisterhood' can actually be achieved amidst a climate of neoliberal and postfeminist logic. They also refuse to understate the destructive potential of these myths about the monstrosity of adolescent femininity. Rather, as we will see, the novels demonstrate how these myths inhibit women's expressions of suffering and divert critical attention away from a profoundly corrupt status quo in which gender-based violence has been normalised.

"The Powerful Illusion of Delicate Girlhood"

In *Dare Me*, competitive cheerleading is a metaphor for the neoliberal incitement to self-regulate and relentlessly work on the body. Addy's capacity for self-governance is certainly underscored from the outset. Emphasising the mechanical qualities of her corporeality, she figures her body as a "new machine" which dutifully accepts her commands. She proudly asserts, "*this is my body, and I can make it do things . . . I can make it spin, flip, fly*" (Abbott, 3; italics in original). As the co-captain of an illustrious cheerleading squad, Addy's social status is privileged and elevated. Yet she specifically accredits this popularity to her heightened capacity for body regulation and control. Figured as individuals in perpetual training, she imagines that her squad is celebrated by the other characters in the social world of the novel for its overt athleticism. Highlighting her exaltation of bodywork, she believes that her peers often gaze with wonder as her team performs their "Herculean" cheer routines.

With first-person narrator Addy functioning as the central point of identification for the reader, female bodily governance is arguably marked as aspirational; it is framed as a pathway to reputation and prestige. However, there is a marked disjunction between Addy's adulation of bodywork and Abbott's visceral descriptions of her body in pain:

> And so it's bleacher sprints for us. Oh, to know such pain. Hammering up and down those bleacher steps to the pulse of an endless whistle. Twenty-one high steps and forty-three smaller steps. Again, again, again, we can feel it in our shins the next day. Our spines, we can feel it everywhere. The bleacher sprints are punishing, and I feel my whole body shuddering – pound- pound-pound – my teeth rattling, its almost ecstatic – pound-pound-pound, pound-pound- pound. By Saturday practice, though, we're already – some of us – starting to look forward to that pain, which feels like something real.
>
> (Abbott, 17–18)

Here, as accentuated by Abbott's use of onomatopoeic sounds, the novel underscores the harsh effects of aesthetic labour on Addy's body. The repetition of these sounds also suggests that this aesthetic labour has become habitual and is an essential part of creating and maintaining an indefectibly feminine exterior. Addy, of course, does not conceive of her brutal bodywork as harmful or as a form of self-harm. Rather, she experiences a kind of masochistic pleasure from it. She overtly acknowledges that it fortifies her materiality – that it allows her to feel connected to her own body and thus to 'feel real'.

On the one hand, by foregrounding Addy's pleasurable response to this bodywork, the narrative appears to promote aesthetic labour as gratifying for the reader. On the other hand, Abbott's visceral descriptions of her narrator's quotidian suffering – ubiquitous throughout her novel – trouble this seeming exaltation of neoliberal and postfeminist ideologies. Drawing attention to how pain and suffering are inherent to inhabiting a 'successful' female body, and of satisfying contemporary ideals of femininity, these descriptions force the reader to consider the punishing nature of contemporary gender norms.

Likewise, Abbott's deployment of a motif of breathlessness or suffocation troubles any straightforward interpretation of the novel's promotion of the 'postfeminist masquerade' as the primary pathway to female pleasure and success. Juxtaposing her 'mirror moments', the narrative underscores how Addy's bodywork enables her to clearly establish and maintain a subjective identity:

> I stand in front of the mirror, my face bare, flushed, taut. Slowly, my hands lifting the sticky nose, dusty brushes, oily wands waving in front of my face, fuchsia streaking up my cheeks, my lashes stiffened to brilliant black, my hair stiff, gleaming, pin-tucked. The perfumed mist, thick in my throat, settling. I look in the mirror. And it's finally me there.
>
> (Abbott, 287)

Before she 'performs' at a football game, Addy is actively engaged in the production of the self. Through this strategic transformation of her body, she fortifies her subjectivity and is granted social visibility.

In contrast, as Addy narrates the process of removing these signifiers of femininity after the game – her glittered lashes, her streaked hair, her sequins – she highlights the fractures in her subjectivity. She suggests that there is a disconnect between her performative identity and her authentic self:

> After a game, it takes a half-hour under the shower head to get all the hairspray out. To peel off all the sequins. To dig out that last bobby pin nestled deep in your hair. After, you stand in front of the steaming mirror, the fuchsia streaks gone, the lashes unsparkled. And it's just you there, and you look like no one you've ever seen before. You don't look like anybody at all.
>
> (Abbott, 3)

Acknowledging her own 'non-existence' outside of this performative identity, Addy believes that once she has removed her 'mask', she is marked by an abject nothingness which excludes her from the dominant social order. By underscoring this nothingness, the novel implies that Addy's adoption of a postfeminist masquerade – in line with McRobbie's assertions – is the only way in which she can successfully operate as a subject in contemporary culture. Nonetheless, Addy's glowing account of the transformation of her body in the above excerpts – as underscored by Abbott's use of overtly positive words such as 'brilliant' and 'gleaming' – obscures the restrictive reality of her performance. It stresses the pleasure involved in Addy's adoption of the masquerade.

However, during a key scene in which Coach French invites Addy into her home and instructs her to pretend to be her – to imagine that they have body-swapped – the prose complicates this reading of Abbott's novel.

> And I'm her. And this is my house, and Matt French is my husband, tallying columns all day, working late into the night for me, for me. And here I am, my tight, perfect body, my pretty perfect face, and nothing could ever be wrong with me, or my life, *not even the sorrow that is plainly right there in the centre of it. Oh, Colette, it's right there in the centre of you, and some kind of despair too, Colette* – that silk sucking into my mouth, the weight of it now, and I can't catch my breath, my breath, my breath.
>
> (Abbott, 66)

As Addy fantasises about what it might be like to *be* Coach French, she highlights how her aspirational mentor possesses all the feminine markers of success as promoted by neoliberal postfeminism: she has a beautiful home, a doll-like daughter, a doting husband and the ideal body. In spite of her awareness of these apparent successes, Addy senses that there is a hollowness at the heart of this fantasy of female perfection. Underscoring the superficiality of the postfeminist masquerade, she suggests that Coach's 'ideal' life is nothing more than an empty facade with sorrow and suffering at its centre.

Addy also begins to experience a choking sensation at the thought of transforming into Collette. As emphasised by her repetition of 'my breath', she becomes overwhelmed with panic. While Coach seemingly 'has it all', her committed adherence to the feminine ideal is evidently figured as stifling; Addy suggests that it has a leaden quality which weighs heavily on her. Thus, by employing this motif of breathlessness, the narrative suggests that Coach's postfeminist masquerade has actually facilitated her symbolic suffocation. These descriptions of Coach's embodied experience of the postfeminist masquerade – as intuited by Addy – trouble the novel's exaltation of neoliberal and postfeminist ideologies. They force the reader to question whether the kind of empowerment that is achieved through a performance of idealised femininity is unfettered from hegemonic power structures or, conversely, if it is facilitating the subordination of women.

Later, the novel more explicitly connects Addy's experience of pain and suffering to her occupation of an adolescent female body:

> I wondered did she look at us that first week and see past the glossed hair and shiny legs, our glittered brow bones and girl bravado? See past all that to everything beneath, all our miseries, the way we all hated ourselves but much more everyone else? Could she see past all of that to something else, something quivering and real . . . ?
>
> (Abbott, 10)

As Addy worries that her low self-esteem will be laid bare under Coach's gaze, the novel emphasises her feelings of powerlessness as a female subject under neoliberal postfeminism. Unable to express her discontent – to articulate these feelings of powerlessness – Addy's perpetual punishment of her body, in the guise of aesthetic labour, might be best understood as an embodiment of her 'illegible rage'. It becomes a way in which she can covertly communicate her suffering. Nevertheless, by including these copious descriptions of female bodies in pain, the novel forces us to consider how the misdirection of female rage against the self – as necessitated by neoliberal and postfeminist ideologies – ensures that women continue to suffer in silence. In other words, these descriptions confront the reader with the possibility that the mediation or misdirection of female rage is enabling hegemonic power structures to remain intact.

While Addy's brutal bodywork is figured as a pathway to self-actualisation in *Dare Me*, Camille Preaker's perpetual punishment of her body is explicitly framed as self-harm in *Sharp Objects*. In contrast to Abbott's protagonist, Camille's attempts to self-actualise have ultimately been ineffectual. Unable to satisfy contemporary ideals of femininity, she frequently engages in self-destructive behaviour. She drinks to excess to obliterate her consciousness – to be "wrapped in black, gone away" – and is a self-proclaimed 'cutter' – "a snipper, a slicer, a carver, a jabber" – who has covered her body with self-inflicted wounds (Flynn, 76). Yet, as we will see, Flynn attempts to re-politicise her protagonist's 'pathology' by providing a socio-political context for its genesis.

As part of an off-the-record interview with Detective Richard, Camille recounts a series of violent incidents from her adolescence. But in the process, she exposes a disturbing attitude towards victimhood and vulnerability:

> I could feel my limbs disconnecting, floating nearby like driftwood on an oily lake. . . . "Once, an eight-grade girl got drunk at a high-school party and four or five guys on the football team had sex with her, kind of passed her around. Does that count?" "Camille. Of course it counts. You know that, right?" "Well, I just didn't know if that counted as outright violence or . . ." "Yeah, I'd count a bunch of punks raping a thirteen-year-old outright violence, yes I sure would." "So it's the age that makes it rape." "It'd be rape at any age." "If I got a little too drunk tonight, and was out of my head and had sex with four guys, that would be rape? Sometimes drunk women aren't raped; they just make stupid choices – and to say we deserve special treatment when we're drunk because we're women, to say we need to be looked after, I find offensive."
>
> (Flynn, 139–41)

Camille frames gang rape as a consequence of flawed decision-making, and a failure of self-control, by the victim. Conforming to a neoliberal and postfeminist culture which reviles vulnerability and dependence, she passionately advocates personal responsibility and self-governance. In doing so, Camille inadvertently highlights how these ideologies – which promote hyper-responsibility – deny women any avenue for the expression of their suffering. They covertly ensure that women become enmeshed in collusion with the very forces which stifle their critical voices and sustain their oppression.

Later, when recalling the experience of losing her virginity, Camille makes a disturbing confession. Exposing herself as the subject of the aforementioned gang rape, she asserts that her 'first time' was also her second, third, fourth and fifth time. The gang rape of a 13-year-old girl which she hypothesised in her conversation with the detective was actually her own experience. Yet, by having Camille acknowledge that the emergence of her compulsion towards self-harm coincided with this sexual assault, the novel refuses to dismiss her self-harming practices as a form of normative gender embodiment. Camille's 'pathology' is not a constituent part of being a woman but a consequence of misogynistic violence. In this context, Camille's sense of weightlessness or corporeal detachment, 'floating', takes on symbolic resonance: underscoring that her internalisation of the neoliberal and postfeminist incitement towards personal responsibility has ultimately left her detached from and unable to articulate her own trauma.

In attempting to make legible what has been made illegible by cultural forces beyond her control, Camille's cutting becomes a way of protesting the stifling of her own voice through a voiceless act. The style of Flynn's narration also supports this reading of Camille's cutting as a form of silent protest. By mimicking some of the quintessential aesthetic tropes commonly associated with 'trauma narratives', it further underscores and concretises the reality of Camille's suffering. Functioning as a kind of metafictional manifestation of a 'traumatised' consciousness, trauma narratives are characterised by their temporal disorganisation and fragmentation. As Cathy Caruth observes, these narratives are "stories of wounds that cry out, that addresses us in an attempt to tell us of a reality or truth that is not otherwise available" (1996, 88).

While Camille has been unable to consciously connect the traumatic events of her youth to the murders of Ann and Natalie, her timelines are evidently disjointed and disrupted. Her 'present' narration is constantly obstructed by her recollections of the past:

> Something was wrong, right here, very wrong. I could picture Bob Nash sitting on the edge of Ann's bed, trying to remember the last thing he said to his daughter. I saw Natalie's mother, crying into one of her old T-shirts. I saw me, a despairing thirteen-year-old sobbing on the floor of my dead sister's room, holding a small flowered shoe. Or Amma, thirteen herself, a woman-child with a gorgeous body and a gnawing desire to be the baby girl my mother mourned. My mother weeping over Marian. Biting that baby.
>
> (Flynn, 173)

Camille's trauma cannot be properly assimilated into her conscious mind. Instead, with the past actively impeding on the present, she appears to be circling around a multitude of traumatic experiences – from her mother's abuse to her sister's death – whilst remaining incapable of articulating the reality of her suffering. Overtly contradicting Camille's explicit repudiation of vulnerability, the text's aesthetic effects emphasise how she has been permanently altered by her assault and foreground one of the novel's central themes: how women are damagingly dissociated from their own suffering by contemporary gender ideologies.

Though Camille evidently cannot speak her trauma, her decision to cut distinctly negative and feminised words into her own skin is particularly notable. It makes tangible what women's bodies are often reduced to in a patriarchal culture – "duplicitous," "inarticulate," "baby," "clit," "perky," "cunt," and "wicked" (75–9). As such, Camille's self-harming practices are reframed as an embodied protest against the social forces which assess her value in terms of the 'usefulness' of her body. By scarring herself with these feminised words, Camille struggles to make public those painful aspects of contemporary femininity which neoliberal and postfeminist ideologies have made it impossible to explicitly articulate. These scars also enable her to remove herself as an object of the male gaze. While various characters emphasise how attractive she had been in her youth, Camille asserts: "Every time people said I was pretty, I thought of everything ugly swarming beneath my clothes" (Flynn, 201). From this perspective, the narrative suggests that Camille's self-harming practice – her destruction and abjection of her own body – has subversive potential. For Camille, it functions as a form of active resistance to the neoliberal and postfeminist incitement towards self-subjection and self-objectification.

Further, it is crucial to note that Camille situates the genesis of her cutting in the context of her compulsion towards narration:

> The problem started long before that, of course. Problems always start long before you really, really see them. I was nine and copying, with a thick polka-dotted pencil, the entire Little House on the Prairie series word by word into spiral notebooks with glowing green covers. I was ten and writing every other word my teacher said on my jeans in blue ballpoint. . . . By eleven, I was compulsively writing down everything anyone said to me in a tiny blue notepad, a mini reporter already. Every phrase had to be written on paper or it wasn't real, it slipped away.
>
> (Flynn, 76–7)

Refusing to be reduced to a docile body, her impulse to narrate is explicitly linked to her desire for agency over her own reality – her desire to reclaim control of her own narrative voice. This process of narrating bolsters Camille's sense of corporeality. Distorting the reduction of women to sign or symbol, it becomes her way of writing herself into existence. Thus, by figuring narrative creation as a form of self-creation, the novel frames Camille's self-harming practices – her cutting of these distinctly feminised words – as a way of mobilising against the oppressive patriarchal ideologies which have enabled her docility.

Nevertheless, as Bordo alerts us, protest can function "paradoxically, as if in collusion with the cultural conditions that produce [it], reproducing rather than transforming precisely that which is being protested" (177). Following Bordo's logic, I would be remiss not to highlight the limitations of arguing for the subversive potential of representations of women's self-harming practices. While Camille's self-mutilation might function as a form of unconscious resistance, it simultaneously risks affirming the idea that the mediation of women's pain and suffering must be managed individually and privately. Through her self-harming practices, Camille is certainly able to express her dissent and dissatisfaction as a female subject. Yet she is only able to do so by destroying her own body. All the while, the hegemonic structures of power which have necessitated her silence remain undisturbed.

The conclusion of Camille's narrative arc further undermines the subversive potential of Flynn's novel. When she discovers that Amma is a serial murderer, Camille suffers a nervous breakdown. As a result, she is forced to live under the care of her editor and his wife. In other words, Flynn concludes her novel with an image of Camille, wholly infantilised, being tenderly tucked into bed by her substitute parents who read her a 'bedtime' story. This discomforting image of Camille certainly emphasises her disempowerment. In spite of her bodily protests, she is no closer to living agentically. But this conclusion might also function as a kind of aesthetic resistance to what Sarah E. Whitney describes as the trope of overcoming, synonymous with postfeminist texts. In these texts, she argues, trauma is often only seen as valuable insomuch as it leads to an "empowered overcoming" (2016, 11). For instance, a character who is assaulted becomes a 'stronger' person because of their experience of violence. This trope powerfully reflects the values of neoliberal and postfeminist thought, suggesting that trauma is a state of mind that can be resolved or 'overcome' individually and without systematic address. However, by refusing to reproduce this narrative trope, Flynn rejects the depoliticisation of women's trauma as an individual issue that should be managed privately. Instead, the conclusion of her novel reminds the reader that there is no easy, 'pop-psych' solution to Camille's trauma.

Mean Girls

Thus far, I have argued that representations of women's 'self-harming practices' in *Dare Me* and *Sharp Objects* underscore how neoliberal and postfeminist ideologies promote the misdirection of female rage against the self. But these novels also highlight how female rage in response to societal injustices has penetrated intimate relationships between women. As we will see, both novels reanimate and modify a key contemporary archetype of monstrous femininity – the 'mean girl' – to critique how these ideologies condition women to project their rage onto the bodies of other women. In doing so, the novels illuminate how these ideologies impede the potential for female solidarity in contemporary culture whilst emphasising the wider political implications of this.

The literary archetype of the 'mean girl' emerged as part of a subgenre of chick lit marketed specifically towards teenage girls: chick lit jr. Coined by Joanna Webb Johnson, the subgenre typically foregrounds adolescent female protagonists and addresses quintessential YA issues such as coming of age, identity and sexuality. In its exaltation of postfeminist ideas about confidence, assertiveness and self-determination, the subgenre exhibits many of the same tropes associated with its adult counterpart. Like chick lit, it often "tries to affirm flawed women, acknowledge insecurities involving physical attributes, and gives lessons in negotiating relationships – usually by showing the wrong way first" (2005, 141–2).

Usually emphasising the shared activity of fashion and shopping, popular examples of the subgenre – including Cecily von Ziegesar's *Gossip Girl* (2002) and Lisi Harrison's *The Clique* (2004) – embrace the pleasures of consumerism. Chick lit jr. also persistently reproduces discourses of female empowerment. Borne out of the girl-power movement – a distinctive element of postfeminist culture – it promotes the idea that a sisterhood of female friends is the place from which the ever-evolving adolescent girl can *truly* draw her strength. The connection between female empowerment and consumerism permeates chick lit and chick lit jr. is almost indistinguishable from its adult counterpart. As Samantha Lindop argues, it promises a nearly identical "all-girl world of fun, sassiness and dressing up in revealing clothes with lots of glitter and makeup in order to please yourself" (2015, 100). But the subgenre substitutes the metropolitan settings usually associated with chick lit for more appropriately juvenile spaces. The novels often follow the trials and tribulations of an every-girl character who is desperately trying to adjust to a new school. As this benevolent heroine attempts to negotiate her burgeoning relationship with a sophisticated 'cool' girl group, she usually falls victim to the genre's monstrous antagonist – the queen bee or mean girl.

In contrast to more traditional forms of aggression which often manifest as physical intimidation or harm, Sara K. Day notes how the behaviour associated with the mean girl generally falls under the category of 'relational aggression' (2017, 136). She opts to harm others via a purposeful kind of manipulation which disarms those around her. This mean girl, a recurring archetype in chick lit jr., often demonstrates an alarming amount of social influence. Through a combination of charisma and deception, she omnipotently reigns supreme. Nonetheless, as Day observes, these novels frequently conclude with her downfall. Social harmony can only be restored once she has received her 'comeuppance' – usually at the hands of the less popular girls she has incessantly tormented (136).

While representations of adolescent girls as excessively 'bitchy', mean and innately competitive towards each other have become common in the popular media, the increasing ubiquity of the mean girl as a cultural figure facilitates the perpetuation of troubling discourses about adolescent womanhood. The idea that there is something *inherent* about girlhood and girls themselves which produce these disturbing behaviours has begun to circulate in our culture with an alarming alacrity. In other words, the line between discursive representations of mean girls and what it is actually like to inhabit an adolescent female body has become blurred. Persistently figured as a fundamental quality of adolescent womanhood, this 'problem' of relational aggression has become individualised. Removed from its cultural context, it has been reframed as an individual issue which requires only a personal solution in the form of behavioural adjustments. As a result, the discourses that work to maintain these attitudes about adolescent femininity continue to go unexamined.

Presenting as a generic hybrid of sorts, *Dare Me* blends the prototypical elements of a murder-mystery plot with some of these key tropes from chick lit jr. From the outset, it situates itself clearly within Lindop's all-girl world. The reader is immediately immersed in descriptions of glitter, sparkles, fuchsia streaks and flailing pom-poms, as Addy narrates a post-game scene in the girls' locker room. Adopting a conventionally 'teenage' dialect, Addy's narrative voice mimics that of the quintessential chick lit jr. protagonist. Her first-person confessional style of narration is overtly juvenile:

> For much of the school year, the rest of the student body views us as something like lacquered lollipops, tiara'd princesses, spirit whores, chiclet-toothed bronze bitches. Aloof goddesses unwilling to mingle with the masses. . . . At the pep rally, they see our swagger, our balls, our badassery.
>
> (Abbott, 76)

It is populated with slang words – 'swagger' and 'badassery' – which casually reflect post-feminist discourses of female empowerment.

Beth's status as the prototypical mean girl of chick lit jr. is cemented early in the novel. As the captain of her squad of "cheerlebrities," she occupies a privileged position in the school's social hierarchy – she is the universally worshipped queen bee. But Beth's dictatorial regime depends on intimidation to fortify her power. She abuses her teammates by denigrating their weight and slut-shaming them for their sexual activities. In line with the hostile behaviours of the archetypal mean girl, Beth's aggression is decidedly 'relational'. She strategically manipulates those around her as a means of weakening their self-esteem. Beth also deliberately attempts to damage the interpersonal relationships between her teammates by recruiting reluctant volunteers to reinforce her abuse – thereby strengthening her own power and influence.

However, in her reading of the novel's conclusion, Leigh Redhead suggests that *Dare Me* ultimately exposes *Addy* as an "unreliable narrator who has hidden her ambition all along" (2018, 118). While Beth nearly dies in a suicide attempt and Coach's husband is arrested for the murder of her lover, it is Addy who emerges triumphant. As Redhead suggests, she is able to "outperform" the other women in order to become the 'top girl' – the new captain of the cheerleading squad (118). For Redhead, this 'reveal' arguably reframes Addy as the novel's primary antagonist; she is the monstrous mean girl whose thinly veiled ambitions have made her a "sociopath" (118).

Following this logic, Redhead appears to suggest that *Dare Me* reaffirms contemporary myths about adolescent femininity by vilifying Addy and pathologising her behaviour. Yet her argument notably disregards how this kind of 'monstrous' or 'sociopathic' behaviour is not specific to Addy. Rather, driven by their unwavering hunger for power, all of Abbott's female characters are decidedly monstrous. This diversion from the prototypical dichotomisation of girls into 'good versus bad' categories of femininity – ubiquitous throughout the chick lit jr. genre – might provide a clue as to the subversive potential of Abbott's novel. By making all of her female characters 'monsters', perhaps Abbott is attempting to illuminate the pathologising effect of neoliberal postfeminism on female subjectivity. In addition, by focusing specifically on intimate relationships between women and girls, the narrative highlights the irreconcilability of these pathologising ideologies with female solidarity.

This notion of female solidarity is introduced early in Abbott's novel. It is Addy's integration into the cheerleading squad which enables her to achieve a sense of intimacy and belonging:

> With Coach Fish, when we would do pyramids, we used to think of it as stacking ourselves. Building it layer by layer. Now we are learning that the pyramid isn't about girls climbing on top of each other and staying still. It's about breathing something to life. Together. Each of us a singular organ feeing the other organs, creating something larger. We are learning that our bodies are our own and they are the squad's and that is all. . . . I feel Mindy beneath me, the sinew of her we are moving as one person, we are bringing Beth up and she is part of us too, and her blood shooting through me, her heart pounding with mine. The same heart.
>
> (Abbott, 20–1)

Here, Abbott's pyramid metaphor underscores the unity of the squad and the solidarity between these girls. Addy's tendency to lapse into the plural 'we' further highlights her avoidance of the singularity of individualism and her privileging of a collective identity. As Addy gradually fortifies her bond with her teammates, the narrative emphasises how their communal bodywork enables them to coalesce into one highly functioning, synchronous unit. Thus, the novel appears to present Addy's cheerleading team as a microcosm of girlfriend culture – as an intimate sisterhood bound to each other through their mutual experience of body regulation.

However, the novel's structural arrangement simultaneously undercuts this notion of female solidarity and sisterhood. Ordered into a series of chapters which situate time exclusively in relation to the squad's 'big game', the novel figures its characters as competitive players and underscores the gamification of their everyday reality. An undercurrent of competitiveness pervades their interactions. They are deeply ambitious and often evince a proclivity for strategic behaviours which undermine the influence of their social 'superiors'.

For example, RiRi's competitive impulse manifests itself as a game of seduction:

> All week, Beth has kept Sarge Will in her sights, determined to take RiRi down. They both agreed: who-ever can get him to do a below-the-waist touch. Beth works the school corridors like a gun-slinger, spurred boots click-clacking. . . . As for RiRi, her cheer skirt hoists heavenward, waistband tugged high enough to show what her mama gave her. The two of them, they're dangerous.
>
> (Abbott, 68)

While neither girl seems particularly interested in pursuing a romantic relationship with Sarge Will, both Beth and RiRi are committed to their competition. Parodically figured as faux cowgirls who are engaging in a to-the-death shoot-out, they strategically exploit their sexuality as a means of establishing who is the most conventionally attractive – who is irresistible. Read in this way, their desire for Sarge Will appears to originate from their feelings of envy and competition towards each other.

Tacy Slaussen – another member of the cheerleading squad – also exhibits this proclivity for competition. When Beth is stripped of her captain title by Coach French and overlooked for the coveted position of the team 'flyer', Tacy immediately exploits the opportunity to elevate her social status. Though her subservience and fragility are repeatedly highlighted throughout the narrative – she is referred to as "that little pink eyed nothing," "the handmaiden," the "servant" and "Beth's baby bitch" – Tacy is wholly committed to usurping Beth's position and becoming the 'top girl' at *any* cost (Abbott, 46–8). In attempting to perform a quintessential flyer 'trick' – during which she is propelled into the air by her teammates – Tacy is recurrently injured and becomes overwhelmed by fear. As Addy notes, she starts sobbing half an hour into their team practice and never stops. Nevertheless, Tacy refuses to yield; she is willing to punish her body, over and over again, in order to self-optimise – in order to become the 'new' Beth.

Likewise, Addy's competitive desire to overthrow 'Captain Beth' is unwavering. Imagining herself as the prestigious team flyer, she envisions her "head clacking against the gym floor . . . spleen shattered . . . legs like barrettes bent back" (Abbott, 46). In spite of Tacy's recurrent and brutal injuries, Addy's hunger for her 'top girl' position has no bounds. As she watches Tacy from the sidelines, she quietly asserts, "me, me, me, it should be me" (Abbott, 46). While both Addy and Tacy are evidently committed to self-optimisation at any cost, Abbott's abject descriptions of their bodies in pain concurrently confronts the reader with a troubling reality: suffering is a constituent part of maintaining a 'successful' female subjectivity.

As the novel progressively exposes the girls' inherent competitiveness, Abbott reanimates and modifies a pivotal recurring metaphor – that of the pyramid which appears to symbolise female solidarity. While an injured Emily observes the team's routine, she is overcome with panic and fear:

> "Addy," she is saying, breathless. "I never saw it before . . . I never saw the stunts. From back there . . . I never saw us." "What do you mean?" I say, a faint ripple in my chest . . . She starts talking, breathless and high, about the way we were stacked, like toothpicks, like Pixy Stix, our bodies like feathers, light and tensile. Our minds focused, unnourished, possessed . . .
>
> *A pyramid isn't a stationary object. It's a living thing . . . The only moment it's still is when you make it still, all your bodies one body, until . . . we blow it apart.*
>
> "I couldn't look," she says. "I had to cover my eyes . . . "Now I see. . . . Standing back," she says, mouth hanging in horror, "it's like you're trying to kill each other and yourselves."
>
> (Abbott, 262)

Evidently, Emily's ability to temporarily operate outside the team unit allows her to recognise the insidious nature of this pyramid – to acknowledge its destructiveness. Troubling a hive mentality, she exposes how the pyramid has unstable foundations; built around adolescent girls' desire for self-optimisation and self-actualisation, it paradoxically enables their subjugation.

In contrast to the sense of unity which underpinned earlier descriptions of the pyramid, this iteration of Abbott's metaphor highlights the irreconcilability of competitive individualism with an authentically supportive sisterhood. Abbott's visceral descriptions of the weightlessness of these girls' bodies – they are as light as feathers and as insubstantial as toothpicks – are also particularly notable. Underscoring their innate fragility and vulnerability, these descriptions further trouble the idea that neoliberal and postfeminist ideologies are unconditionally empowering.

With its incessant references to vision and voyeurism, a sense of being watched – of being under an omniscient gaze – permeates Abbott's novel. This recurring motif draws attention to the ways in which female sociality can generate networks of peer-surveillance, policing feminine behaviour in line with neoliberal and postfeminist ideals. While the narrative establishes their aptitude for bodily governance from the outset, the squad's self-monitoring practices are markedly heightened by the arrival of Coach French. With every feature perfectly calibrated – from the precise arches of her eyebrows to the sharp edges of her sleek bob to her taut, drum-tight physique – Coach French personifies the neoliberal ideal of aesthetic entrepreneurship; she is flawlessly in control of her own body. Under the weight of her gaze, the girls are incited to intensify their self-regulations.

For example, when Coach singles out Emily before a training session – publicly berating her for her weight gain – Addy quickly adjusts her own behaviour; she begins to snack exclusively on egg whites, almonds and spinach in an effort to pare her waist "down to nothing" like her mentor (30). Enmeshed in a network of peer surveillance, Winch's gynaeopticon, Coach's regulatory gaze evidently has a catalytic effect on Addy's bodily governance. As Coach repeatedly scrutinises those around her, she is incited to scrutinise herself. She becomes hyper-vigilant of her entire body to the point that she can feel its progressive compression.

Addy's subjection to the girlfriend gaze also triggers her feelings of insufficiency and guilt. When she binges on cinnamon snack puffs prior to cheerleading practice, she fears exposure; she believes that the failure to successfully self-regulate is written on her body. With fat coded as a symbol of laziness and a lack of willpower – as a symptom of a mismanaged life – Addy strategically intensifies her self-surveillance and self-governance. Thus, by exploiting the motif of voyeurism, the narrative highlights how the girlfriend gaze can facilitate body regulations by inducing feelings of disgust and shame.

However, Addy is not merely a passive object of the girlfriend gaze. Rather, she actively *returns* Coach's gaze; she becomes increasingly obsessed with analysing and evaluating her every movement. For Addy, Coach French is irrefutably aspirational; she has the 'perfect' body, the 'perfect' family, the 'perfect' life. As an embodiment of idealised femininity, Addy is motivated to physically mimic Coach French; she alters her gait and repeatedly straightens her posture to match her aspirational instructor. With Coach framed as her role model, the novel underscores how Addy's girlfriend gaze contributes to the construction of her normative feminine identity. It enables her to mimetically enhance her own performance of the feminine ideal.

While the girlfriend gaze amplifies Addy's *bodily* governance, it simultaneously influences her desires. Utterly indifferent to the opposite sex, Addy admits that she has never given Jordy Brennan – or any of the boys in her school – more than a fleeting thought. Yet, when Coach remarks on Jordy's attractiveness, she begins to consider him as a prospective partner and vividly imagines their sexual interactions. Explicitly aroused by these fantasies in a way that feels wholly unfamiliar to her, Addy experiences sexual pleasure for the very first time. By adopting Coach's desirous gaze, she is initiated into the realm of womanhood as an empowered sexual agent.

But the novel underscores how this 'empowering' girlfriend gaze can simultaneously function as a tool of conservative governance. It can facilitate the policing of female sexuality in line with normative femininity. In a redeployment of an overtly misogynist lexicon, the squad frequently mock each other's sexual activities. They refer to each other as 'whores', 'tarts' and 'cocksuckers' from the outset. Under the guise of humorous banter, they publicly shame each other for their sexual transgressions. Though the girls understand this 'banter' as a sort of intimate discourse between friends, the narrative concurrently highlights how it functions as a form of verbal policing. With slut-shaming sublimated into an acceptable mode of social interaction, the girls' 'banter' essentially establishes a 'sexual hierarchy' whilst regulating how they express and explore their own sexuality.

Beth's and Addy's evasion of their romantic feelings for each other certainly affirms this idea that the girlfriend gaze polices female sexuality. Enmeshed in the gynaeopticon, these girls are complicit in monitoring their teammates' bodies and behaviour while being aware that they are similarly under this omniscient, watchful eye. Yet, throughout the course of the novel, there is an inferred sexual tension between them which culminates in a moment of passion; privately, they share a kiss. While in this moment, the girls imply that they have feelings for one another; they ultimately prioritise their sense of belonging to their group. In order to appear 'normative', they opt to apathetically engage in sexual activities with boys. With their same-sex desire foreclosed, the narrative emphasises the pernicious effects of the internalisation of a girlfriend gaze. Beth and Addy must repudiate their 'abnormal' desires and align themselves with heterosexual femininity so that they can successfully integrate into the squad.

Abbott's 'girl' characters are chronically competitive and perpetually passive-aggressive, and her novel risks re-affirming the cultural conception of adolescent femininity as inherently monstrous. Yet by highlighting how their 'pathological' behaviour has been motivated by their desire to satisfy neoliberal ideals of femininity – to self-optimise and become the 'top-girl' – the novel simultaneously emphasises the pathologising effect of the dominant ideology on female subjectivity. As I have demonstrated, the novel underscores how these ideologies are incongruous with female solidarity, actively impeding the intimate bonds between women. But the novel also gestures towards an even more insidious consequence: that these ideologies have corrupted the *affect* of friendship.

This corruption is clearly perceptible during a key scene in which Addy voyeuristically watches Emily 'purge' after 'binging':

> All those posters and PSAs and health-class presentations on body image and the way you can burst blood vessels in the your face and rupture your esophagus if you can't stop ramming those Hostess snowballs down your throat every night, knowing they'll have to come back up again, you sad weak girl. . . . And there's Emily, keening over the toilet bowel after practice, begging me to kick her in the gut so she can expel the rest, all that cookie dough and Cool Ranch, the smell making me roil. Emily, a girl made entirely of donut sticks, cheese powder and Haribo. I kick, I do. She would do the same for me.
> (Abbott, 13–14)

Addy is clearly disgusted by Emily's 'weakness', her inability to control her eating habits and strive for self-optimisation. In a disturbing parody of the proverbial 'you are what you eat', she reduces her body to the sum of its intake and explicitly equates her weight gain with a decrease in her market value. Still, Addy demonstrates an awareness that women's eating habits are obsessively scrutinised in contemporary culture and her narrative is brimming with casual references to diet foods, 'thinspiration' websites and disordered eating habits. The sarcastic tone she adopts when discussing these disordered eating habits – in conjunction with the disturbing and visceral language she uses to describe this punishing behaviour – indicates her feelings of anger and discontent about them.

Yet Addy *misdirects* her rage away from the patriarchal structures which necessitate this punishing behaviour, opting to physically assault Emily by kicking her in the stomach. From this perspective, the narrative suggests that networks of peer-surveillance play a pivotal role in the mediation and misdirection of female rage. While diet culture – privileging and demanding thinness – functions as a tool of patriarchal governance that creates impossible standards of feminine beauty, Addy and Emily are unable to challenge these hegemonic ideals. Instead, as facilitated by the gynaeopticon, the girls are forced to resolve their rage about societal injustices on the bodies of other women through violence.

More troublingly, the narrative suggests that Addy *feels* righteous about this act of physical violence against her friend. She does not identify this act as harmful or cruel. Rather, by bolstering Emily's self-governance, Addy understands it as a display of solidarity and encouragement which strengthens the bond between them. Blurring the lines between cruelty and intimacy, her act of violence is recoded as a disturbing display of affection. Thus, the novel demonstrates how the affective quality of friendship has been crucially altered by the dominant ideology. 'Friendliness', from Addy's perspective, is practically indistinguishable from peer regulation.

While Abbot's characters exemplify the contemporary figure of the 'mean girl', they also evoke a much older archetype of monstrous femininity: the witch. Barbara Creed argues that the witch figure is marked by her wiliness and cunning and is "an implacable enemy of the symbolic order" (1993, 56). She often employs her evil powers – which are seen as an intrinsic part of her 'feminine nature' – to control gullible men. Prototypically, the witch is depicted as a decrepit, old woman – a 'hag'. But as Sady Doyle observes, contemporary reiterations of this monstrous archetype articulate a pervasive dread about the prominence and perceived power of adolescence girls in Western culture (2019, 218). Popularised in films such as Andrew Fleming's *The Craft* (1996), these adolescent witches are motivated by a thinly veiled rage. Tired of being silenced and subordinated, they exploit their supernatural gifts in order to reclaim their lost power and disrupt the patriarchy.

An uneasy anxiety about adolescent female power notably permeates Abbott's novel. From the outset, we are warned by Addy that there is "something dangerous about the boredom of teenage girls" (Abbott, 3). The novel employs a 'witchy' lexicon to heighten this threat posed by adolescent womanhood: Beth's innate ability to influence others is likened to a witchy hex; Addy is accused of being "some kind of Wicca" and the squads' synchronised menstrual cycles are understood as a manifestation of the "witchiness of girls" (Abbott, 95–105). Abbott's use of the thriller format – which prototypically engenders feelings of discomfort in reader – further bolsters the disquietude about adolescent femininity pervasive in her narrative. The driving force of the plot is the question of who murdered Sarge Will, and the reader is encouraged to suspect that either Beth or Addy is responsible for this crime.

By implicating these girls in a violent murder and insinuating their guilt throughout, the narrative risks affirming the monstrosity of adolescent femininity and perpetuating those myths. It also makes the reader complicit in the condemnation of Beth and Addy. In attempting to solve the mystery at the centre of the novel, the reader is forced to doubt the innocence of these girls, continually questioning the reliability of their narrative. But one particularly troubling episode undermines this straightforward interpretation of Abbott's novel, suggesting that she has cleverly *exploited* the thriller format to stress to the reader the political consequences of these myths.

When the squad attends an alcohol-fuelled party with men from the Marine Corps, Addy finds Beth asleep in her car with her underwear and clothing removed. As Beth struggles to articulate a coherent sentence, Addy notices that her thighs are covered in bruises.

Consequentially, she begins to interrogate Beth, who accuses Sargent Prine – disturbingly nicknamed 'Mauler' – of sexually assaulting her. Later, once Beth has sobered up, Addy continues her cross-examination:

> "Beth," I whisper, tucking the throw blanket tighter around her, "is it true? Is it true Prine did things to you? Made you do things?" Her eyes don't open, but I know she knows I'm there. I feel like I've tunnelled my way into her dream, and that she'll answer me there. "I made him make me," she murmurs. "And he did. Can you believe it?" Made him make me. Oh Beth, what does that even mean? I picture her taunting him. Doing her witchy Beth things.
>
> (Abbott, 132)

Here, like the 'Emily' incident, the lines between cruelty and intimacy are blurred. While Addy clearly demonstrates her affection for her friend – tenderly wrapping her in a blanket – her repeated questioning of Beth feels, at the very least, accusatory. She firmly places the blame for the elided attack on the victim. But, underscoring once more the corruption of the affect of friendship, Addy perceives her actions as inherently good, a display of solidarity which will assist Beth in 'successfully' self-regulating and thus preventing further attacks.

Encouraged by Addy to take personal responsibility for her choices, Beth reiterates her complicity in her own assault. Internalising a misandrist discourse which perpetuates the idea that women and girls have a near supernatural influence over the opposite sex, Beth excuses Prine's inability to control his sexual urges. She acquiesces to the idea that she placed him under a 'witchy spell', or hex, and that she possesses mystical 'seductive' powers making her 'responsible' for the assault. While these myths about the monstrosity of adolescent femininity are culturally produced fictions, Beth evidently accepts them as 'truth'. Yet the novel highlights how the myths have real-world consequences for girls. They have disempowered Beth by ensuring that she holds herself accountable for the actions of her abuser.

The revealing gap between Beth's perspective and the narrative perspective underscores how these myths are facilitating female disempowerment. Though Beth is overcome by feelings of personal responsibility after the assault, Abbott's disturbing descriptions of her body in pain – acutely emphasised by the copious bruises on her thighs – are impossible for the reader to ignore. These descriptions actively undermine Beth's bravado whilst solidifying her status as a victim. In short, they confront the reader with the reality of the violence she has endured. That Matt French – Coach's husband – is ultimately exposed as the murderer of Sarge Will further supports this interpretation of *Dare Me*. Culminating in their absolution, the novel reassures the reader that these adolescent girls are not omnipotent monsters.

"I Wish I'd Be Murdered"

The primary antagonist of Flynn's *Sharp Objects* – Amma Crellin – also resembles the quintessential mean girls of chick lit jr. As the prettiest and most popular girl in her high school, she is figured as the 'queen bee' to a group of 'adoring' followers. With a distinctly Machiavellian principle defining all her social interactions, Amma admits that she would rather be feared than be loved by her peers. Like Abbott's Beth, her privileged position in the social hierarchy of her 'clique' is maintained by consistent manipulation and abuse to control and demean those around her.

To assert her power and authority, Amma regularly 'pimps' out her friends to random teenage boys and then mocks and taunts them afterwards for their sexual activities. She even nonchalantly changes their names at will. In order to demonstrate her dominance and ensure her unrivalled status as queen bee, she informs Kelsey – a more submissive member of her friend group – that she must exclusively refer to herself as 'Jodes'. Amma also repeatedly recruits reluctant volunteers from *within* her girl gang to assist her in her quotidian bullying of more vulnerable targets – specifically an overweight little girl.

As with *Dare Me*, this depiction of Amma as a prototypical mean girl risks reaffirming troubling myths about the monstrous omnipotence of adolescent females. However, I propose a more complex reading of her novel. At the level of prose style, rather than character or story, Amma's descriptions of her purported empowerment are populated with striking contradictions and disjunctions, undermining any straightforward interpretation of her potential for power as female subject under neoliberal postfeminism.

Motivated by a desire for power, Amma appears to believe that adhering to the postfeminist masquerade is her surest pathway to empowerment. From the outset, she is figured as an expert performer of the feminine masquerade; she carefully reproduces certain culturally prescribed modes of femininity – including youthfulness, passivity and vacuousness – whilst consistently adjusting her performative behaviours in order to heighten her appeal to specific 'audiences'. For example, when in the presence of her mother Adora and stepfather Alan, Amma performs a kind of childish docility. In order to eclipse Camille and secure her parent's absolute and unwavering attention, she throws puerile tantrums and allows herself to be infantilised. This performative behaviour is consciously and deliberately chosen:

> "Camille, I must apologise to you for last night," Alan started. "Amma is going through one of those stages." "She's very clingy," my mother said. "Mostly in a sweet way, but sometimes she gets a bit out of hand." . . . "I'm sorry you had to see me that way, Camille." Amma said. "Especially since we don't really know each other. I'm just going through a stage." She flashed an overdone smile.
>
> (Flynn, 83–4)

Employing a lexicon stolen directly from her parents, Amma exposes a prior juvenile outburst as nothing more than an attention-seeking performance used to provoke the affections of her parents.

Amma also expressly figures *herself* as Adora's little doll:

> The girl was in a childish checked sundress, matching straw hat by her side. She looked entirely her age – thirteen – for the first time since I'd seen her. Actually, no, she looked younger now. Those clothes were more appropriate for a ten-year-old. She scowled when she saw me assessing her. "I wear this for Adora. When I'm home. I'm her little doll." "And when you're not?" "I'm other things."
>
> (Flynn, 54)

By allowing her mother to style her in immature clothing better suited to a prepubescent girl – to routinely play 'dress-up' with her – she knowingly becomes a passive object of beauty and play. Moreover, in gesturing towards the transience of her doll-like role, Camille underscores the ease with which Amma can adopt a multitude of 'masks' to support her agenda.

In stark contrast, Amma's performances outside of her 'dollhouse' are more lascivious. As underscored by her choice of provocative and revealing clothing – she opts to trade her mother's childish sundress for a mini-skirt, platform sandals and a tube top – Amma exhibits a discomforting amalgamation of overt sexuality with an infantile naivety reminiscent of a long-standing literary motif: the Lolita. As the titular adolescent heroine of Vladimir Nabokov's (1955) novel, Lolita's childishness and youthful innocence were figured as the primary sources of her sexual appeal. It was her 'babyishness' which appeared to provoke Humbert Humbert's uncontrollable erotic desires.

While, as Samantha Lindop highlights, Nabokov's use of first-person narration ultimately exposed his protagonist as a cunning and despicable paedophile who knowingly targeted 'nymphets' between the ages of 9 and 14; later adaptations of his controversial novel blurred the lines between predator and prey (95). Specifically, director Stanley Kubrick's (1962) adaptation framed Lolita as a sexual provocateur – as an obnoxious, manipulative, lollipop-sucking seductress who was wholly cognisant of her effect on men.

In line with Kubrick's reimagining of the Lolita character, Amma eroticises her childish innocence to disarm the men in her hometown. Recounted from Camille's perspective, her interactions with Detective Richard are particularly revealing:

> Amma leaned into the driver's window, cleavage teasing the boy . . . "Hey, Dick," Amma called. She was sucking on a red oversized Blow Pop. "Dick, when are you going to take us for a ride?" Amma asked, plopping down in the dirt in front of us, her legs pulled up to reveal a glimpse of her panties.
>
> (Flynn, 144–5)

Drawing on an iconic image from Kubrick's promotional poster – in which actress Sue Lyons sucked seductively on an oversized red lollipop – Flynn constructs an overt parallel between her antagonist and the Lolita character. As with Kubrick's Lolita and Humbert Humbert, Detective Richard is destabilised by Amma because he is unable to determine whether she is cognisant of her provocations. While her pointed use of double entendres – Detective Richard becomes 'Dick', for example – certainly suggests flirtatiousness, the scope of her naivety is ultimately left open to interpretation.

Detective Richard is so disarmed by this confusing interaction that he quickly abandons his interrogation of Amma. From this perspective, the coalescence of Amma's infantile naivety with her provocative sexuality appears to bolster her power as a female subject. It allows her to deflect any suspicion of her involvement in the murders of Ann and Natalie. Yet Flynn's deployment of this intertextual reference gestures towards an alternative reading of Amma's purported omnipotence. Like Kubrick's Lolita, Amma is able to feel powerful only by making herself an object of the male gaze. With her 'dominance' over men contingent on this self-objectification, the reader is forced to consider to what degree Amma's omnipotence is actually illusory.

While Amma demonstrates a marked capacity for self-possession in her ability to fluidly morph between these archetypes of femininity – the passive doll and the flirtatious ingenue – her performances neatly encapsulate the contradictory demands placed on women and girls by neoliberal postfeminism. On the one hand, Amma partakes in a kind of self-sexualisation which underscores how 'heterosexiness' still holds immense social currency for the contemporary female subject. Simultaneously, Amma is forced to negotiate the complex pushes and pulls of these ideological conditions by ensuring that while she appears 'sexy' she does not appear 'slutty'. As exhibited earlier, her sexuality must be carefully contained so as not to be interpreted as aggression. By drawing attention to how Amma must accommodate these unwritten rules as part of her postfeminist masquerade, the narrative gestures towards the limitations of her purported empowerment. If Amma is still obliged to satisfy restrictive ideals of femininity, how empowered can she truly be?

These limitations are more clearly perceptible when Amma discusses her sexuality with Camille:

> "Sometimes if you let people do things to you, you're really doing it to them." Amma said, pulling another Blow Pop from her pocket. Cherry. "Know what I mean? If someone wants to do fucked-up things to you, and you let them, you're making them more fucked up. Then you have the control. As long as you don't go crazy."
>
> (Flynn, 233–4)

The unusual way that Amma describes her past sexual encounters with boys certainly blurs the boundaries between activity and passivity – between domination and submission. Enmeshed within a distinctly neoliberal and postfeminist rhetoric of choice as the primary marker of empowerment, Amma struggles to find a way to express how she has been affected by patriarchal structures which necessitate female subordination whilst concurrently retaining her status as an empowered agent. She oscillates between a version of herself where she is in control of her sexuality and a version of herself where she is the passive recipient of disturbing or violent sexual advances. Amma also reiterates that any attempt to resolve these innate contradictions has the potential to be pathologising – to drive someone crazy.

Amma struggles to reconcile her feelings of subservience with the image of herself as an inherently powerful and privileged subject perpetuated by neoliberal and postfeminist discourses. Nevertheless, the disjunction between Amma's confident assertions of 'girl power' and her descriptions of her *embodied* experience of 'girl power' calls into question the authenticity of her empowerment. It forces the reader to consider if Amma has been constrained by these purportedly enabling ideologies – by the pervasive dissemination of these discourses of female freedom.

The *kind* of femininity to which Amma aspires – which she explicitly recognises as aspirational – further undermines any straightforward interpretation of her monstrous omnipotence. Throughout the course of the narrative, Amma romanticises death and figures the Dead Girl as the ultimate ideal of femininity. With idols such as Princess Diana and Persephone – the queen of the dead – she believes that "when you die, you become perfect" (85). Amma's exaltation of this Dead Girl figure illuminates an alarming contradiction: despite the proliferating discourses about female empowerment, passivity continues to be the most highly valued 'feminine' quality in contemporary culture.

Amma may be an adept performer of stereotypes of femininity. But she is also aware that her adherence to the postfeminist masquerade relegates her to the realm of passivity and denies her any adequate outlet for her rage:

> "I've got to get out of here," Amma said with the exhausted affectation of a pampered housewife. "I'm bored all the time. That's why I act out. I know I can be a little . . . off . . . Just, you know, lashing out. You know, I know you know. You know sometimes you need to hurt." She said it as if she were selling a new hair product. "Camille?" Her voice quiet and girlish and unsure. "You know how people sometimes say they have to hurt because if they don't, they're so numb they won't feel anything? What if it's the opposite? What if you hurt because it feels so good? Like you have a tingling, like someone left a switch on in your body. And nothing can turn the switch off except hurting? What does that mean?"
>
> (Flynn, 237–41)

Here, Amma explicitly links the requirement of feminine coherence and mastery, prerequisites of the postfeminist masquerade, to her feelings of constraint and confinement. In contrast to neoliberal and postfeminist rhetoric of girl power, she underscores how this requirement is actually subordinating; it has necessitated a suffocating kind of passivity from which she feels there is little hope of escape. Thus, having sacrificed her critical voice as a prerequisite of her entry into the dominant social order – as part of this postfeminist masquerade – Amma begins to misdirect her rage towards other women.

But unlike the prototypical mean girl, Amma's aggression towards others is not exclusively relational. Rather, she is exposed as a serial killer who targets very particular victims: adolescent girls who flagrantly transgress social boundaries and wilfully reject prescribed gender norms. Ann Nash – Amma's first victim – is described as a rambunctious nine-year-old girl who has a distinctly wild or feral quality to her appearance. With short, self-cut hair and perpetually mud-stained clothing, she is portrayed as an innate 'tomboy'. Similarly, Natalie Keene – Amma's second victim – is marked by her 'otherness'. She is figured as a "goofy kid . . . just kind of a weirdo" – an outsider whom Camille imagines would have been labelled as difficult (Flynn, 160).

These girls had also displayed a proclivity for angry outbursts prior to their murders. With "serious, scary-time tempers," the girls were notorious for their volatility (Flynn, 202). In an interview with Meredith, a local girl from the town, Camille learns that they had even attended etiquette lessons with Adora to teach them how to mediate their rage. Refusing to take up the postfeminist masquerade – to adopt a mollified performance of the ideal feminine – both Ann and Natalie savagely responded to Adora's attempts to realign their behaviour and train the 'wildness' out of them. Provoked towards violence, they had bitten her so hard that she was scarred with their teeth marks and required stitches. By contextualising their physical aggression as a response these etiquette lessons, the narrative crystallises the girls' rejection of contemporary gender norms. Instead, their biting can perhaps be understood as an attempt to articulate their rage at the regulatory practices of femininity. That Amma specifically targets *these* adolescent girls – girls who refuse to conform to contemporary gender norms – is particularly notable. It frames her as an agent of patriarchy, enforcing the patriarchal ideologies which she has clearly internalised.

While this depiction of Amma might be interpreted as an affirmation of the monstrosity of adolescent femininity, there is an evident parodical tone to Flynn's prose. Her depiction of Amma as a mean-girl-turned-psychopathic-murderer is so overwrought and ridiculous that it often verges on burlesque. With Amma's monstrosity exaggerated to ludicrous effect, Flynn appears to be parodying the archetype of the mean girl and thus drawing attention to its artifice. Disrupting the 'hyperreality' of this cultural archetype – the blurring of the boundaries between embodied femininity and discursive constructions of adolescent femininity – Flynn's use of parody makes comically visible the absurdity of contemporary discourses about young women's omnipotence. Rather than reproduce these problematic discourses, she redeploys and exaggerates this archetype in order to challenge and debunk myths about monstrous femininity.

Flynn's postmodern aesthetics shape *Sharp Objects* as a kind of literary 'collage'. The novel combines disparate plot types – the 'high school' comedy of manners with the prototypical murder mystery – and incongruous genres – chick lit jr. with detective fiction and the gothic. Signalling a textual self-consciousness, Flynn's copious references to novels from the literary canon suggests a mixing of 'high' art with popular fiction. While these 'Frankenstein' aesthetics risk epistemic chaos, they simultaneously draw attention to the process of narrative 'creation'. In doing so, they remind the reader that the social world of Flynn's novel is not reflective of reality but is an artificial construction. By extension, these aesthetics suggest that we should be prepared to read Amma not as realistic character but as a discursively produced archetype. In other words, at the level of prose, Flynn's novel challenges the hyperreality of these archetypes of monstrous femininity by emphasising their artificiality.

Flynn cleverly utilises another long-standing literary motif to further emphasise the farcicality of these popular discourses about adolescent women: the dollhouse. Derived from Henrik Ibsen's *A Doll's House* (1879), the dollhouse has become a recurring cultural symbol for both repressive domesticity and the regulatory constraints of idealised femininity more generally. Drawing on this recognisable metaphor, Flynn's novel repeatedly suggests that Amma has been confined within her own enervating dollhouse. Figured as Adora's little doll, she has been rendered docile and forced to perform a traditionally feminine role. Yet, throughout the course of the narrative, Amma habitually plays with a *literal* doll's house which – from its upholstery to its basic design – is an *exact* replica of the home she shares with Adora. By working on this doll's house, Amma is able to create and experience a fantasy of perfection – to exercise control and assert her power in a way that she is unable to accomplish in reality. Thus, while the dollhouse can symbolise Amma's desire for power, it concurrently gestures towards the illusory nature of the power she has achieved as part of her recurring performances.

The disturbing 'items' Amma utilises as accessories to adorn her doll's house are particularly illuminating. She creates its 'authentic' marble floor using teeth she extracted from both Ann's and Natalie's corpse and constructs a braided, chocolate-coloured rug out of the hair of her third and final victim – Lily Burke. On the one hand, Amma's choice of 'decorations' makes her complicit in the objectification of women and girls; she ultimately reduces the value of her victims to the sum of their body parts. Moreover, by using these body parts to create and sustain her fantasy of perfection – as exemplified by her doll's house – the narrative implies that Amma's pursuit of power is contingent upon the downfall of other women and girls.

On the other hand, the implausibility of this episode is impossible to ignore. In stark contrast to the naturalism of Ibsen's *A Doll's House* – which realistically dealt with similarly contentious social issues – Flynn's deployment of the dollhouse metaphor is utterly fantastical; it seems more appropriate to a frightening fairy-tale. While the idea that Amma would construct a dollhouse from the body parts of other girls is certainly unsettling, it is so comically overwrought that it verges on absurd. In contrast to the prototypical mean girl whose behaviour is at least grounded in identifiable social relations and institutions (friendship, high school), Amma's monstrous antagonism towards other women – her outer directed rage – is grotesquely surreal and exaggerated to the point of parody. Consequentially, Flynn's narrative highlights the ridiculousness of these monstrous myths about adolescent girls and their purportedly innate competitiveness. By confronting its readers with the artificiality of these myths, the novel forces us to consider a crucial question: are these culturally produced fantasies encouraging the misdirection of female rage against other women and thus allowing existing gender hierarchies to remain intact?

Flynn also gestures towards the political consequences of the prevalence of these myths of the monstrous feminine. Like Amy Elliot Dunne – the 'monstrous' protagonist of Flynn's later novel *Gone Girl* (2012) – Amma is exposed as a murderer whose skill at social performance has allowed her to commit her crimes without raising suspicion. But her capacity to get away with murder is contingent on a wider culture of misogynistic violence. Throughout the course of the narrative, a series of theories is posited about a potential serial killer who is terrorising the town of Wind Gap. For example, Bill Vickery, the town's sheriff, suggests that "some looney crazy man" must have committed the murders – some guy who "forgot to take his pills" (14). Likewise, Detective Richard asserts that the assailant must be some "sick baby killer bastard" because he "can't picture a woman" as the perpetrator of these violent crimes (24). While these assumptions certainly suggest the quotidian nature of misogynistic violence, they concurrently gesture towards an equally disturbing idea: that the proliferation of these myths of the monstrous feminine are actively diverting attention away from a profoundly corrupt status quo in which gender-based violence has become an assumed aspect of women's everyday reality.

Flynn deploys another key archetype of the monstrous feminine – the phallic mother – to a similarly polemical effect. According to Creed, representations of the phallic mother rarely deviate from the traditional formula: her 'perversity' is almost always grounded in possessive or dominating behaviour towards her offspring, usually her male child (139). As an extension of the myth of woman as castrator, the phallic mother's inordinate maternal devotion is often figured as her most frightening attribute; it threatens to symbolically engulf her child whilst blurring the boundaries of their autonomous subjective identity.

Introducing her protagonist's narrative arc within the context of a monstrous mother narrative, Flynn opens her novel with Camille's investigation of an abusive women who had locked her four children in a faeces-covered room with little food while she "smoked pipe" (1). Thereafter, the reader is continually confronted with 'bad mother' figures – from Joya, Camille's cold and unaffectionate grandmother, to the nameless, absent mother of a local child who allows her prepubescent son to play with guns. But Adora is the most overt reanimation of the archetypal castrating mother. Consumed by her desire for omnipotence, she consistently exerts her power over her children in order to bring them under her control.

While this depiction of Adora animates long-standing myths about monstrous maternity, Flynn implements a subtle yet crucial subversion: Adora's unsettling urge to tyrannise her daughters notably manifests as Munchausen Syndrome by Proxy (MSbP). Coined by John Money and June Werlwas in the *Journal of the American Academy of Psychiatry and the Law* in 1976, MSbP is a syndrome in which carer figures – usually mothers – create symptoms of illness in children or dependants in a quest for attention, emotional satisfaction or absolute control. Encompassing an oddly warped dialectic of harm and care, it allows the perpetrator to *publicly* perform their maternal devotion whilst *privately* damaging and abusing their progeny. From this perspective, MSbP might be best interpreted as a kind of masquerade – as a performance through which a woman can satisfy patriarchal ideals of maternity like self-sacrifice and compassion.

Committed to fulfilling these patriarchal ideals, the narrative emphasises how Adora's yearning to be acknowledged as the perfect mother is her primary motivation for poisoning her daughters. In her recollections of the past, Camille certainly highlights Adora's dedication to her 'good mother' performance. She details how Adora would pantomime as a playful, doting mother in public but would quickly discard that mask once in her private domain. Through this recollection, the narrative implies that Adora is aware of the potency of the maternal ideal – that she recognises its value in a patriarchal culture. Yet, like Amy Elliot Dunne, it is the desire to satisfy these gendered ideals which makes Adora a monster. As such, Flynn disrupts any straightforward interpretation of Adora as a reductive reanimation of the quintessential phallic mother. Rather, she exploits MSbP to highlight the insidious effects of patriarchal ideals of maternity – to underscore how these ideals, which dictate women's behaviour in line with a culturally approved set of regulations, have created an unliveable pressure that has the potential to be pathologising.

Flynn's overwrought depiction of Adora's abhorrent behaviour also supports her disassemblage of the myths of the monstrous feminine. Adora's 'monstrosity' is at times so explicit that it reads as a parody. Invoking recognisable myths of the monstrous feminine, Adora is described by Detective Richard as a "fairy tale wicked witch of a woman" (298). Similarly, the nurse who treated Marian as a child likens Adora to a horrifying figure from the Brother's Grimm. Like Amma, Adora's 'wickedness' is persistently overemphasised. For example, in what appears to be a play on a breast-feeding scenario – where the child eats and sucks from its mother's breast – Camille highlights the magnitude of Adora's devouring presence:

> I remember by mother, alone in the living room, staring at the child almost lasciviously. She pressed her lips hard against the baby's apple slice of a cheek. The she opened her mouth just slightly, took a tiny bit of flesh between her teeth, and gave it a little bite.
> (Flynn, 124)

Here, coveting the child as a form of sustenance, Adora's capacity for a monstrous kind of consumption – one which threatens to annihilate the subject – is unmistakably apparent. In fact, it is so over the top that it borders on ridiculous. Thus, by drawing attention to the absurdity of Adora's behaviour, Flynn's exaggerated descriptions underscore the artificiality of the archetype of the monstrous mother.

Nevertheless, by concurrently rationalising Adora's monstrosity in genealogical terms, Flynn's novel risks undermining its own clever subversions. Specifically, by figuring Adora's malignant behaviour as a direct consequence of her fraught relationship with her abusive mother, the novel obscures the pathologising effect of patriarchal constructions of maternity. Importantly, this appears to be a recurring pattern in Flynn's work. As with *Gone Girl*, *Sharp Objects* has an unmistakably feminist viewpoint. At the same time, it articulates a rather conventional 'generational' narrative: Adora Crellin and Amma Crellin are the monstrous products of monstrous parents. And so Flynn's novel locates the blame for monstrous female behaviour firmly within the individual, deflecting readers' attention away from the punishing nature of neoliberal postfeminism.

Both Abbott and Flynn are indubitably critical of contemporary gendered ideals. As we have seen, their novels repeatedly draw attention to the pernicious effects of those ideals on women. Simultaneously, however, the novels reify hegemonic gender ideologies by reproducing individuating narratives which obfuscate the socio-political factors deleteriously impacting their female protagonists. As such, there is a constant tension in these novels between subversion and reiteration. This tension, I propose, indicates something crucial: a cultural break with, but not total detachment from, neoliberal postfeminism and its rhetoric.

Reference List

Abbott, Megan. *Dare Me*. Picador, 2012.
Bordo, Susan. *Unbearable Weight: Feminism, Western Culture, and the Body*. University of California Press, 1993.
Bride Wars. Directed by Gary Winick, Twentieth-Century Fox, 2009.
Caruth, Cathy. *Unclaimed Experience: Trauma, Narrative and History*. Johns Hopkins University Press, 1996.
Creed, Barbara. *The Monstrous Feminine: Film, Feminism, Psychoanalysis*. Routledge, 1993.
Day, Sara K. "Mean Girls End Up Dead: The Dismal Fate of Teen Queen Bees in Popular Culture." *Bad Girls and Transgressive Women in Popular Television, Fiction and Film*, edited by Julie Chappell and Mallory Young, Palgrave Macmillan, 2017, pp. 135–157.

DiVello, Adam. *The Hills* (Done and Done Productions). MTV, 2006–2010.
Doyle, Sady. *Dead Blondes and Bad Mothers: Monstrosity, Patriarchy and the Fear of Female Power*. Melville House Printing, 2019.
Flynn, Gillian. *Gone Girl*. Crown Publishing Group, 2012.
Flynn, Gillian. *Sharp Objects*. Orion, 2006.
Gill, Rosalind, et al. *Aesthetic Labour: Rethinking Beauty Politics in Neoliberalism*. Palgrave Macmillan, 2017.
Harris, Anita. *Future Girl: Young Women in the Twenty-First Century*. Routledge, 2004.
Harrison, Lisi. *The Clique*. Little, Brown Books for Young Readers, 2004.
Ibsen, Henrik. *A Doll's House*. 1879.
Johnson, Joanna Webb. "Chick Lit Jr: More Than Glitz and Glamour for Teens and Tweens." *Chick Lit: The New Woman's Fiction*, edited by Suzanne Ferriss and Mallory Young, Routledge, 2005, pp. 141–158.
Lindop, Samantha. *Postfeminism and the Fatale Figure in Neo-Noir Cinema*. Palgrave Macmillan, 2015.
Lolita. Directed by Stanley Kubrick, Metro-Goldwyn-Mayer, 1962.
McRobbie, Angela. "Notes on the Perfect: Competitive Femininity in Neoliberal Times." *Australian Feminist Studies*, vol. 30, no. 83, 2015, pp. 3–20. doi: 10.1080/08164649.2015.1011485.
McRobbie, Angela. *The Aftermath of Feminism: Gender, Culture and Social Change*. Sage Publications, 2008.
Mean Girls. Directed by Mark Waters, Paramount Pictures, 2004.
Money, John and June Werlwas. "Folie à Deux in Parents of Psychosocial Dwarfs: Two Cases." *Journal of the American Academy of Psychiatry and the Law*, vol. 4, no. 4, 1976, pp. 351–362.
Nabokov, Vladimir. *Lolita*. Olympia Press, 1955.
Orgad, Shani and Rosalind Gill. "Safety Valves for Mediated Female Rage in the #MeToo Era." *Feminist Media Studies*, vol. 19, no. 4, 2019, pp. 596–603. doi: 10.1080/14680777.2019.1609198.
Redhead, Leigh. "Teenage Kicks: Performance and Postfeminism in Domestic Noir." *Domestic Noir: The New Face of 21st Century Crime Writing*, edited by Laura Joyce and Henry Sutton, Palgrave Macmillan, 2018, pp. 115–135.
Star, Darren. *Sex and the City* (Darren Star Productions). HBO, 1998–2004.
The Craft. Directed by Andrew Fleming, Columbia Pictures, 1996.
von Ziegesar, Cecily. *Gossip Girl*. Bloomsbury Publishing, 2002.
Whitney, Sarah E. *Splattered Ink: Postfeminist Gothic Fiction and Gendered Violence*. University of Illinois Press, 2016.
Winch, Alison. *Girlfriends and Postfeminist Sisterhood*. Palgrave Macmillan, 2013.

Conclusion

All the Rage

In 2014, popular American singer Beyoncé performed a medley of her greatest hits at the MTV Video Music Awards (VMA). As part of this performance, she stood still before a gigantic screen and listened to a recorded voice asserting:

> We teach girls to shrink themselves, to make themselves smaller. We say to girls "You can have ambition, but not too much. You should aim to be successful, but not too successful. Otherwise, you will threaten the man."

The recording was sampled from a lecture delivered in London in 2012 by the novelist Chimamanda Ngozi Adichie and broadcast as a TEDx talk. Beyoncé was gradually joined on stage by a large group of female dancers. As Adichie's speech concluded with a definition of the word 'feminist', the group on stage moved closer together until they stood shoulder to shoulder in unison. Their physical closeness felt intimate, signalling a kind of togetherness or camaraderie. Bolstering those feelings of solidarity, the women were shadowed in darkness and practically indistinguishable. Their careful arrangement made manifest Beyoncé's amplification of Adiche's key message: 'we should all be feminists'. Lest that message be misconstrued, her performance concluded with an indubitably political statement: the word 'feminist' in bright, white lights projected on the huge screen and visually dominating the stage.

Throughout this performance, Beyoncé was depicted as aspirational for the audience. The camera persistently lingered on her flawless makeup, glamorous outfit and toned physique, while her command of the stage drew attention to her confidence and self-assurance. As such, the feminist rhetoric she unabashedly embraced was concurrently coded as aspirational, rebranding feminism as 'cool' or even 'sexy'. This differed markedly from how feminism was represented in popular culture during the early millennial period. Synchronous with the entrenchment of postfeminism, those popular representations figured feminism as angry, cynical and man-hating. Thus, to publicly identify as a feminist was to mark oneself as vituperative or hypersensitive, desperately clinging to 'antiquated' notions about women's subjugation.

Characterised by its 'double entanglement' of feminist with anti-feminist rhetoric, postfeminist discourse took feminism into account, stressing that gender equality had been achieved, only to repudiate it as a redundant relic of the past – an obstacle to women's pursuit of pleasure. However, typified by Beyoncé's VMA performance, feminism began to undergo a significant shift in popular representation during the mid-2000s. An omnipresent force, it became spectacularly visible throughout popular culture. Like Beyoncé, several powerful, high-profile women publicly declared themselves as feminists. Actress Emma Watson, for example – best known for her role as Hermione Granger in the popular film franchise *Harry Potter* (2001–11) – became a UN Goodwill ambassador and the face of their HeForShe campaign, urging men to join the feminist movement. Watson later created a 'feminist' book club, available to the public on popular website GoodReads, encouraging women of all ages and ethnicities to embrace feminism. Gloria Steinem's memoir *My Life on the Road* (2015) was notably the club's first book of choice.

In music, songs like Kesha's 'Woman' (2017) and Daya's 'Sit Still, Look Pretty' (2015) employed a distinctly feminist rhetoric to endorse female empowerment and body positivity. Likewise, there was a resurgence of feminist discourse in the popular media, with blogs and websites including Feministing, Feminist Current, Crunk Feminist Collective and Jezebel offering a gendered perspective on current affairs. Further underscoring its popularity, feminism even became a marketing sensation. While high-end designer brands like Christian Dior and Prabal Gurung produced slogan t-shirts, ranging in price from $195 to $710, declaring "We Should All Be Feminists" and "This Is What A Feminist Looks Like," online fashion retailer ASOS sold affordable 'feminist-as-fuck' necklaces to their eager consumers.

In response to the obvious appetite for feminism, production companies started to commission 'feminist' re-boots of popular film franchises, including *Ghostbusters* and *Ocean's Eleven*, with all female casts. Meanwhile, conversations about gender inequity were revived in the public sphere. During her acceptance speech at the 2015 Oscars, for example, actress Patricia Arquette used her time on stage to criticise the continued disparities of pay between the genders. Similarly, Under Armour, an American sport equipment corporation, used their 'I Will What I Want' advertising campaign to denounce gender imbalances in sport. Highlighting the physical prowess of Misty Copeland, a principal ballerina at the American Ballet Theatre, the campaign promoted an understanding of male and female athletes as equals, worthy of comparable commendation.

In 2013, when I was studying for an MA in Gender, Sexuality and Cultural Studies, I was asked by my professor if I considered myself a feminist. At the time, I was working on a project not dissimilar to this book. That project interrogated popular representations of feminine passivity and feminine malevolence in the nineties, attempting to elucidate the deleterious impact of those regressive representations on women. It was, in other words, a wholeheartedly feminist project. Nevertheless, I refused to identify as a feminist, to publicly adopt that label. Embarrassed and ashamed of the title, I declared instead that I was simply interested in 'gender theory' (as if those things were mutually exclusive).

Despite taking place less than ten years ago, this recollection feels utterly antediluvian. Feminism, once taboo for my generation, is now everywhere in our current cultural imaginary. It is, as Jennifer Baumgardner and Amy Richards so effectively put it, "like fluoride . . . simply in the water" (2000, 17). That seems like, and is, a cause for celebration. This popular iteration of feminism, visible across television series, in film and on social media, has certainly amplified the voices of women and re-centralised women's issues in the public sphere. Troubling the postfeminist assumption that feminism is no longer needed, the revival of popular feminism has foregrounded the pervasive gendered inequity in our culture.

By rebranding feminism as 'fashionable' or 'trendy', popular feminism has encouraged more and more women to proudly and publicly identify as feminists. It has also significantly altered the *affect* of feminism. In contrast to those feelings of shame I attached to the word, 'feminism' now engenders a wholly different set of affective responses, such as pride and pleasure, in women. Nevertheless, it is important to acknowledge that popular feminism exists on a continuum, sharing many of the same characteristics of the neoliberal and postfeminist ideologies interrogated in this book. And so, like critic Sarah Banet Weiser, I am sceptical about the subversive potential of popular feminism, recognising that it is constituted through the self-same neoliberal ideals as its problematic postfeminist 'predecessor'.

Undermining postfeminist rhetoric of girl power, this current manifestation of feminism insists on women's vulnerability under contemporary patriarchy and overtly challenges their subordination. At the same time, as Weiser observes, this new feminist wave does not always confront or subvert the status quo. Instead, following neoliberal logics, popular feminism offers individual solutions to those asymmetries of power, encouraging women to be more confident *within* pre-existing economic and political spheres (2018, 4). This is most clearly discernible in global advertising campaigns such as Always's' #LikeAGirl and Dove's Be Real. These kinds of campaigns usually highlight the pernicious effects of hereto-patriarchy on women, like low self-esteem and body issues, utilising a feminist lexicon to convey this message. But their 'remedy' for those ailments is often de-politicised, motivating women to overcome their 'limiting beliefs' by dispelling all negative emotions and adopting an attitude of self-assurance – however superficial that attitude might be. All the while, the socio-political structures which engendered those feelings continue to evade critique.

Rosalind Gill is similarly dubious about popular feminism, highlighting how it is governed by the same *affective* rules as postfeminism – rules which are critiqued throughout this book. This commodified and corporate-friendly version of feminism is palatable and has broad appeal. Unlike second-wave feminism, typically characterised as angry or vitriolic, it is "a feminism that is actually encumbered by its desire not to be angry, not to be 'difficult', not to be 'humourless'" (2016, 618). And so, while popular feminism permits women to publicly denounce gender inequities, these criticisms can only be expressed in an affable, 'friendly' way, inhibiting any real challenge to hegemonic structures of power. As Zeisler neatly summarises:

> The aspects of feminism currently given voice in pop culture are the most media-friendly ones, the ones that centre on heterosexual relationships and marriage, on economic success that doesn't challenge existing capitalist structures, on the right to be desirable yet have bodily autonomy . . . it is a glossy, feel-good feminism that pulls focus away from deeply entrenched forms of inequality.
>
> (2016, 4–5)

In other words, popular feminism functions as a kind of hollow shell, its feminist veneer concealing an emptiness within and failing to effectuate any real structural changes.

Despite these conspicuous shortcomings, I believe that it would be unproductive to totally dismiss popular feminism as nothing more than a modified version of postfeminism, similarly 'neoliberalised'. Instead, I propose that the increased visibility of feminism in popular culture, the revitalisation of feminist ideologies, contributed to the conditions of possibility for the contemporary resurgence of women's anger in the public sphere. To be clear, this is not to say that women haven't always been angry or frustrated about gender inequity. But by platforming feminism and making it 'accessible' again, popular feminism created the optimal conditions for *articulating* this anger.

Against the long-standing sublimation of female rage, a women's march opposing the Trump administration ruptured the 'feelings rules' of postfeminist popular culture in January 2017, making legible their deep-rooted anger about societal injustices. With 'pink pussy hats' – designed to challenge Trump's infamous "grab 'em by the pussy" remark – these women coalesced on the streets, united by their mutual feelings of frustration and discontent. On visually arresting posters, the marchers exploited familiar popular culture references to challenge sexism and gender inequity, expressing their dissatisfaction with the profoundly corrupt status quo. Their messages included: 'I Don't Want to Wear Glass Slippers, I Want to Break Glass Ceilings', 'The Women Strike Back', 'Girls Just Want to Have Fun-damental Human Rights' and 'This Episode of the Handmaid's Tale Sucks'.

Attended by millions, The Women's March originated in Washington, DC, but quickly expanded its reach through 'sister' protests all over the word. In Poland, for example, women banded together to dispute the tightening of abortion regulations under the Law and Justice government. Likewise, women's movements erupted in Italy, Spain and Portugal, lambasting the ubiquity of gendered violence and the weakness of existing legislation, demanding more effective laws, and rigorous application of those laws, to protect women. Adopting a long-established mode of politics – taking to the streets – to challenge gender inequity, these marches signalled a crucial shift away from the relentless focus on individualism, synonymous with neoliberal postfeminism, that characterised the first decade of the twenty-first century. On the contrary, the protesters embodied a revived feminist political collectivity – a coalition of women, unified by their rage, who were rejecting the perpetual privatisation of their suffering and demanding structural changes.

As women progressively coalesced online to share their experiences of sexism and misogyny, more and more high-profile men – including NBC news anchor Matt Lauer, popular comedian Louis C.K. and celebrated film producer Harvey Weinstein – were publicly accused of sexual misconduct and removed from their positions of power. These stories seemed to capture public attention about gendered violence in an unprecedented way. In hindsight, it certainly felt like we were on the cusp of a fundamental shift. The sheer number of women divulging those frightening stories was ineluctable, attesting to an epidemic of gender-based violence and marking the abuse of women as intolerable.

Reflecting a collective consciousness moulded by neoliberal ideologies, the #MeToo movement took something individual – 'my story' – and subverted the *form*, connecting women with one another globally. As such, there was a 'sisterly' feeling permeating throughout the culture, a sense of togetherness that had felt long since lost. At the same time, this online movement had a kind of 'feedback loop' function, altering the *affect* of popular feminism. Female anger, persistently repudiated and dismissed as feminine hysteria, is now palpable throughout contemporary media culture; 'all the rage', it has itself become popular. As evidenced by the increasing ubiquity of furious on-screen heroines, from Offred in *The Handmaid's Tale* (2017–present) to Marvel's *Jessica Jones* (2015–2019), rage is quickly becoming the dominant generic affect of 'women's' popular culture. This signals a radical break with the mandatory optimism of neoliberal postfeminism.

Still, as we have seen throughout this book, those 'ugly feelings' – rage, discontent, anxiety and pain – were always there, sublimated but festering beneath the surface like an unhealed wound. *Twilight* (Meyer, 2005–2008) and *Fifty Shades* (James, 2011–2012) conclude their narratives with their female protagonists' transformation into the hegemonic ideal of neoliberal postfeminism. As we saw, these transformations are presented as pleasurable and aspirational for the series's readers, an effect reinforced by Meyer's and James's adaptation of the popular romance formula. Nevertheless, affects like discontent, vulnerability, unhappiness, fear, anxiety and pain are ubiquitous in the trilogies, drawing attention to the limitations of those hegemonic gender ideologies.

As I demonstrated in Chapters 1 and 2, both Anastasia and Bella struggle with low self-esteem, consumed with worries about their appearance and enervated by punishing beauty ideals. Persistently pushing against their feelings of subjugation, they were also overwhelmed and perplexed by the asymmetries of power in their relationships, recognising that their fantasies of romantic reciprocity were artificial. And so, by tracking moments of affective dissonance in these novels, burrowed into the fiction and emerging in weird forms, I argued that the reader was forced to consider the benevolence of neoliberal and postfeminist ideologies – particularly the rhetoric of choice as a marker of empowerment. These dissonances, I proposed, confronted the reader with the possibility that those hegemonic ideologies sanctioned the abuse of women by silencing their critical voices and privatising their solutions to gendered violence.

Like feminism, however, Anastasia's and Bella's 'ugly feelings' were not permissible in these texts and had to be camouflaged. Consequentially, their struggles are easily resolved by the novels' conclusions, the status quo reinstated in the shape of a prototypical happy ending. From this perspective, the emergence of domestic noir might be interpreted as a kind of turning point in women's fiction, whereby those feelings of disillusionment with neoliberal postfeminism were registered more explicitly at the level of plot. While anger and discontent had a latent presence in *Twilight and Fifty Shades*, sublimated by the dominant ideology, the novels discussed in Chapters 3 and 4 make manifest that disaffection. In characters like Amy Elliot Dunne, Rachel Watson, Camille Preaker, Amma Crellin, Beth and Addy, readers were finally granted a vehicle for *overtly* addressing and confronting their frustrations.

As we have seen, both *Gone Girl* (Flynn, 2012) and *The Girl on the Train* (Hawkins, 2015) re-deploy key tropes from the romance genre to shatter its idealised images of domestic bliss and female empowerment, disrupting neoliberal and postfeminist fantasies of the good life. These fantasies, we saw, were not only discordant with reality but also toxic and dangerous – possessing the potential to pathologise women and licence violence against them. While those novels foregrounded female protagonists who were beginning to recognise their oppression, becoming increasingly angry and embittered, *Dare Me* (Abbott, 2012) and *Sharp Objects* (Flynn, 2006) centralised women's rage. This rage, however, was often misdirected – turned inwards against the self or outwards towards other women. As was demonstrated in Chapter 4, I interpreted this misdirection as a strategy for averting critical attention away from dominant systems of power, effectuated by neoliberal postfeminism. These diversions, I argued, depoliticised and privatised women's suffering. They also crucially contaminated the intimate relationships between women, corrupting the affect of friendship.

Female rage, once quiescent or inert, becomes more clearly perceptible in the progression of this book, mirroring the trajectory of feminism in the postmillennial period. No longer a residual ideology, feminist rhetoric is omnipresent – ubiquitous throughout popular culture. More pertinently, it often manifests as feminist anger. But the question must be asked: can this anger be harnessed for meaningful political change? Can we cultivate and sustain a collective feminist rage to disrupt those dominant systems of power, catalysing a systematic overhaul?

Advocating for the use of anger as an energising resource with feminist potential, Audre Lorde argues:

> Every woman has a well-stocked arsenal of anger potentially useful against those oppressions, personal and institutional, which brought the anger into being. Focused with precision, it can become a powerful source of energy serving progress and change.
> (1981, 8)

Driven by women's rage, movements like #MeToo and The Women's March certainly brought widespread public awareness to the quotidian reality of gender-based violence in our culture, challenging the depoliticisation of women's suffering and reframing it as a structural issue. More recently, however, some critics have appraised those movements as futile or fruitless, intimating that women have not successfully mobilised their rage, like Lorde proposed, to effectuate systematic changes.

Quoted in *The Guardian* in 2019 (Perraudin, 2019), Zelda Perkins, a former assistant of Weinstein, lamented that "while people are beginning to speak and the water is stirring, I don't think that the changes are as big as people would have hoped in the two-year period." Feminist critic Jilly Boyce Kay is similarly sceptical about the efficacy of #MeToo. Perturbed by the continued depth, reach and power of misogyny in contemporary culture, Kay highlights how despite the overwhelming volume of stories of sexual violence against women circulating throughout the popular media, Brett Kavanaugh was still confirmed as an associate justice of the Supreme Court in the United States in 2018 in defiance of feminist opposition (2019). His confirmation by the US Senate, she argued, effectively trivialised the accusations of sexual assault levelled against him by Christine Blasey Ford and thereby undermined all of those victims who had come forward as part of the #MeToo movement to tell their stories of gendered violence.

Western women's right to reproductive freedom has also come under renewed threat. In June 2022, for example, Republican conservatives in the US Congress successfully overturned *Roe vs. Wade*, the 1973 Supreme Court judgement which lifted restrictions on access to abortion in America. Likewise, despite thousands of women taking to the streets in protest, the government of Poland issued a near-total ban on abortion in 2020, signalling a regression of Polish women's reproductive rights. These events, not isolated or unique, are mere samples of the continued institutionalisation of misogyny in our culture. Still, as I discovered while working on this book, feminism is highly mobile and constantly in flux. It moves in and out of the popular consciousness so rapidly that it is often difficult to track in real time. As such, I'm hesitant to dismiss the recent feminist movements as failures, believing that any definitive answer about their efficaciousness would be premature. Although it is admittedly difficult not to feel deterred by the increased visibility of misogyny – especially in the wake of #MeToo and The Women's March – I refuse to hastily succumb to despair. Rather, moments like the passing of Coco's Law have only reinforced my certitude in the uses of anger for feminist gains.

Commemorating Nicole 'Coco' Fox Fenlon, a 21-year-old woman who took her own life after years of bullying on social media, Coco's law criminalises online harassment, stalking and 'revenge porn' in Ireland. Drafted in 2017, the bill re-surfaced in the popular media in 2020 following the leaking of explicit images of young women – many of whom were underage – on a discord server without their consent. While these images, shared in the thousands, were intended to humiliate and degrade their subjects, those women refused to be silenced and took to social media to vent their anger and demand new legislation. One victim, Megan Sims, started an online petition, signed by over 40,000 people, calling for the Irish government to prohibit "image-based sexual abuse."

Sims was not alone in this endeavour. Thousands of victims, enraged by the sharing of their images, began to actively tweet elected officials pressuring them to legislate Coco's law. They also cleverly exploited their online platforms to connect with media representatives, further disseminating their demands and publicly articulating their rage. Like #MeToo, these women utilised online spaces to share their individual stories with one another. Linked by the mutuality of those experiences, they forged a kind of sisterhood. Consequentially, on 18 December 2020, Coco's law was passed in the Seanad, giving credence to the notion that women's anger, when harnessed into something collective, *can* destabilise the status quo.

The 'Coco's law movement' demonstrates just how significantly feminism has metamorphosed in the postmillennial period. In contrast to those postfeminist discourses repudiating feminism as archaic and censorious, feminism is not only 'au courant' but also commonly recognised as a crucial facet of modern women's daily lives. Empowered by feminist rhetoric, those Irish women, pushing for legislative change, exploited the tools available to them to effectuate systemic change. Subverting the individuation of their suffering, they shared *personal* stories to create something *collective*, signalling a crucial break with – but not total detachment from – neoliberal postfeminism. By mapping the trajectory of feminism during the postmillennial period and underscoring its increased tangibility in contemporary popular fiction, this book delineates the genesis of that break. In doing so, it functions as a crucial vehicle for understanding the evolution of popular feminism and specifically the conditions that contributed to its emergence.

Reference List

Abbott, Megan. *Dare Me*. Picador, 2012.
Baumgardner, Jennifer and Amy Richards. *Manifesta: Young Women, Feminism, and the Future*. Farrar, Straus and Giroux, 2000.
Beyoncé. MTV Video Music Awards. 24 Aug. 2014, The Forum, Inglewood, California.
Daya. "Sit Still, Look Pretty." *Daya*, Red Records, 2015. *Spotify*, open.spotify.com/album/6hZQdRjpTaKiZ3Z6wqNlEz?highlight=spotify:track:0Mlm5SrNK34Jqn8Rk1Gs3g.
Flynn, Gillian. *Gone Girl*. Crown Publishing Group, 2012.
Flynn, Gillian. *Sharp Objects*. Orion, 2006.
Gill, Rosalind. "Post-Postfeminism?: New Feminist Visibilities in Postfeminist Times." *Feminist Media Studies*, vol. 16, no. 4, 2016, pp. 610–630. doi: 10.1080/14680777.2016.1193293.
Harry Potter and the Philosopher's Stone. Directed by Chris Columbus, Warner Bros. Pictures, 2001.
Harry Potter and the Chamber of Secrets. Directed by Chris Columbus, Warner Bros. Pictures, 2002.
Harry Potter and the Prisoner of Azkaban. Directed by Alfonso Cuarón, Warner Bros. Pictures, 2004.
Harry Potter and the Goblet of Fire. Directed by Mike Newell, Warner Bros. Pictures, 2005.
Harry Potter and the Order of the Phoenix. Directed by David Yates, Warner Bros. Pictures, 2007.
Harry Potter and the Half-Blood Prince. Directed by David Yates, Warner Bros. Pictures, 2009.
Harry Potter and the Deathly Hallows - Part One. Directed by David Yates, Warner Bros. Pictures, 2010.
Harry Potter and the Deathly Hallows - Part Two. Directed by David Yates, Warner Bros. Pictures, 2011.
Hawkins, Paula. *The Girl on the Train*. Doubleday, 2015.
James, E.L. *Fifty Shades Darker*. Vintage Books, 2012.
James, E.L. *Fifty Shades Freed*. Vintage Books, 2012.
James, E.L. *Fifty Shades of Grey*. Vintage Books, 2011.
Jessica Jones. Created by Rosenberg, Melissa, Marvel Television. Netflix, 2015–2019.
Kay, Jilly Boyce. "Anger, Media and Feminism: The Gender Politics of Mediated Rage." *Feminist Media Studies*, vol. 19, no. 4, 2019, pp. 591–615. doi: 10.1080/14680777.2019.1609197
Kesha. "Woman." *Rainbow*, 2017. open.spotify.com/album/1IYVB8NfiRqhdZlTxjspNh?highlight=spotify:track:1kJtfldK9F7XmsSiSNlbth.
Lorde, Audre. "The Uses of Anger." *Women's Studies Quarterly*, vol. 9, no. 3, 1981, pp. 7–10.
Meyer, Stephenie. *Breaking Dawn*. Atom, 2008.
Meyer, Stephenie. *Eclipse*. Atom, 2007.
Meyer, Stephenie. *New Moon*. Little, Brown Company, 2006.
Meyer, Stephenie. *Twilight*. Atom, 2005.
Perraudin, Frances. "#MeToo Two Years On: Weinstein Allegations 'Tip of the Iceberg', Say Accusers." *The Guardian*, 14 Oct. 2019, www.theguardian.com/world/2019/oct/14/metoo-two-years-weinstein-allegations-tip-of-iceberg-accusers-zelda-perkins-rosanna-arquette.
Steinem, Gloria. *My Life on the Road*. Penguin Random House, 2015.
The Handmaid's Tale. Miller, Bruce, MGM Television. HBO, 2017–present.
Weiser, Sarah Banet. *Empowered: Popular Feminism and Popular Misogyny*. Duke University Press, 2018.
Zeisler, Andi. *We Were Feminists Once: From Riot Grrrl to Covergirl, The Buying and Selling of a Political Movement*. Public Affairs, 2016.

Index

2008 economic crash 13

Abbott, Megan 4, 96–100, 104–10, 117, 123; *see also Dare Me*
abject, the 64–5
abortion 38, 122, 124
abuse 4–5, 16, 27, 30, 33, 53–4, 56–8, 67, 74, 87, 101, 104, 110, 122–3; *see also* domestic abuse; emotional abuse; intimate partner abuse; sexual abuse
Adichie, Chimamanda Ngozi 119
adolescence 20, 100, 109
aesthetic labour 46, 50–1, 93, 98–9
affective dissonance 15, 46–56, 61–2
affective politics 47
agency 1, 13, 15, 19, 28, 32, 34, 39, 44–5, 47, 49–51, 61, 65, 67, 71, 79, 81, 85, 89, 93, 102; sexual 60; *see also* agency pendulum; narrative agency
agency pendulum 47
alcoholism 67, 82–3, 85
Always's #LikeAGirl 120
Angel 27–8
anorexia 10, 73, 94
antifeminism 3, 24, 26
Aristotle 64
Arquette, Patricia 120
Austen, Jane 26
authoritarianism 31, 57, 74, 86
autonomy 9, 13, 24, 32; bodily 121

Backlash 9
BDSM 43–5, 49, 54, 58–9
Beauty and the Beast 57–8
beauty-and-the-beast narrative 57–8
beauty standards 50–1
Beyoncé 119–20
binge drinking 82, 94
biological clocks 12–13
Bluebeard 12
bodily autonomy 121
body dysmorphia 10
body positivity 120

body regulation 97, 105, 107
bodywork 2–3, 46–7, 49, 93, 97–8, 100, 105
Bride Wars 95
Bridget Jones's Diary 8–9, 68–9
Bronte, Charlotte 11, 27, 85; *see also Jane Eyre*
Bronte, Emily 58; *see also Wuthering Heights*
Brothers Grimm 117
Buffy the Vampire Slayer 27–8
bulimia 73, 94
bullying 111, 124
Bushnell, Candace 8, 68; *see also Sex and the City*
Byronic hero 14, 26

capitalism 121; late 81; *see also* consumer capitalism
castrating mother 116
chastity 24
chauvinism 75
cheerleading 96–7, 104–7
chick culture 68
chick lit 4, 7–10, 12–13, 15–16, 68–70, 103; *see also* chick lit jr.
chick lit jr. 16, 103–4, 110, 114
chick noir *see* domestic noir
"chick-whip" 43
choice 9, 14, 20–1, 26, 31–4, 38, 40, 45, 47, 49, 54, 56, 60, 70, 100, 110–11, 115, 120; discourse of 32–4; as empowerment 3, 14, 21, 31, 34, 123; life 20, 88–9; rhetoric of 14, 21, 32, 40, 113, 123
Christie, Agatha 84
C. K., Louis 122
Clique, The 103
Close, Glenn 65
Coco's Law (Ireland) 124–5
collective social justice 53
commodity feminism 47, 53
competitive individualism 93, 95, 106
consent 33, 44, 47, 53–62, 124
conservatism 3, 65
consumer capitalism 39
consumer culture 46

consumerism 3, 34, 46–8, 76, 103
'Cool Girl' 66, 68–74, 76–7, 80, 94
Copeland, Misty 120
Coppola, Francis Ford 27
corporeality 51, 87, 97, 102
courtship novel 26
Craft, The 109
crime fiction 4, 16, 77, 89–90; feminist 90
crime genre 86, 90; *see also* true crime
cruel optimism 76
cult: sadomasochistic 2; sex 1
cutting 94, 101–2

Dare Me 4, 16, 96–100, 104–11
dark fantasy *see* paranormal romance
David de Morrissey series 27
Daya 120
'Dead Girl' 75–80, 85–7, 89, 113
depoliticisation 33, 67, 73, 95; of violence 16, 89; of women's suffering/trauma 97, 102, 123–4
detective fiction 13–14, 114
de Villeneuve, Gabrielle-Suzanne Barbot 57; *see also Beauty and the Beast*
Diana, Princess 113
diet culture 109
dollhouse 111, 115
Doll's House, A 115
domestic abuse 83
domesticity 11, 13, 20, 22, 115
domestic noir 4, 10–15, 61, 123
domestic thriller *see* domestic noir
Dominus Obsequious Sororium (DOS) 1–5
doppelgänger *see* female double
Dove 'Be Real' campaign 121
Dracula 27
Dreyer, Carl 27; *see also Vampyr*
Dulos, Jennifer 75
Du Maurier, Daphne 11–12, 85, 89; *see also Rebecca*
Dunham, Lena 44; *see also Girls*

Edmondson, Sarah 1–3; *see also* NXIVM
emotional abuse 56
erotica 4, 43, 45
erotic love 24

Faludi, Susan 9, 65; *see also Backlash*
fantasies 4, 6, 12, 30, 39, 44–5, 71, 76–7, 80–1, 83, 85–7, 89, 99, 107, 115, 123; female 44; of good life 76, 80, 83, 85–7; heterosexual male 71; revenge 6; sexual 44, 59–60; wish fulfilment 7
Fatal Attraction 65–6; *see also* Close, Glenn
feelings rules 17, 47–8, 56, 61, 90, 121
female anger 94, 122; *see also* female rage; women's anger

female beauty, ideals of 94
female disempowerment 110
female double 15, 51, 85
female empowerment 3, 15, 24, 26, 28, 32–3, 40, 61, 71, 103–4, 113, 120, 123
female friendship 16
female monsters 15–16, 64, 67, 73–5, 89
female monstrosity 64, 67
female obedience 59
female power 64, 109
female psycho-killer 65
female rage 16, 93–117, 121, 123
female sexuality 7, 9, 19, 24–5, 44–5, 47, 60, 68, 107–8
female sexual pleasure 45
female solidarity 97, 103, 105–6, 108
female subjugation 45, 59
female submission 45, 59–60
female subordination 10, 12, 113
female victimisation 7, 79
female/women's melancholia 81
feminine beauty 28, 35, 38, 46, 51, 109
feminine ideal 51, 70–1, 80, 86, 99, 107
feminine identities 9, 67, 95–6, 107
feminine subjectivity 40, 46, 61, 69, 94
femininity 9, 21, 24, 34, 47, 51, 64, 71–2, 81, 93, 95, 104, 113–14; abject 85; adolescent 16, 97, 104, 108–10, 114; archetype of 15, 79; chaotic 50; constructions of 95; contemporary 15, 69–70, 73–4, 101; conventional ideals of 10; failed 67, 81, 85; hegemonic ideals of 13; heterosexual 47, 108; idealised 14, 16, 47, 70–2, 78–9, 93–4, 96, 99, 107, 115; ideals of 51, 66, 70, 73, 78, 81–3, 85–6, 89, 95–6, 98, 100, 112; masquerade of 15, 77, 80, 87; misogynistic conception of 67; monstrous 15–16, 97, 103, 109, 114–15; neoliberal ideals of 108; normative 65, 84, 93, 95–6, 107; passive 79; postfeminist ideals/version of 67, 70; prescribed 111; regulatory 75, 114; signifiers of 98; stereotypes of 69, 113; successful 24, 71–2, 87; traditional 9
feminism 3–4, 7, 9–10, 13, 21, 24, 40, 51–4, 60, 65, 69, 119–21, 123–5; contemporary 73; liberal 7; heterosexual 47; *see also* antifeminism; commodity feminism; neoliberal postfeminism; popular feminism; postfeminism; second-wave feminism
feminists 7, 43–6, 119–20
feminist solidarity 89
femme fatale 13–14
Fenlon, Nicole 'Coco' Fox 124
Fielding, Helen 8–9, 68; *see also Bridget Jones's Diary*
Fifty Shades of Grey series 6, 15, 40, 43–62; *Fifty Shades Darker* 43, 49–51, 55; *Fifty*

128 *Index*

Shades Freed 43, 59–60; *Fifty Shades of Grey* 43, 48–50, 52–7, 59–60
Flynn, Gillian 4–5, 15–16, 66–8, 70, 73–5, 78–80, 89–90, 96, 100–2, 110, 112, 114–17; *see also Gone Girl*; *Sharp Objects*
Ford, Christine Blasey 124
Foucault, Michel 45, 95; panopticon 49, 95
freedom(s) 1, 13, 19–20, 25, 52, 54, 85, 93; female 113; feminist 9; reproductive 124
frenemies 24, 95–6
Freud, Sigmund 6, 64
Furies 64

gang rape 35, 100
gender-based violence 3, 7, 15, 17, 40, 46, 67, 77, 79, 86, 89–90, 97, 116, 122, 123–4
gendered violence 3–4, 28, 56, 79, 86, 89, 122–4
gendered wage gap 2
gender equality 13, 119
gender ideologies 13, 15–16, 51, 67, 70, 74, 87, 89; hegemonic 4, 13–17, 90, 117, 122
gender issues 3
gender norms 19, 59, 75; archaic 30; conservative 19; contemporary 67, 71, 73, 85, 98, 114; neoliberal 80; oppressive 47; postfeminist 80; prescribed 114; regressive 19; restrictive 80; retro-sexist 28, 33, 36, 52, 67; traditional 36, 65, 79
gender performativity 70
gender politics 8
gender roles 12; heteronormative 28; oppressive 15, 34; prescribed 85; regressive 74; retro-sexist 26, 36; traditional 12, 23, 25, 28, 34, 39, 66, 74, 93
girlfriend culture 96, 105
girlfriend gaze 95–6, 107–8
girlhood 103; delicate 97–102
Girl on the Train, The 4, 66–7, 80–90, 123
'girl power' 3, 8–10, 112–14, 121
girl-power movement 103
Girls 44
Gone Girl 4, 15, 64–80, 89–90, 115, 117, 123
Gone with the Wind 58
Gossip Girl 103
Green, Anna Katherine 84
Greer, Germaine 6–7
gynaeopticon 95–6, 107–9

Handmaid's Tale, The 122
happy ending 37, 39–40, 62, 68, 123
'Hard' romance 5
Hardy, Thomas 60; *see also Tess of the D'Urbervilles*
Harlequin Enterprises Ltd. 5
Harlequin romance 4–5, 7–8, 15, 44, 61
Harrison, Lisi 103; *see also Clique, The*

Hawkins, Paula 4–5, 15–16, 66–7, 80–90, 123; *see also Girl on the Train, The*
HeForShe campaign 120
hegemonic masculinity 29, 33, 71, 74, 94
hegemonic power structures 16, 54, 95–7, 99, 102, 121
heroine 5–13, 15, 20, 26, 28, 30–1, 58, 67–9, 79, 103; adolescent 112; chick lit 9–10, 13, 15, 68, 70; fairy-tale 78; Harlequin 5, 7, 11; on-screen 122; pure 5; romantic 8, 10, 20, 57; teenage 20; virginal 5
Herter, Lori 27; *see also* David de Morrissey series
heteronormativity 59, 83
heterosexuality 59
heterosexual love 6
heterosexual male dominance 45
heterosexual relationships 8–9, 12, 59, 68, 121
Hills, The 95
historical romance 5
Holloway, Natalie 78

Ibsen, Henrik 115; *see also Doll's House, A*
identity 20, 39, 50–51, 85, 103; autonomous 116; collective 105; crisis 65; feminine 9, 67, 95; neoliberal 76; normative feminine 107; performative 98; postfeminist 76; social 39; subjective 51, 76, 85, 98, 116
ideology(ies): antifeminist 26; conservative social 23; dominant 4, 15, 40, 47, 56, 61, 72, 108–9, 123; feminist 121; gendered 16, 74; hegemonic 15, 40, 46, 48, 54, 61–2, 86, 123; hetero-patriarchal 60; pathologising 105; phallocentric 64; *see also* gender ideologies; neoliberal ideologies; patriarchal ideologies; postfeminist ideologies
individualisation 79, 88; of relational aggression 104; of structural issues 47; of women's suffering 16, 97; of women's rage 16
individualism 2–3, 16, 60, 72, 105, 122; competitive 93, 95–6, 106
injustice 2, 14, 94, 103, 109, 121
Interview with the Vampire 27
intimate partner abuse 31
intimate partner violence 66
intimate terrorism 84–90
Irish fae 64

James, E. L. 4, 15, 43, 45, 51–2, 55–9, 61, 122; *see also Fifty Shades of Grey* series
Jane Eyre 11, 27
Jessica Jones 122
'just-say-no' rhetoric 54

Kavanaugh, Brett 124
Kesha 120
'kink' 43, 45, 59

Kinsella, Sophie 13; *see also Shopaholic and Baby*
Kubrick, Stanley 112; *see also Lolita*

Lauer, Matt 122
liberation 34, 45, 47, 71, 77; sexual 8, 10, 25, 47, 60–1; women's 14, 61, 65
Lolita (book and film) 112
Lorde, Audre 123–4

Mack, Alison 1
malaise 61, 81
male castration anxiety 64
male domination 12, 14, 28, 31, 45, 58, 60, 71, 87; *see also* patriarchal domination
male gaze 60, 101, 112
male sexual aggression 14, 28
male sexual pleasure 45
male violence 14, 28, 33, 61, 86–7, 89; eroticisation of 14, 31; naturalisation of 29–30, 32; romanticisation of 29–30; sanctioning of 30, 56; threat of 28, 61; victims of 86–7
managerial state 2
manipulation 14, 16, 33, 36, 52, 54, 56, 67, 79, 82, 86, 103–4, 110
marriage/matrimony 10–11, 13, 20–3, 25–6, 36, 43, 58–9, 66, 68, 80–2, 121
marriage thriller *see* domestic noir
masculinity 28, 30; 'bad' 74–5; 'essential' 30; gendered ideals of 83; 'good' 74–5; 'normative' 14, 28; traditional ideals of 28; *see also* hegemonic masculinity
masochism 20; *see also* sadomasochism
maternity/motherhood 10–11, 13, 20, 34, 43, 58, 81, 116–17
mean girls 16, 97, 103–11, 114–15
Mean Girls 95
#MeToo movement 94, 122, 123–4
Meyer, Stephenie 4, 14, 19–21, 23, 25–6, 28–33, 35–9, 58, 122; *see also Twilight* series
misogyny 2, 4, 66–7, 72–5, 100, 107, 115–16, 122, 124
Mitchell, Margaret 58; *see also Gone with the Wind*
modern gothic novel 11–12
modern gothic romance 4, 14–15, 26–7, 61
modesty 8, 24
monogamy 13
monstrosity 15–16, 36–7, 65, 67, 81, 114, 117; of adolescent femininity 97, 109–10, 114; female 64, 67; woman's 65; *see also* monstrous feminine; monstrous mother
monstrous feminine 64, 115–17
monstrous mother 116–17
'Mr Right' 7, 69
MTV Video Music Awards (VMA) 119

Munchausen Syndrome by Proxy (MSbP) 96, 116
murder mystery 96, 114
Murnau, F. W. 27; *see also Nosferatu*

Nabokov, Vladimir 112; *see also Lolita*
narrative agency 77, 84, 86
narratives 7–11, 16, 19, 21, 24–6, 28, 30, 32, 57–8, 65, 68, 77–9, 81, 86–7, 89–90, 101, 117, 122; chick lit 7–8, 10; contemporary crime 86; crime 88–9; domestic noir 11–14; fantasy 83; missing women 78; modern gothic 12; redemption 27; romance 6, 8, 26; romantic 7, 12; true crime 77; vampire 27; of victimhood 79; of violence 79; *see also* narrative agency; trauma narratives
negative emotions 3, 47, 87, 94, 121
neoliberal ideologies 2, 16, 46, 70, 73–4, 76, 79, 81, 83, 86, 89–90, 93–5, 97–101, 103, 107, 121–3
neoliberalism 2–3, 46, 72–4
neoliberal postfeminism 3–5, 15–17, 21, 34, 38, 40, 46, 49–50, 53, 56, 61, 67, 71–2, 76, 79, 81–2, 84, 90, 93, 95, 99, 105, 111–12, 117, 122–3, 125
'new-wife-versus-old-wife' trope 89
norms 30, 36, 72, 75, 85, 97; class 75; feminine 64; gendered 76; patriarchal 3, 25; *see also* gender norms
Nosferatu 27
nostalgia 83
NXIVM 1–2, 17

online harassment 124
optimism 69, 76; mandatory 3, 87, 122
Other, the 64
otherness 64, 81, 114

paranormal romances 26–34
passivity 5–6, 8, 24, 36, 47, 59, 65, 85, 111, 113–14, 120
patriarchal domination 96
patriarchal ideologies 64, 102, 114; hetero- 60
patriarchal order 66
patriarchy 4, 16, 36, 45, 54, 65, 75, 93–4, 97, 109, 114, 121; hetero- 121; neoliberal 38, 40, 61
peer regulation 95, 109
peer-surveillance 107, 109
Persephone 113
personal responsibility 3, 15, 32–4, 46, 54, 56, 100–1, 110
Peterson, Laci 78
phallic mother 116
Piesse, Bonnie 1–3; *see also* NXIVM
Poland 122, 124
popular feminism 120–2, 125

popular romance formula 4, 7–8, 38, 43, 122
popular romance genre 5, 7
pornography 45
postfeminism 2–3, 24–6, 35, 52, 119, 121; *see also* neoliberal postfeminism
postfeminist disorders 73, 94–5
postfeminist ideologies 2, 4, 10, 16, 24, 26, 28, 35, 46, 69–70, 73, 76, 79, 81, 83, 86, 89–90, 93–5, 97–101, 103, 107, 121, 123
postfeminist masquerade 93–9, 111–14
postmillennial period 5, 14–15, 40, 47, 52, 90, 123, 125
power dynamics 96; contemporary gendered 60; traditional gendered 28; violently gendered 14, 31
powerlessness 2, 35, 39, 51, 99
pregnancy 38–9, 65, 78
Pride and Prejudice 26
'Prince Charming' 14, 27, 34, 76
privatisation 2; of feelings/suffering 2–3, 17, 87, 122–3

queen bee 103–4, 110–11

Radcliffe, Ann 26
Raniere, Keith 1
rape 3, 10, 66, 100; culture 30; *see also* gang rape
Reagan, Ronald 2, 65
Rebecca 11–12, 85, 89
regency romance 5
relational aggression 103–4
relationships 11–13, 20, 25, 29, 32–3, 35–7, 40, 44, 48–9, 52–6, 58–61, 65, 68–9, 76–7, 80, 83, 96, 103, 117, 123; abusive 20, 30, 56, 58; BDSM 54; committed 70; contract 48–1, 54, 58–9; conventional 58; dominant–submissive 59; heterosexual 8–9, 12, 15, 59, 68, 121; interpersonal 104; intimate 31; intimate, between women 8, 16, 97, 103, 105, 123; long-term 21; monogamous 9, 12; romantic 9, 12, 24, 27, 44, 83, 105; sadomasochist 43; traditional 59
reproductive freedom 124
retreatism 10, 13
retro-sexism 10, 20, 24, 26, 28, 33, 36, 52, 67, 69
'revenge porn' 124
Rice, Anne 27; *see also Interview with the Vampire*
Richardson, Samuel 6; *Clarissa* 6
Roe v. Wade 124
romance *see* 'Hard' romance; Harlequin romance; historical romance; modern gothic romance; paranormal romances; popular romance formula; popular romance genre; regency romance; romance genre; sci-fi romance; 'womance' (woman-centre romance)

romance genre 7, 9–10, 12–15, 26, 30–1, 45, 57, 61, 123; gothic 28; paranormal 28; *see also* popular romance genre; 'womance'
romantic reciprocity 76–7, 123
Romeo and Juliet 26

sadomasochism 1, 44–5
safeword 54
sci-fi romance 5
second-wave feminism 3, 6, 9–10, 21, 23, 40, 52, 65, 69, 121
seduction 6, 55, 105
self-actualisation 36, 38, 46, 49, 51, 100, 106
self-care 3, 46–8
self-control 1, 37, 67, 71, 80–1
self-discipline 2, 37, 72–3, 80, 94
self-esteem 2, 20, 36, 56, 68, 99, 104, 121
self-governance 38, 48–9, 65, 71, 80, 82, 97, 107, 109
self-gratification 23–4, 36, 47, 52, 60
self-harm 38, 73, 95, 98, 100–3; *see also* cutting
self-improvement 48, 68
self-monitoring 3, 9, 35, 73, 93, 107
self-mutilation 102; *see also* self-harm
self-objectification 60, 101, 112
self-optimisation 23, 46, 48, 93, 95–6, 106, 108
self-ownership 85
self-punishment 1
self-regulation 2, 38, 46, 48–9, 80, 97, 107, 110
self-sexualisation 47, 112
self-subjection 101
self-surveillance 72–3, 107
Serial 77, 86
serial killer 96, 102, 114–15
Sex and the City 8, 68, 95
sexism 47, 66, 122; *see also* retro-sexism
sex trafficking 1
sexual abuse 124
sexual assault 53, 100, 124
sexual attack 3
sexual difference 64
sexual fantasies 44, 59–60
sexual harassment 2
sexual misconduct 122
sexual politics 8
sexual surrender 44
Sharp Objects 4, 16, 96, 100–3, 110–17, 123
Shopaholic and Baby 13
Sims, Megan 124
sisterhood 4, 8, 16, 89, 97, 103, 105–6, 124
slut-shaming 104, 108
Smart, Elizabeth 78
Smithon women 6–7
social media 120, 124
social order 27; dominant 27, 66, 93–4, 98, 114
social roles 12–13
stalking 31, 57, 124

Steinem, Gloria 120; *My Life on the Road* 120
Stevenson, Robert Louis 55; *The Strange Case of Dr Jekyll and Mr Hyde* 55
Stoker, Bram 27; *see also* Dracula
subordination 1, 6, 10, 12, 14, 20–1, 31, 61, 64, 87, 94, 99, 113, 121
subservience 106, 113
suffering 2–3, 14, 17, 21, 30, 38, 40, 56, 61, 87–8, 97–102, 106, 122, 125; female 4, 7–9, 73, 94–5; *see also* women's suffering
systemic change 125

Tess of the D'Urbervilles 60
Thatcher, Margaret 2, 65
"top girls" 93, 96, 104, 106
traditionalism 7, 9–10, 13, 20–1, 26, 76, 85
trauma narratives 83, 101
true crime 77–8, 86
True Detective 86
true love 5, 7–8, 24, 30, 33, 38, 69
Trump, Donald 2, 121
Twilight series 4–6, 14–15, 19–40, 43, 58, 61, 90, 122–3; *Breaking Dawn* 19, 21–3, 25, 36–40; *Eclipse* 19, 22, 25, 29, 31–4, 37; *New Moon* 19, 29–30, 33, 35, 37–8; *Twilight* 19, 25, 35–6
Twin Peaks 86

'ugly feelings' 17, 122–3
UK 2–3, 5, 65
uncanny double 15, 85
Under Armour 'I Will What I Want' advertising campaign 120
USA 2–3, 5, 65, 77, 124
US Congress 124
US Senate 124
US Supreme Court 124

Vampire Academy 28
Vampire Diaries, The 28
vampires 26–37
vampirism 26, 34–6, 39
Vampyr 27
victim blaming 56
victimhood 2, 4, 15, 21, 34, 38, 40, 53, 79, 88, 100
violence: acts of 65, 67, 79, 109; depoliticisation of 16, 89; of men 14, 16, 32; misogynistic 100, 115–16; physical 28, 109; normalisation of 30; romanticisation of 30; sexual 54, 124; sexualised 4; against women 4, 16, 33, 67, 79, 89–90, 109, 123–4; *see also* abuse; gender-based violence; gendered violence; intimate partner violence; male violence; rape; sexual assault
virginity 5, 25, 100
von Ziegesar, Cecily 103; *see also* Gossip Girl
Vow, The 1–2
voyeurism 107–8

Watson, Emma 120
Weinstein, Harvey 122, 124
welfare state 2
Whedon, Joss 27–8; *see also* Angel; *Buffy the Vampire Slayer*
witch figure 109–10, 113, 117
'womance' (woman-centre romance) 8
women's anger 94, 121, 124
women's empowerment 3, 93
Women's March, The 121–2, 124
women's sexual gratification 9, 24–5, 45, 47, 49, 60
women's suffering 7, 17, 35, 38, 102; depoliticisation of 97, 102, 123–4; individualisation of 16, 97; *see also* women's trauma
women's trauma 102
World Health Organization 3
Wuthering Heights 26, 58